THE
DOWNSIZING
OF AMERICA

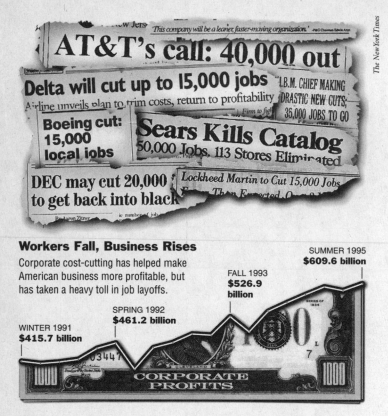

AT&T's call: 40,000 out

'This company will be a leaner, faster-moving organization.' —AT&T Chairman Edwin Artzt

Delta will cut up to 15,000 jobs
Airline unveils plan to trim costs, return to profitability

I.B.M. CHIEF MAKING DRASTIC NEW CUTS; 36,000 JOBS TO GO

Boeing cut: 15,000 local jobs

Sears Kills Catalog
50,000 Jobs, 113 Stores Eliminated

DEC may cut 20,000 to get back into black

Lockheed Martin to Cut 15,000 Jobs

Workers Fall, Business Rises

Corporate cost-cutting has helped make
American business more profitable, but
has taken a heavy toll in job layoffs.

SUMMER 1995
$609.6 billion

FALL 1993
**$526.9
billion**

SPRING 1992
$461.2 billion

WINTER 1991
$415.7 billion

CORPORATE
PROFITS

Quarterly figures at annual rate, seasonally adjusted 1995 dollars.
Source: Bureau of Economic Analysis

THE
DOWNSIZING
OF AMERICA

The New York Times

TIMES **T** BOOKS

RANDOM HOUSE

Downsizing graphic created for The New York Times *by James Denk.*

Copyright © 1996 by The New York Times Company, Inc.
All rights reserved under International and Pan-American
Copyright Conventions. Published in the United States by Times Books,
a division of Random House, Inc., New York, and simultaneously
in Canada by Random House of Canada Limited, Toronto.

ISBN: 0-8129-2850-4

Manufactured in the United States of America
9 8 7 6 5 4 3 2
First Edition

Acknowledgments

THE WRITERS GET the bylines, and most deservedly so. But this six-month project could not have seen the light of print without the contributions of many other people at *The New York Times*. Glenn Kramon and Paul Fishleder were involved from start to finish in conceiving and editing the articles for the pages of *The Times* and now for this somewhat longer book. Tom Redburn was also important in shaping the series. The page design and graphics of the original seven-part newspaper series, which appeared March 3–9, 1996, were the work of Joe Zeff and Pat Lyons, and the photography was coordinated and edited by Lonnie Schlein. The poll was conceived and interpreted by Mike Kagay, the paper's director of news surveys, and his staff. Josh Barbanel performed the statistical analyses that were needed to count and describe the casualties of the downsizing of America.

This book was supported in part by a grant from the Alfred P. Sloan Foundation, which seeks to stimulate new thinking about the role of the corporation in American society and about the changing relationship between work and families.

Contents

Introduction

BACK IN THE SPRING of 1995, we began to talk about making sense of what seemed a troubling and enigmatic period for the American worker. Something strange had happened the year before. Despite the fact that the nation's economy was strong halfway into the term of the Democratic president, Bill Clinton's party had lost its hold on Congress in stunning fashion. Like everyone else, we wondered what factors were behind it. At the same time, we could hear on many fronts that people were bitter, anxious, disenfranchised.

We sensed that their sullenness was related, in ways not fully portrayed, to an acute job insecurity. The staggering waves of layoffs that began washing over the country in the late 1970s as corporations merged, downsized, and re-engineered had failed to retreat. And those waves seemed to be crashing over an ever-widening spectrum of Americans—no longer strictly the much-battered blue-collar worker, but increasingly the once-impervious highly educated middle- and upper-class managers and professionals, people who never thought they would face want.

Workers have always lost jobs in America to the churning cycles of the economy, and more jobs were being created than eliminated, but never before had layoffs persisted with such tenacity and in such magnitude in an expanding economy. The picture appeared even more discouraging than that. For two decades, people had also seen their wages level off or decline, and now dispossessed workers were frequently finding that the replacement jobs available to them paid appreciably less than their lost positions. Everywhere, people were working longer hours and feeling expendable. The aggregate effect seemed to be a deep-seated pessimism in many Americans, causing people to question what dreams of possibility were available to them and to succeeding generations.

These developments were so broad and abstract that trying to picture them was like peering at the sky through a thick gauze pad. In the summer of 1995, in an effort to illuminate what was going on, we decided to attempt to determine exactly who was in this growing army of layoff veterans, and how job insecurity had affected the psyche and behavior of Americans. Reporters for *The New York Times* had written extensively about downsizing for years, of course, but we felt we had never captured fully its effect on American society. We wanted to portray anecdotally and statistically what was happening to the American people in a time that seemed to defy easy comprehension. We wanted to view the transformation underway not through unsentimental economic barometers like productivity indicators but through the prism of the lives of the millions caught up in it. We wanted to take a close look at individuals, families, workplaces, communities, and politics.

The picture we found is not a pretty one. To be sure, there are many chief executives and economists who argue that downsizing is for the national good, simply part of the ultimately salubrious forward march of capitalism. Let the efficient displace the less efficient. Take a good look at the improving economic indicators, they say, and you'll see we're doing quite well, thank you.

Almost two hundred years ago, the same argument might have been made when the peasants in England were shunted off the land and left to toil in misery in the slums. It was good for the economy, maybe, but it also precipitated the wrenching social ills that fill the sorrowful pages of Charles Dickens.

In the spring of 1996, the argument that what is happening is for the better is easy enough to make from the vantage point of an executive suite or a tenured chair, where job insecurity seems remote and next week's paycheck is a given. But it wasn't our task to judge this argument. What we sought was only to document real suffering, psychic as well as material, among millions of Americans.

PART I

The Price of Jobs Lost

Louis Uchitelle and N. R. Kleinfield

DRIVE ALONG the asphalt river of Interstate 95 across the Rhode Island border and into the pristine confines of Connecticut. Stop at that first tourist information center with its sheaves of brochures promising lazy delights. What could anyone possibly guess of Steven A. Holthausen, the portly man behind the counter who dispenses the answers?

Certainly not that for two decades he was a loan officer whose salary had risen to $1,000 a week. Not that he survived three bank mergers only to be told, upon returning from a family vacation, that he no longer had his job. Not that his wife kicked him out and his children shunned him. Not that he slid to the bottom step of the economic ladder, pumping gas at a station owned by a former bank customer, being a guinea pig in a drug test and driving a car for a salesman who had lost his license for drunkenness. Not that, at 51, he makes do on $1,000 a month as a tourist guide, a quarter of his earlier salary. And not that he is worried that his modest job is itself fragile, and that he may have to work next as a clerk in a brother's liquor store.

That, however, is his condensed story, and its true grimness lies in the simple fact that it is no longer at all extraordinary in America. "I did not realize on that day I was fired how

Andrea Mohin / The New York Times

Steven Holthausen, once a loan officer, dispenses tourist tips at a highway stop in Connecticut. "I lost both my family and my job. That is not where I wanted to be at this point in my life," he said.

big a price I would have to pay," Mr. Holthausen said in a near whisper.

More than 43 million jobs have been erased in the United States since 1979, according to a *New York Times* analysis of Labor Department numbers. Many of the losses come from the normal churning as stores fail and factories move. And far more jobs have been created than lost over that period. But increasingly the jobs that are disappearing are those of higher-paid, white-collar workers, many at large corporations, women as well as men, many at the peak of their careers. Like a clicking odometer on a speeding car, the number twirls higher nearly each day.

Peek into the living rooms of America and see how many are touched:

Nearly three-quarters of all households have had a close encounter with layoffs since 1980, according to a new poll by *The New York Times*. In one-third of all households, a family member has lost a job, and nearly 40 percent more know a relative, friend, or neighbor who was laid off.

One in 10 adults—or about 19 million people, a number matching the adult population of New York and New Jersey combined—acknowledged that a lost job in their household had precipitated a major crisis in their lives, according to the *Times* poll.

While permanent layoffs have been symptomatic of most recessions, now they are occurring in the same large numbers even during an economic recovery that has lasted five years and even at companies that are doing well.

In a reversal from the early 1980s, workers with at least some college education make up the majority of people whose jobs were eliminated, outnumbering those with no more than high school educations. And better-paid workers—those earning at least $50,000—account for twice the share of the lost jobs that they did in the 1980s.

Roughly 50 percent more people, about 3 million, are affected by layoffs each year than the 2 million victims of violent crimes (reported murders, rapes, robberies, and aggravated assaults). But while crime bromides get easily served up—more police, stiffer jail sentences—no one has come up with any broadly agreed upon antidotes to this problem. And until Patrick J. Buchanan made the issue part of the presidential campaign, it seldom surfaced in political debate.

Yet this is not a saga about rampant unemployment, like the Great Depression, but one about an emerging redefinition of employment. There has been a net increase of 27 million jobs in America since 1979, enough to easily absorb all the laid-off workers plus the new people beginning careers, and the national unemployment rate is low. The sting is in the nature of the replacement work. Whereas twenty-five years ago the vast majority of the people who were laid off found jobs that paid as well as their old ones, Labor Department numbers show that now only about 35 percent of laid-off, full-time workers end up in equally remunerative or better-paid jobs. Compounding this frustration are stagnant wages and an increasingly unequal distribution of wealth. Adjusted for inflation, the median wage is nearly three percent below what it was in 1979. Average household income climbed 10 percent between 1979 and 1994, but 97 percent of the gain went to the richest 20 percent.

The result is the most acute job insecurity since the Depression. And this in turn has produced an unrelenting angst that is shattering people's notions of work and self and the very

---

The New York Times POLL

Whether they lost a job themselves or saw a relative or friend thrown out of work, nearly three quarters of American adults say they have been touched to some degree by a layoff in the last 15 years.

■ In the past 15 years, was there any time that you were laid off permanently or your job was eliminated?

I have been laid off
20%

If not anyone in your household, how about someone you know well, like a close friend, relative or neighbor?

Someone I know well
38%

If not you, how about a member of your household?

Someone in my household
14%

TOTAL AFFECTED BY A LAYOFF:

Me or someone close to me
72%

promise of tomorrow, even as President Clinton proclaims in his State of the Union Message that the economy is "the healthiest it has been in three decades" and even as the stock market had rocketed to 81 new highs in the year ending March 1, 1996.

Driving much of the job loss are several familiar and intensifying stresses bearing down upon companies: stunning technological progress that lets machines replace hands and minds; efficient and wily competitors here and abroad; the ease of contracting out work, and the stern insistence of Wall Street on elevating profits even if it means casting off people. Cutting the payroll has appeal for gasping companies that resort to it as triage and to soundly profitable companies that try it as preventative medicine against a complicated future. The conundrum is that what companies do to make themselves secure is precisely what makes their workers feel insecure. And because workers are heavily represented among the 38 million Americans who own mutual funds, they unwittingly contribute to the very pressure from Wall Street that could take away their salaries even as it improves their investment income.

The job apprehension has intruded everywhere, diluting self-worth, splintering families, fragmenting communities,

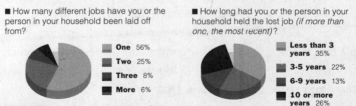

Asked of people whose households have experienced a layoff in the past 15 years (34 percent of the total):

■ How many different jobs have you or the person in your household been laid off from?

- One 56%
- Two 25%
- Three 8%
- More 6%

■ How long had you or the person in your household held the lost job *(if more than one, the most recent)*?

- Less than 3 years 35%
- 3-5 years 22%
- 6-9 years 13%
- 10 or more years 26%

Based on telephone interviews with 1,265 adults conducted Dec. 3 to 6 nationwide. People who did not answer or did not know are included in totals but not labeled.

altering the chemistry of workplaces, roiling political agendas and rubbing salt on the very soul of the country. Dispossessed workers like Steven Holthausen are finding themselves on anguished journeys they never imagined, as if being forced to live the American dream of higher possibilities in reverse.

Many Americans have reacted by downsizing their expectations of material comforts and the sweetness of the future. In a nation where it used to be a given that children would do better than their parents, half of those polled by *The Times* thought it unlikely that today's youth would attain a higher standard of living than they have. What is striking is that this gloom may be even more emphatic among prosperous and well-educated Americans. A *Times* survey of the 1970 graduating class at Bucknell University, a college known as an educator of successful engineers and middle managers, found that nearly two-thirds doubted that today's children would live better. White-collar, middle-class Americans in mass numbers are coming to understand first hand the chronic insecurity on which the working class and the poor are experts.

All of this is causing a pronounced withdrawal from community and civic life. Visit Dayton, Ohio, a city fabled for its civic cohesion, and see the detritus. When Vinnie Russo left his job at National Cash Register and went to another city, the eighty-five boys of Pack 530 lost their cubmaster, and they still don't have a new one. Many people are too tired, frustrated or busy for activities they used to enjoy, like church choir.

The effects billow beyond community participation. People find themselves sifting for convenient scapegoats on which to turn their anger, and are adopting harsher views toward those more needy than themselves.

Those who have not lost their jobs and their identities, and do not expect to, are also being traumatized. The witnesses, the people who stay employed but sit next to empty desks and wilting ferns, are grappling with the guilt that psychologists label survivor's syndrome. At Chemical Bank, a department of fifteen was downsized to just one woman. She sobbed for two days over her vanished colleagues. Why them? Why not me?

The intact workers are scrambling to adjust. They are calculating the best angles to job security, including working harder and shrewder, and discounting the notion that a paycheck is an entitlement. The majority of people polled by *The Times* said they would work more hours, take fewer vacation days, or accept lesser benefits to keep their jobs.

Even the most apparent winners are being singed. A generation of corporate managers have terminated huge numbers of people, and these firing-squad veterans are fumbling for ways to shush their consciences. Richard A. Baumbusch was a manager at CBS in 1985 when a colleague came to him for advice: Should he buy a house? Mr. Baumbusch knew the man's job was doomed, yet felt bound by his corporate duty to remain silent. The man bought the house, then lost his job. Ten years have passed, but Mr. Baumbusch cannot forget.

One factor making this period so traumatic is that since the Second World War people have expected that their lives and those of their children would steadily improve. "It's important to recall that throughout American history, discontent has always had less to do with material well-being than with expectations and anxiety," said David Herbert Donald, a social historian at Harvard. "You read that 40,000 people are laid off at AT&T and a shiver goes down your back that says, 'That could be me,' even if the fear is exaggerated. What we are reacting against is the end of a predictable kind of life, just as the people who left the predictable rhythms of the farm in the 1880s felt such a loss of control once they were in the cities."

As the clangor from politicians over the jobs issue has begun to be heard, aspirants to public office may find an audience in that group of households in which a lost job produced a major crisis.

The *Times* poll revealed something of their signature. Only 28 percent, versus 44 percent of the entire population, say they are as well off as they imagined at this juncture of their lives. The vast majority feel the country is going in the wrong direction, and they are more pessimistic about the economy. They are more likely than the overall population to be divorced or separated. They are better educated. Politically, they are more apt to label themselves liberal. They are more likely to favor national health insurance, and to say that curbing government programs like Medicare, Medicaid, and welfare is a misguided idea. And more than 63 percent, compared with 47 percent in the whole population, want the government to do something about job losses.

Wherever one turns one encounters the scents and sounds of this sobering new climate. Ask Ann Landers. Last year, when she adopted a stone-hearted view in her column to a laid-off worker, lecturing him that he had a "negative attitude," she was swamped by 6,000 venomous letters, one of the largest responses to any of her columns. "They were really giving me the dickens," Ms. Landers said. "This is the real world, girl. Now I am trying to be supportive." People run into acquaintances and don't ask how their job is, but whether they still have it. Surf the Internet or flick on the comedy channels and take in the macabre jokes. Sales clerk: "What size are you?" Customer: "I'm not sure. I used to be a 42 Regular. But that was before I was downsized." Wife: "But why'd they fire you?" Husband: "They said something about the company making too much money. If the business tanks, they said they'd call me back." Such graveyard humor is pervasive in Scott Adams's popular comic strip, *Dilbert*, about a 1990s computer engineer who quakes under a gruff and hectoring boss. In one strip, Dilbert competes with Zimbu, a monkey, for a job, and loses. In another, the boss informs Dilbert that he is about to become involved in all aspects of the company's production. "Dear Lord," Dilbert realizes. "You've fired all the secretaries." Raw material arrives daily in the form of E-mail from demoralized workers.

In an effort to somehow cauterize the emotional damage of the dismissals, managers have introduced a euphemistic layoff-speak. Employees are "downsized," "separated," "severed," "unassigned." They are told that their jobs "are not going forward." The word *downsize* didn't even enter the language until the early 1970s, when it was coined by the auto industry to refer to the shrinking of cars. Starting in 1982, it was applied to humans and entered in the college edition of the American Heritage Dictionary.

Meanwhile, the word *layoff* has taken a fresh meaning. In the past, it meant a sour but temporary interruption in one's job. Work was slow, so a factory shift would be laid off. But stay by the phone—the job will resume three weeks or three months from now when business picks up. Today, layoff means a permanent, irrevocable goodbye.

A Portrait of the Victims

Imagine the downsized posed shoulder to shoulder for an annual portrait, some sort of dysfunctional graduation picture. Mostly young, male, blue-collar workers dominated the glossies of the 1980s. Now, white-collar people stare out from every row. Many more of them are women and those whose hair flashes with gray. Instead of factory clothes, far more wear adornment appropriate for carpeted offices.

At his office in the Labor Department's Bureau of Labor Statistics, Thomas Nardone, an associate commissioner, keeps a chart that tracks the correlation between income and layoffs. In the 1980s, the chart shows, the higher the income, the less frequent the layoffs. Now the two lines rise in tandem. Blue-collar workers constituted the bulk of the layoffs in the 1980s, but as companies have slashed their costs more deeply,

1981-83: Factory Hands in the Heartland

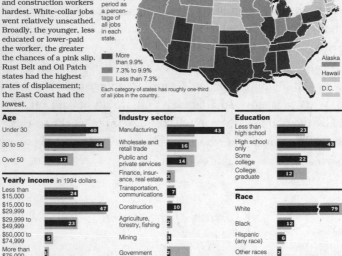

LAYOFFS in the early '80s hit factory, mine and construction workers hardest. White-collar jobs went relatively unscathed. Broadly, the younger, less educated or lower-paid the worker, the greater the chances of a pink slip. Rust Belt and Oil Patch states had the highest rates of displacement; the East Coast had the lowest.

Total jobs eliminated in three-year period as a percentage of all jobs in each state.

■ More than 9.9%
■ 7.3% to 9.9%
□ Less than 7.3%

Each category of states has roughly one-third of all jobs in the country.

Alaska
Hawaii
D.C.

Age
Under 30 — 40
30 to 50 — 44
Over 50 — 17

Yearly income in 1994 dollars
Less than $15,000 — 24
$15,000 to $29,999 — 47
$29,999 to $49,999 — 23
$50,000 to $74,999 — 5
More than $75,000 — 1

Industry sector
Manufacturing — 43
Wholesale and retail trade — 16
Public and private services — 14
Finance, insurance, real estate — 8
Transportation, communications — 7
Construction — 10
Agriculture, forestry, fishing — 2
Mining — 3
Government — 2

Education
Less than high school — 23
High school only — 43
Some college — 22
College graduate — 12

Race
White — 79
Black — 12
Hispanic (any race) — 6
Other races — 2

What the Bar Charts Show

PERCENTAGE OF OVERALL LABOR FORCE
PERCENTAGE OF ELIMINATED JOBS

The charts illustrate how hard each category of worker was hit by layoffs. If the two bars are the same length, the category had layoffs in proportion to its size. A black bar longer than the gray means the group experienced more than its proportionate share of job losses; a gray bar longer than the black means it had less than its share. Figures may not add to 100 percent because of rounding.

and as technology has obviated the need for office workers and middle managers, the concentricity of the layoffs opened up in the 1990s to include white-collar people. Whereas those with no more than high school educations used to be hardest hit, now it is frequently people with college degrees, even advanced degrees.

The job insecurity reaches beyond corporations. Government is also scaling back, although not as drastically as corporations, erasing many of the jobs that historically elevated the poor. Between 1979 and 1993, 454,000 public service jobs vanished. Academia is contributing to the dislocation by paring its rolls and increasingly leaving college teachers in jeopardy by denying them tenure. Doctors, once leading the way

1991-93: Office Workers on the Coasts

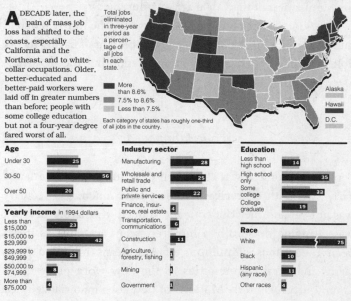

A DECADE later, the pain of mass job loss had shifted to the coasts, especially California and the Northeast, and to white-collar occupations. Older, better-educated and better-paid workers were laid off in greater numbers than before; people with some college education but not a four-year degree fared worst of all.

Total jobs eliminated in three-year period as a percentage of all jobs in each state.

■ More than 8.6%
■ 7.5% to 8.6%
□ Less than 7.5%

Each category of states has roughly one-third of all jobs in the country.

Alaska
Hawaii
D.C.

Age
Under 30 — 25
30-50 — 56
Over 50 — 20

Yearly income in 1994 dollars
Less than $15,000 — 23
$15,000 to $29,999 — 42
$29,999 to $49,999 — 23
$50,000 to $74,999 — 8
More than $75,000 — 4

Industry sector
Manufacturing — 28
Wholesale and retail trade — 25
Public and private services — 22
Finance, insurance, real estate — 4
Transportation, communications — 6
Construction — 11
Agriculture, forestry, fishing — 1
Mining — 1
Government — 1

Education
Less than high school — 14
High school only — 35
Some college — 22
College graduate — 19

Race
White — 75
Black — 10
Hispanic (any race) — 11
Other races — 4

along the smug path to American bounty, are succumbing to the cost-containment convulsions in health care.

What so many middle-class workers are experiencing for the first time is achingly familiar to poorer people. Job security never seemed to apply to them. Indeed, those at the lower end of the economic ladder are slipping even further. Rene Brown is a thrice-downsized woman who is still in her forties. Since the start of the 1980s she has been downsized out of an $8.50-an-hour job at a meatpacking plant, a $7.25-an-hour job in a bank mailroom, and a $4.75-an-hour job loading newspapers. She now earns $4.25 cleaning office buildings in Baltimore. Ms. Brown, who is married without children, has done this menial work for three years, without a raise. She is annoyed that, despite a high school diploma and a year of community college, she cannot find a way back up the income ladder. If her wage were only higher, she said, it would "make the humiliation of this job at least endurable."

The poor are losing out in another way. The newly pinched middle class has grown increasingly intolerant of having its tax dollars applied to social programs benefiting the disadvantaged.

What Happened

People, of course, always lost their jobs. In the nineteenth and early twentieth centuries, it didn't take much; job security was not yet an American concept. Indeed, the nature of work was changing drastically a hundred years ago, just as it has been today. Tens of millions of Americans migrated from farms and rural communities to the new work growing up around urban centers. Millions of new jobs materialized, for example, in the auto industry, in highway construction, in the expanding network of railroads and commuter lines and, above all, in the shift from cumbersome steam-powered equipment to sophisticated factory machinery powered by electricity. That shift ushered in mass production. The giant department store and the big retail chain also appeared in this era, elbowing out smaller enterprises. The advertising industry was born and office jobs mushroomed.

Huge fortunes were amassed overnight and mansions appeared along the beaches of Newport. Poverty, child labor, twelve-hour days, and unhealthy working conditions were huge problems, of course. And there was also a lot of insecurity, as workers discovered that the familiar guarantees of life on the farm and in their small towns were gone. Skilled craftsmen who once thought they were masters of their own destiny awoke—like middle managers today—to discover that their talents were suddenly redundant. But there was a saving grace: A worker forced off a job much more often than not found himself in another that paid as well or better, if not right away, then within a year or two. Indeed, the incomes of most Americans kept rising, and millions of families, for the first time, acquired the multitude of inexpensive consumer goods made possible by mass production.

The Great Depression brought a temporary halt to this progress, but the Second World War ushered in an unprecedented era of economic growth. Demand for workers soared. The postwar years led many people to the succoring belief that they had an almost divine right to a very particular American dream entailing a home, a secure job, and a raise every year. An unwritten social contract, codified in part by strong labor unions, came into being, under which managers and workers pledged their loyalty to one another. Leaving a job became a major decision, one made more often by the workers than their bosses. And if a worker left, or was fired, the odds of landing another job at similar or better pay were very much in the worker's favor. "We had a vision then that life was good, and a conviction you could make it even better," said Michael Piore, an economist and historian at the Massachusetts Institute of Technology. "Now that conviction is gone."

The booming economic growth that fed this optimism slackened in the early 1970s, and the American economy has remained stuck at a lower volume. Not since the middle of the nineteenth century, in fact, has the economy grown so slowly for so long; even the Depression, while far more devastating, lasted only a decade. The vigor that had lifted so many families to higher incomes subsided. There were many reasons. Intensified competition from foreign producers with lower labor costs—and from American companies offering low wages—withered the demand for workers with pretensions of earning even fifteen or twenty dollars an hour. Adding to the burden,

The New York Times POLL

Some people see storm clouds of economic uncertainty on every horizon: They fear a layoff in the next year, an empty bank account when they retire, and a poorer future for their children. These worries stop many Americans from feeling secure economically, especially those who have been through a layoff. And most people think the widespread threat of layoffs is here to stay.

◼ How worried are you that in the next 12 months you or someone in your household might be out of work and looking for a job for any reason?

◼ Very worried
15%
◼ Somewhat
worried
31%

◼ How worried are you about not having enough savings for retirement?

RESPONDENTS WHO ARE NOT RETIRED

◼ Very worried
35%
◼ Somewhat
worried
42%

the steady and pronounced progress of technology kept taking tasks from human beings and giving them to machines, undermining the bedrock notion of mass employment. Whereas the General Motors Corporation employed 500,000 people at its peak in the 1970s, twenty years later it can make just as many cars with 315,000 workers. Computer programs rather than lawyers prepare divorce papers. If 1,000 movie extras are needed, the studio hires only 100 and a computer spits out clones for the rest. Behind every ATM flutter the ghosts of three human tellers. Cutbacks in military spending and mergers that shrunk two companies into one also helped to make American workers less and less needed.

By the late 1970s, the convergence of these trends prompted companies to sanction large-scale layoffs. At first, the job losses occurred largely in beleaguered smokestack industries. Now the most modern and prosperous industries

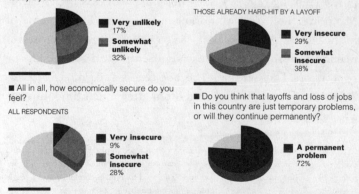

■ In America, each generation has tried to have a better life than their parents, with a better living standard, better homes, better education and so on. How likely do you think it is that today's youth will have a better life than their parents?

Very unlikely
17%
Somewhat unlikely
32%

THOSE ALREADY HARD-HIT BY A LAYOFF

Very insecure
29%
Somewhat insecure
38%

■ All in all, how economically secure do you feel?

ALL RESPONDENTS

Very insecure
9%
Somewhat insecure
28%

■ Do you think that layoffs and loss of jobs in this country are just temporary problems, or will they continue permanently?

A permanent problem
72%

People who did not answer or did not know are included in totals but not labeled. For respondents who worry they may be laid off, "soon" means the next 12 months. "Already hard-hit by a layoff" means people who said they or someone in their households had been laid off at least once in the last 15 years, and that the layoffs had caused major crises in their lives (10 percent of all respondents).

like telecommunications and electronics are shedding jobs regularly—companies like Sun Microsystems, Pacific Telesis, and IBM. Media companies, including *The New York Times*, are also doing so. Labor Department statistics show that more than 36 million jobs were eliminated between 1979 and 1993, and an analysis by *The New York Times* puts the number at 43 million through 1995.* Many of the jobs would disappear in any age, when a store closes or an old product like the typewriter yields to a new one like the computer. What distinguishes this age are three phenomena: white-collar workers are big victims; large corporations now account for many of the layoffs; and a large percentage of the jobs are lost to "outsourcing"—contracting work to another company, usually within the United States.

Far more jobs are being added than lost. But many of the new jobs are in small companies that offer scant benefits and less pay, and many are part-time positions with no benefits at all. Often, the laid off get only temporary work, tackling tasks once performed by full-timers. The country's largest employer, renting out 767,000 substitute workers each year, is Manpower Inc., the temporary-help agency. In this game of musical jobs, people making $150,000 resurrect themselves making $50,000, sometimes as self-employed consultants or contractors. Those making $50,000 reappear earning $25,000. And these jobs are discovered often after much time, misery, and personal humiliation.

* The Bureau of Labor Statistics conducts surveys on job displacement of adults 20 and over every other year, generally in January or February, and asks about prior years. To compensate for varying recall accuracy, overlapping surveys have been combined into a single consistent series by *The New York Times* using a moving-average technique. 1994 and 1995 figures are *New York Times* projections based on past trends and annual figures for unemployment and the labor force. Survey results and estimates based on them are subject to sampling error, which may be substantial for small states and demographic groups.

The Rationale for Cutting

Most chief executives and some economists view this interlude as an unavoidable and even healthy period during which efficiency is created out of inefficiency. They herald the downsizings, messy as they are, as necessary to compete in a global economy. The argument is that some workers must be sacrificed to salvage the organization.

Sears, Roebuck and Company felt its very existence threatened in a world of too many stores and too many ways for people to buy what Sears sold for less. Cost cutting, in the form of 50,000 eliminated jobs in the 1990s, was part of the response. "I felt lousy about it," Arthur C. Martinez, Sears's chairman, said. "But I was trying to balance that with the other 300,000 employees left, and balance it with the thousands of workers in our supplier community, and with 125,000 retirees who look to Sears for their pensions, and with the needs of our shareholders." At the Newport News, Virginia, shipyard of Tenneco Inc., a diversified manufacturer, 11,000 out of 29,000 jobs have been shed since 1990, largely because of technological efficiencies like automated welding. It's also true that the Pentagon is buying fewer ships. Dana G. Mead, Tenneco's chairman, boasts that Newport News is now as efficient as any shipyard in the world. Four workers operating robots can cut all the ribs of a tanker, a task that had required twenty-one and took longer. "We put in automation to get more competitive," Mr. Mead said, adding that the change won important tanker and submarine contracts. "Then how many workers you build back depends on the rate the commercial business grows, and what the Navy decides to build." Robert E. Allen, the AT&T chairman who has recently been turned into something of a symbol of corporate avarice for authorizing the elimination of 40,000 jobs, said that intensifying competition left him without choices. He said that with the Baby Bells free to invade AT&T's long-distance stronghold, AT&T's bloated staff of middle managers is no longer affordable. "The easy thing would be to rest on our laurels and say we are doing pretty well, let's just ride it out. The initiative we took is to get ahead of the game a little bit." Also intrinsic to the new message is that the lion's share of raises and bonuses must be channeled to those judged most talented and diligent. This new standard of "pay for performance" has made a growing divide among incomes a hallmark of the layoff era. In essence, a new notion of growth and job creation has emerged in which, rather than an expanding economy benefiting all, only the stellar performers—or those providentially in the right careers—come out ahead.

At the same time, some layoffs seem rooted in economic fashion. An unforgiving Wall Street has given its signals of approval—rising stock prices—to companies that take the meat-ax to their costs. The day Sears announced it was discarding 50,000 jobs, its stock climbed nearly 4 percent. The day Xerox said it would prune 10,000 jobs, its stock surged 7 percent. And thus business has been thrust into a cycle where it is keener about pleasing investors than workers.

How this all plays out is a matter of debate. Some contend that through these adjustments American companies will recapture their past dominance in world markets and once again be in a position to deliver higher income to most workers. Others predict that creating such fungible workforces will leave businesses with dispirited and disloyal employees who will be less productive. And many economists and chief executives think the job shuffling may be a permanent fixture, always with us, as if the nation had caught a chronic, rasping cough.

The Hardest Hit

The tally of jobs eliminated in the 1990s—123,000 at AT&T, 18,800 at Delta Airlines, 16,800 at Eastman Kodak—has the eerie feel of battlefield casualty counts. And like waves of strung-out veterans, the psychically frazzled downsized workers are infecting their families, friends, and communities with their grief, fear, and anger. The metabolic changes taking place in the country are only beginning to be understood, but there is no missing the deep imprint on the life of Steven Holthausen, the loan officer turned tourist guide. His high-velocity slide has caused him to go into his soul with calipers. He is suffused with anger, much of it toward himself. Why, he berates himself over and over, did he give so many evenings and weekends to his employer? Why didn't he see that his job was doomed? And then when the dismal news came that July day in 1990, he took it as he felt an executive should, coolly accepting the unfeeling reality of modern economics. Accepting it, that is, until he learned that his duties had been assumed by a 22-year-old at a fraction of his pay.

Once laid off, he not only withdrew from work, he withdrew from sight. He had been co-chairman of the trustees of a church in Westbrook, Connecticut, as well as vice chairman of the police advisory board. He left both posts. No longer a banker, he felt he had lost the requisite dignity to participate in civic activities. "You feel the community has lost its respect for you," he said. For almost a year, Mr. Holthausen scraped by on severance pay, on meager commissions earned as a free-lance mortgage broker and on unemployment insurance. The fact that the unemployment pay was taxed made him resent the government. If the federal budget were balanced by scaling back spending, he reasoned, less of his skimpy income would be taken from him. Accordingly, Mr. Holthausen voted for Ross Perot in 1992, warming to his pledge to cure the deficit. He now considers himself a budget-balancing Republican, although he has yet to settle on a candidate.

He lives alone with his torments in a humble apartment owned by a brother. He sat stock-still as he ruminated on the tatters of his family. Even while he was a banker, tensions underlay the marriage. When he was fired, the couple sought therapy. At the sessions, he beseeched his wife to help him regain his shattered confidence. He found her unsympathetic. Six months later, she ordered him out. Soon after, she filed for divorce and, after years of not working, found a job as a medical secretary. His two teenage children avoided him. Their view, he felt, was that he must have shortcomings or he would not be jobless. Recently, Mr. Holthausen said, his daughter, a high school senior, has become more empathetic after seeing the parents of classmates go through similar ordeals.

"The anger that I feel right now is that I lost both my family and my job," he said. "That is not where I wanted to be at this point in my life." In a society in which identity is so directly quantified by work, the psychological fall involved in losing a job is leading many to stress-induced illnesses. "What makes it so hard for people is very often these situations come about very suddenly," said Dr. Gerd Fenchel, the head of the Washington Square Institute for Psychotherapy and Mental Health in New York, who has seen his caseload swell with downsized workers. "We have a diagnosis called post-traumatic stress syndrome that applies to this. It leaves a trace that people can't get rid of. I'm seeing a lady who for years was employed by an organization and was well liked but was fired. She has been in depression for two years. Her expression now is, 'If the Lord calls, I'm ready.'"

The impact of job loss on marriages varies. The divorce rate, according to several studies, is as much as 50 percent higher than the national average in families where one earner, usually the man, has lost a job and cannot quickly find an equivalent one. Often the wife loses patience. On the other hand, many families where both husband and wife are employed seem to be drawing closer to muster their energies against the common enemy of job insecurity.

The effect on community unity seems more straightforward. In city after city, downsized people are withdrawing from the civic activities that held communities together. Sociologists report that involvement has tumbled at PTAs, Rotary clubs, Kiwanis clubs, town meetings, and church suppers. Bowling leagues are unraveling, even though more people are bowling than ever. The reason is they are visiting alleys not as part of corporate or community leagues, but singly or with a friend. "The 'we' has become a 'me,' or at least a narrower 'we,' " said Robert D. Putnam, a Harvard professor who has documented this contracting participation. He fingers downsizing as a culprit, although not as insidious as television.

In some communities, downsizing has spawned a distrust of big companies headquartered locally for generations, and that has translated into a greater reluctance to support projects favored by those companies. In Cincinnati, for example, the prominent corporate fathers—Procter & Gamble, General Electric, Cincinnati Milacron, Federated Department Stores—once got their way in civic affairs. But recent stands by the corporations—in support of a new arts center, two new sports stadiums, and a shift to a strong mayor-led government—have faced strenuous opposition. And some connect that to bitterness about downsizing. "Loss of trust on the job level extends into the community," said Dennis Sullivan, a

former president of Cincinnati Bell. Many citizens are investing less of their energies in organizations promoting civic
good and more in narrower groups directly concerned with
business. Joseph Kramer, vice president of the Greater
Cincinnati Chamber of Commerce, notices that trend and
worries about it. "What is lost," he said, "is broader concern
about the community."

At the same time, the job insecurity is unleashing a "floating anger that is attaching itself to all sorts of targets as a form
of scapegoating," said Daniel Yankelovich, president of DYG
Inc., a polling firm. Polls have shown this anger directed at
targets as diverse as immigrants, blacks, women, government,
corporations, welfare recipients, computers, the very rich,
and capitalism itself. Some experts say that part of the growth
in membership of so-called hate groups is traceable to disaf-
fected downsized workers. The floating anger is also influenc-
ing people's attitude toward politics. Pollsters say it is making
centrist politics harder to practice and making people less

The New York Times POLL

On top of jobs wiped out entirely, workers also face shrinking jobs:
cuts in pay or curtailed work hours. Uncertainty is driving people to
spend less and take second jobs. Some of the laid-off never get
unemployment checks; benefits run out too soon for many who do
get them.

■ In the past three years, have you or
someone in your household been forced to
work fewer hours or to take a cut in pay?

ALL HOUSEHOLDS WITH SOMEONE
WORKING OR LOOKING FOR A JOB

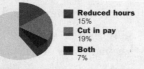

■ Reduced hours
15%
■ Cut in pay
19%
■ Both
7%

■ In recent years, has uncertainty or
insecurity about your economic future
caused you to cut back your day-to-day
spending?

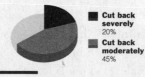

■ Cut back
severely
20%
■ Cut back
moderately
45%

faithful to any one party, less likely to vote, and more willing to entertain the idea of a third party. But at the same time, according to the *Times* poll, those who have gone through a traumatizing layoff are more likely to say that curbing government programs like Medicare, Medicaid, and welfare is a misguided idea, and that the government should do something to halt the loss of jobs.

Adapting to New Times

The downsizing has set off unmistakable currents of adjustment. Increasing numbers of families are scaling back their lifestyles. Two-thirds of those in the *Times* poll said that in recent years queasiness about their economic future had com-

■ In the past three years, have you or someone in your household had to take on an extra job?

ALL HOUSEHOLDS WITH SOMEONE WORKING OR LOOKING FOR A JOB

Took an extra job
34%

RESPONDENTS WHO WORRY THEY MAY BE LAID OFF SOON

Took an extra job
59%

Asked of people whose households have experienced a layoff in the past 15 years (34 percent of the total):

■ As a result of the layoff, did you or someone in your household take money out of any retirement account that required you to pay a penalty?

Took money out
15%

■ As a result of a layoff, did you or someone in your household receive unemployment checks? Did the checks run out during the layoff?

Got checks, but they ran out
29%

Got checks, did not run out
28%

pelled them to curtail their day-to-day spending. One-fifth said the cuts had been "severe."

Many of the dispossessed are stepping up their involvement in new networks rooted in job pursuit. There are assemblages like "Xerox-ex" for laid-off Xerox workers and "Out of the Blue" for former IBM employees. There are age-specific groups like the 40 Plus Club in New York for people over 40 who have lost jobs. And there are arrangements like the job-seekers club at the Trinity Episcopal Church in Princeton, New Jersey.

Some are fulfilling dreams by initiating their own businesses and otherwise tapping into some new inner serenity. After twice losing jobs at computer companies in six years, Marilyn Collins, a 52-year-old computer systems expert, got fed up feeling she was "dispensable" and joined her husband in the small New York direct-mail consultancy he had founded. Since her arrival, the once marginal business has flourished.

Eighteen months ago, Kenneth Russell, 41, quit his aerospace engineer's job at Northrop just ahead of a sure layoff. He and his wife, a nurse, sold their home in Palmdale, California, and moved to Arlington, South Dakota. They make pottery. The corporate life meant income of $110,000. The pottery life netted $15,000 last year (this year is going much better). "It is fantastic," he said. "We have much better friends, because there is no inordinate competition between people as there was in the corporate stuff. There are no false pretenses, you don't have to try to impress anyone. It is very real."

Living in Denial

There remain, however, other downsized workers who resist reining in their lives, as if denying what has happened. Just as many people who grew up in the Depression took a long time to shake their fear that hard times would return, today many who grew up in the 1950s and '60s are refusing to accept that a period they see as enduringly golden is over. Increasingly, these people are financing their living costs and adornments through every dollar available to them, including penalized withdrawals from their retirement accounts.

More than six months after losing his six-figure job at Barnett Banks Inc. in Jacksonville, Florida, Robert Miller is yielding only reluctantly to the likelihood that, at 52, he will never again command his past income. He continues to live with his wife and two children in a $700,000, six-bedroom home in a rarified gated community on Sawgrass Island in Ponte Vedra. His severance is dwindling, and soon he will be drawing on savings. "I worked hard for that house," Mr. Miller said. "I hate to use the word *deserve*, but it is human nature to feel that way." No job leads have materialized. His wife, Debbie, who had not worked, has joined with six other women to begin a computer database that will sell church-related information. Only recently have the Millers even contemplated moving. They have their eye on another gated community, where they might scale back to four bedrooms.

The Stunned Survivors

The new mood manifests itself in myriad ways, perhaps most surprisingly in the impact on those left behind in the office.

The woman is soft-voiced, introspective, married with children. She has rowed the corporate boat straight and narrow for years now. This has lifted her well up the ranks of middle management at a large pharmaceutical company. She earns more than $80,000. A still bigger company acquired hers. Clinging hard to her job, she would not speak for attribution. Instead, she shared her diary.

Entry: "A huge cloud of uncertainty hangs over each employee. Officially, we still haven't been told a thing about the acquisition and must learn about it from the newspapers. The sleepless nights begin."

Entry: "Every day I have lunch with my friend G, a great guy with a good sense of humor and rock solid values hard to find in industry. He will probably have to relocate out of state. This is ironic because the company just moved him here twenty months ago from halfway across the country. We will probably not see each other again."

Entry: "The company has been sold. It would be sick to suggest that this merger—which will result in the loss of thousands of jobs—is in the best interests of employees."

Entry: "My friend M was told that there were two lists: those who would be offered jobs and those who wouldn't. Her name was on the second list. Are they crazy?"

Entry: "My boss left last month. There's no one left to report to."

Entry: "I ran into B today. He wasn't offered a job and is devastated. He is scared he may not be able to pay his kids' college tuition and may have to ask them to transfer to local schools. Any sense of joy I had at being on the 'Schindler's list' of employees who've got jobs with our new parent corporation has been wiped out by experiences like this."

Entry: "I have been here four months and am convinced that I will never fit into this cold foreign corporate culture. I'm reminded of the old adage 'Be careful what you wish for,' since just a few months ago, I was praying they'd offer me a job here."

Many adaptable workers are accepting without sentiment the fact that their company does not owe them as much as people used to expect. Increasingly, like pool players lining up shots, these workers are figuring out the best angles to job security.

Diane Sirois is a curly-haired, irrepressible 39-year-old who assembles the most popular retractable tape measure at the Stanley Works, a hand-tool maker in New Britain, Connecticut. She keeps a studious eye on where the safest jobs are. After the company automated the assembly of the tape measure, she learned to operate one of the intricate new machines, which have the gee-whiz look of a sprawling toy train set. Her reasoning went like this: If there are layoffs, the machinery she runs would be the last to be shut down; under union rules, during a layoff, she could not be bumped by someone unless that worker could learn to operate the machinery in a week's time. It took her three months to master it. "Job security is why I bid for this job," she said flatly. "There are people here who have gotten used to sitting on their tails and repeating the same small task hour after hour, and they don't want to change, even to save their jobs."

Other workers simply agree to more work. In the *Times* poll, 82 percent said they would work longer hours if it would help preserve their job. Some part-timers, among them women who had cut their hours to spend more time raising children, feel pressure to go full time so they won't be viewed as marginal and expendable.

Many workers are returning to school. High school graduates in their mid-twenties, for example, are flocking to community colleges in unprecedented numbers, having discovered that their limited schooling prevents them from landing jobs that pay much above the minimum wage.

Andrea Mohin / The New York Times

Diane Sirois, an employee at the Stanley Works, learned to use a complicated machine to assemble tape measures because she thought it would help protect her job.

Behavior in the office is taking on bizarre twists. Leslie Perlow, a University of Michigan business school professor who studied a team of twelve software engineers at a Xerox office near Rochester, New York, found that the engineers, gripped by job insecurity, felt driven to show off their prowess before their peers and bosses. They spent the bulk of their workday in meetings and crisis sessions, some that were little more than stages where they could advertise their abilities. Not until after five o'clock did they get around to what they were paid for: inventing software. "They felt they were rewarded for individual heroics, and their crisis meetings gave them an outlet for heroics," Ms. Perlow said. "The layoff atmosphere exacerbated this need to 'show' performance." A lot of workers no longer think of their jobs as entitlements. Robby Smith is a 34-year-old engineer at Maitland & Hoge Enterprises, a Houston oil and gas consulting firm that did some downsizing. While Mr. Smith sees no likelihood that his job is at risk, he hastens to point out, "I don't take employment for granted. It is not a right, so to speak, granted by education and experience. That is an attitude I have developed over the past few years." Indeed, he made it a condition of being interviewed that his comments not sound in any way arrogant, so that his boss might conclude that Mr. Smith feels immune from layoffs.

Caught up in a cyclical business, Mr. Smith works hard at establishing his value to the company. Because he supports many projects, he feels less vulnerable to a loss of business. The fact that he does not yet have an engineering degree (he is shy a few courses) has meant that he makes less than the others who do what he does. He considers that a plus for him; if the company needed to find savings, it would get more out of laying off a higher-paid employee. Like the downsized themselves, Mr. Smith keeps his eye trained on his personal balance sheet. He is part of a two-earner family; his wife is an assistant school principal. They have a 2-year-old daughter. They have stopped using all but one credit card. When they buy a car, they finance it through his wife's father instead of the bank. All debt is considered suspect.

Other workers are simply redefining their *raison d'etre*.

To find Mark Featherstone in the small hours of a Monday morning, it is necessary to journey to the nearly deserted cafeteria of the Willow Creek Community Church in South Barrington, Illinois. Mr. Featherstone is a 37-year-old software engineer at Motorola. He has no explicit reason for thinking his job is in jeopardy—Motorola has in fact been adding jobs—but rather than this buoying him, he still feels cornered. Thus he was here at a "Dads Group," rooting for the emotional sustenance he used to get at work. He said he was seeking "a peace within myself instead of the rush of the job." The church has watched its membership grow rapidly, in large measure because of job insecurity. Mr. Featherstone likes his work, but feels the company constantly demands more of him. Every day in the papers, he reads headlines about layoffs, and he waits for the day that the type spells out Motorola. Three years ago, Motorola instituted a point system to rate its software engineers, a now commonplace management tool. Mr. Featherstone finds the rating system stressful. "They are putting a number on everyone," he said. "Everyone may be doing a good job, but someone has to be in the bottom ten percent of the ratings. If there are layoffs, they would be the ones."

The View of the Firing Squads

It was time, no question. On a cool, pale afternoon, Charles Allen stepped across Fifth Avenue and entered St. Patrick's Cathedral to attend noon mass. He knows the rite by heart. He goes every day. Daily mass is an old habit with new meaning for him. Things are on his mind. One signpost of this era is the multitude of executives who decided who would go. As a $90,000-a-year banking executive, Mr. Allen had to fire his share. Many, to his mind, were not competent and got their just outcomes. One, however, will not vacate his mind.

As an officer in charge of operations of the Standard Chartered Bank, Mr. Allen had to dispose of one of the three currency traders in the Toronto branch. The consensus choice happened to be a woman who was indisputably the top performer, but had the weakest political bonds. "I knew that she was the best in the department," he said. "But she had not networked. And I had to inform her that she was terminated. And she looked at me with tears in her eyes and said, 'But, Charlie, you know better.' I will never forget what she said and how she looked that day." Each afternoon at mass, he looks to put the past and the present in perspective. "It is a mark on my character," he said. "I feel a lesser person." There is a sullen irony to Mr. Allen's story. He lost his own job last May and now wanders with the dispossessed.

As senior managers find themselves making almost pro forma decisions to detonate the careers of thousands of workers, a new management issue has engulfed them: how to prettify a message to their employees and to themselves that is inherently harsh. Some executives are essentially resorting to camouflage to cope. Top managers at the Stanley Works have shucked their suits and ties and adopted sweaters and slacks, one reason being that they don't want to advertise their roles in these days of downsizing. Layoffs have reached 2,000 people. Most senior executives insist that they are at the mercy of brutal and irresistible forces. Inside many executive suites, there is an almost "will of God" justification invoked.

Rationalization of a larger good plays a crucial part in enabling senior executives to accept what they do. R. Alan Hunter, the husky president of Stanley, sat in the company cafeteria recently, in a dark sweater and turtleneck. "Is it better to have 100 people in a world-class plant or 120 in a plant that is not world class and might not survive?" he said. "You have to consider what is best for the shareholders and the organization." He nodded at the commonly heard lament that businesses are firing their own customers. But he said this did not enter into his thinking because he didn't know where to insert it in the equation. "We know that if Americans have less money to spend, that is not going to help us," he said. "But that is so broad and huge an issue, it is difficult to bring into the decisions."

Many companies subscribe to the logic that if they share more information with employees, then that absolves them of blame. Stanley recently began inviting all 19,000 workers to quarterly state-of-the-business meetings intended to offer blunt appraisals of how Stanley's tools are performing in the global market. This should mean, Mr. Hunter said, that no employee will feel taken by surprise if he loses his job. This in turn should mean, he said, that management has acted responsibly.

Studies and anecdotal evidence suggest that employer commitment to diversity has eroded in this wobbly environment. Many women, minorities and older workers express anxiety that they are more vulnerable. The most pronounced effect appears to be on minorities. Employment and earnings of blacks relative to whites have unquestionably declined since the 1970s, according to Labor Department data. Economists ascribe this to an array of forces in addition to the downsizing. One rationale of managers is that, with fewer people on the team, keeping the best performers is more vital than satisfying diversity guidelines. But also, with fewer good jobs around, "prejudice is easier to practice," said Harry J. Holzer, a labor economist at Michigan State University.

Mr. Hunter of the Stanley Works has it hardest when he returns home. He said he never tells his two children about laying off workers. His wife asks, however, and that is when phrases catch in his throat. "She'll say, 'Why are you doing it?' " he said. "I can answer that more easily to a Stanley employee than to my wife." He tells her of the need to be competitive, and she nods. Yes, when she goes shopping, she says, she certainly likes bargains.

The Children

There is one final cast of characters in this unspooling drama, and they are the characters of tomorrow. When workers come home with frayed nerves and punctured expectations, what are the children to make of it? The layoffs and the rejiggered lives have caused parents to search themselves for some new song of hope to sing to their children. What is the path to security anymore? What are the safe jobs? What, in short, is an American dream worth dreaming?

In the unlovely apartment of John Castner in North Arlington, New Jersey, all conversations seem to lead to work and its meaning. For much of his accounting career, Mr. Castner traced the predictable path of better work and pay. Starting in 1989, he was swept into the downsizing grinder. Last April, he lost his third job in six years. Now, at 47, he makes do with intermittent work. A widower, he lives with his two children, Julie, 14, and Stephen, 11. "I say to my kids, not only will you have to look for jobs anywhere in the United States, but in Singapore and Hong Kong. You are competing against kids from other countries." He tells them it is no longer enough to be very good, it is imperative to be a star. He feels it vital that they attend a "brand-name college," certainly not the Trenton State stenciled on his own diploma.

His children said they have not been embarrassed by their father's lost jobs any more than they are by neglected ink stains on their hands. After all, many of their friends have downsized parents. Julie, in particular, seems to have been forced into a response common to a lot of middle-class children—growing up earlier in a way reminiscent of what happens to poor children on shoestring budgets and deprived of intact families. She did not try out for the basketball team so she can hold an after-school job as a day-care counselor. "I don't mind work," she said. "It's fun." Despite her adolescence, she demonstrates an adult's knowingness and fortitude. "I wish my father had a job, but since he doesn't, you kind of get a little smarter and think about what you have to do more. How you have to go about, like, choosing a profession. And school is more important, a lot more important. In my school, it is kind of like the in thing to be really smart."

2

A New and Unnerving Workplace

N. R. Kleinfield

IT WAS AN ICY, pastel day and in the harried midmorning hours the sidewalks were clotted with workers parading into One Chase Manhattan Plaza, a sterile tower of ponderous coolness just off Broadway and hard by Wall Street. The blustery wind pulled the folds of jacket sleeves back. On the ground floor of the Chase banking headquarters sprawls a bustling, high-energy branch that employees reverently know as the Mother Branch. A bushy-browed man with a brisk manner who works at the Mother Branch looked around uneasily. "We approach that building with trepidation," he said. "It all seems like a quiz show. Who will win? Who will lose? Do you know the missing letters of the puzzle so you can come back to play again next week?"

It was not the place he wanted it to be or had known it to be. Within a matter of weeks, the tower would no longer be a headquarters of anything, because the Chase Manhattan Corporation was in the final throes of being swallowed by the Chemical Banking Corporation. The combination would be presided over from Chemical's Park Avenue headquarters and would constitute the country's largest bank, moving nothing less than $1 trillion a day. And as these things go, it would also mean 12,000 fewer people would have jobs. It is a numbingly familiar economic drama in recent years, but the script still has shock when it comes to one's own company.

All of this was testing the man's faith. A co-worker sidled past him, a small bouncy woman with glistening cheeks. She wore dark glasses, tilted upward, resting in her platinum hair. She gave a cordial wave and called, "Talking to your headhunter?"

"I wish," the man said.

"Well," she said. "Welcome to another deflating day at Downsize Manhattan Bank."

Like many corporate environments, Chase is a workplace in transition, a company in which old certainties about work no longer apply. The change is carrying a heavy price. A huge insecurity complex has taken root in the bank's employees. The deracinated workers feel forlorn, if not outright hostile. They speak of distraction, bitterness and, perhaps most of all, bewilderment. They are baffled about where their loyalties should lie—and where their employer's loyalty lies. Anxiety stalks the corridors.

To be sure, quite a number of workers also express optimism, an optimism sometimes a front for blinkered denial. Some younger workers don't really believe that an employer owes them much beyond a desk, an ID card, and a paycheck. They are ready and willing to play a game with unclear rules. Certain irrepressibly assured individuals of all ages see something hygienic about downsizing, an efficient way to cleanse sloth—so long as they remain untouched.

Farewell, Mother Chase

Employees called it Mother Chase. It began in 1799 as the Manhattan Company, not to lend dollars but to supply potable water to a New York swept by yellow fever. The disease was carried into the city by ships arriving from the tropics, and frantic citizens had petitioned the City Council for relief. With its spare capital, the new company opened a bank—"an office of discount and deposit," as it was called. The bank at once prospered. Nevertheless, overdrafts and forgeries were commonplace, and the Manhattan Company was thought to be the first bank to have company officers produce a list of businessmen who "merit discount and can safely be trusted," a rudimentary credit department. The water business, however, did not do so well. And thus in 1808, the Manhattan Company sold its unprofitable water works to the city.

In 1955, the company merged with Chase National Bank in what was then the biggest consolidation in the history of American banking. Chase National had been founded in 1877 by a former schoolteacher and had become the bank of the Rockefeller family. It liked to brag that it survived the Great Depression without laying off a single employee.

Jobs at Chase were once as secure as civil service posts. But it has been clear for at least a decade that banks are a capsizing industry. They have been buying and merging with one another, first sporadically and now in a veritable stampede, hemorrhaging jobs in the process. In 1995 alone, there were a dozen mergers among banks each valued at more than a billion dollars. Just four years ago, Chemical itself united with Manufacturers Hanover Trust. The stewards of these banks invoke the need for efficiencies to stave off rival banks, as well as the tide of retailers, car makers, and brokerage houses that offer their own credit cards and banking-type services. They speak of the escalating speed of technological change and the importance of holding the fickle attentions of Wall Street. Rarely do they address the extent to which consolidations result from lost revenues due to inferior management.

Chase itself addressed the marketplace with a certain arrogance, putting little emphasis on customer service, behaving as if people were somehow required to bank at Chase. Infighting was widespread. The bank's structure was so hierarchial that employees actually refused to return phone calls of anyone of lower rank. Management seemed never to have heard of the notion of expense control. Burdened with sluggish performance, Chase began eliminating jobs in the mid-1980s, moving from a high of 47,480 in 1986 to the still shrinking 33,500 in early 1996. Pressure on the bank intensified when Michael F. Price, a mutual fund manager, became Chase's biggest shareholder in April 1995 and admonished Chase to elevate its stock price. Four months later, Chase sold itself to Chemical for $10 billion, a deal that was consummated on March 31, 1996.

Within three years, management predicts that 100 of the two banks' 480 branches will be shuttered and 15 percent of the 74,000 jobs will cease to exist. Although the new entity will bear the more illustrious Chase name, Chemical is clearly in command. Indeed, many profoundly depressed Chase employees interpret the deal as a sellout and surrender by senior management. They view it as the death of the Chase they cherished and the rebirth of a bigger Chemical with a new identity. Thomas Labrecque, Chase's chief executive, has been demoted to president of the new entity, which will be led by Walter Shipley, Chemical's chief executive. Already, quite a number of employees are referring to Mr. Labrecque as "Judas."

One joke going around Chase:

Question: What do you call a Chase worker who is down-sized?

Answer: Chemical waste.

"No More Santa Claus"

With mechanical efficiency, the woman leaned across her desk, gathered up some loan papers and arranged them in a familiar order. She drew a deep breath and slowly let it out. "It's not the bank I started to work for," she said, insisting on the anonymity most fretful employees required for their insights about their unraveling situations. "They used to call it Mother Chase. They don't call it that anymore. Everything is about insecurity, not making enough."

Throughout the Chase rank and file, there is a kind of vitriol more often associated with the Internal Revenue Service. Its seeds were planted prior to the merger, during the years co-workers were going out the door and task forces were judging the necessity of jobs. Some felt there was something lurid or corrupt about it all—an immoral waste of energy somehow.

Like many others, the loan woman didn't think the layoffs at Chase would come out immutably fair. In her words, "It's not only how well have you done your job, but how well you did your political piece." She was not political. That worried her. "Chase has always been my identity," she said. "Chase is part of my name. But I'm not going to roll over and die because I don't work for the new Chase. Yet if this keeps up, who's going to go to work anymore? Why bother? Why get out of bed?"

She took a call, got rid of it, stared into space. Wrestling with their gloom, workers have begun to seize on customs in the most improbable places as suddenly relevant to them. One couple, shaken by the Chase tremors, recently concluded that America might have to become like India, where extended families rather than corporations minister to people. "You feel like you want to work in Japan or Sweden," the loan woman said. "Work in a place where they take care of their people and their crippled. It's like a lost era here. It's like growing up. There's no more Santa Claus."

Chase, in the lingo of human resources, no longer wants to be a parent to its employees. It wants to be their best friend. In step with other large companies, Chase has replaced a paternal-istic organization that guaranteed a job and a raise and a pension with one that tries to assist the employee by sharpening skills that will enhance career success, but will not guarantee any-thing. In the mid-1980s, it simply discontinued perks like employee picnics and dances, as well as a sacrosanct monetary benefit, a profit-sharing plan to which the bank usually con-tributed 15 percent of a worker's salary. That benefit was suc-ceeded by less-lucrative stock-option plans (basing payment on the company's fortunes) and 401(k) retirement plans to be managed by the employee. And the company began outsourcing innumerable jobs—guards, messengers, check processing.

Not surprisingly, employee discontent escalated, and Chase eventually concluded that it had to do something to address this angst. To a certain extent, it felt the solution lay in a cof-fee cup. In early 1993, Chase did something many companies were doing at the time: It engaged everyone in a mass exercise to compose a statement of values and goals. It called the effort Vision Quest. Chase thought it would make everyone feel warmer about the company and their role in it. The result was a set of five not unobvious "critera for winning": customer focus, teamwork, respect for one another, quality, and professionalism. The rather nebulous goal decided on as a new leitmotiv was to appeal to the bank's three constituents—employees, customers, and shareholders—and become the employer, provider, and investment of choice. "We spread that vision statement all over the world," said John Farrell, the head of human resources for both the old and new Chase. "It's down on the wall in our lobby." Managers beseeched their charges: "Live the values" and "Link to the vision."

Mr. Farrell scooped up a Styrofoam coffee cup and twirled it in his fingers. The precepts were inscribed right on the cup. The cups are stacked up at coffee stations throughout Chase. The idea was, every time you had some coffee you drank the values, too. Chase was aggressive about workers adopting the principles. "People who didn't live the values, who stayed in their silo, were fired and that was made very public," Mr. Farrell said. "If people weren't being respectful to other people, they were zapped."

The expression "employer of choice" was converted into a spread of programs, including stock ("Vision shares") for every employee, flexible work arrangements enabling compressed work weeks and, most notably, Career Vision. Begun in 1994 as the embodiment of the new covenant between employer and employee, Career Vision offers self-assessment tests, career forums, training in skills like teamwork, and a network of workers who will let you trail them to see what they do. The intention was for this to serve as a handhold on a new way of life. The idea was to shift the burden of managing a career onto the employee. The company's role would be to offer workers tools to expand their skills so that they remained employable, whether at Chase or elsewhere. Anyone at any level could use the tools, but none was mandatory.

Now there are Career Development Centers, like the one at Two Chase Manhattan Plaza. There are counselors at the ready. There is a makeshift career library, actually just two stout bookcases containing some tapes, Chase training manuals, and a familiar run of self-help career nostrums: "The Age of Paradox," "Swim with the Dolphins," "Knock 'Em Dead," "Anger at Work," "The Age of Unreason," "Don't Shoot Yourself in the Foot." All of this, though, means a chameleon-like change for workers, one particularly tough for longtime employees having trouble accepting the justness of it. Chase could not say whether it was succeeding. "It's too early to say," Mr. Farrell said. "We're continuing to tweak it."

Clearly, though, this feel-good approach was having a hard time of it in an environment of lost jobs. A lot of employees regarded it as little more than "happy talk" and as some sort of political campaign intended to mask the fact that their jobs were being pillaged. The whole corporation creaked under the weight of the merger. "They were constantly surveying us to see how we felt," a marketing manager said. "Your compensation was even partly tied to employee satisfaction. The third-quarter survey determined your bonus. I would tell people, don't be stupid enough to say you were unhappy on that survey. But the truth is, we were unhappy. At one meeting, the senior marketing guy screamed at us, 'I'm sick and tired of you guys complaining. If you're unhappy, leave.' We were shocked. We got yelled at for being unhappy. That made us even more unhappy."

A goodly number of workers were openly bitter about what they saw as a cartoon substitute for security and decent pay. In any event, with their jobs in doubt, they felt uncomfortable spending days away from their duties trying to psychoanalyze themselves. As one Chase vice president expressed it, "To a lot of us, Career Vision is like the Energizer Rabbit clickety-clacking through Bosnia."

A Survivor's Cynicism

In effect, he had become a white-collar factory worker. Punch him in. Watch him run when the evening bell sounds. He is a business analyst at Chase, ten years with the company. He had been through smaller downsizings in 1987 and 1991. One group he was in was entirely eradicated. The sepulchral air was getting to him. "Everyone is extremely guarded and paranoid," he said. "From the official communications, we're getting more babble, quotes from speeches and rah-rah stuff, and we're beyond that."

Even though the chances are good he will keep his job, he has been transformed. One disturbing truism of the new workplace is that downsizing has its insidious effect on survivors, too. "The merger has eliminated for me a certain motivation and all risk-taking, because this boy was a risk-taker," he said. "I went into areas that no one else wanted to go into. I did a lot of confrontation and tried my best to make it constructive and changed things. I shoot for the moon and I settle for a little rock. I'm not doing that anymore. We've all become soldiers. We will obey whatever is said and will not challenge. Since the merger, it's just a nine-to-five job for me."

A manager in another department said the mood had changed in other ways, too: "People are a lot less amenable to being absorbed into the work culture. It's pay me, don't play with me. Don't give me an employee picnic. They're acting like independent contractors. And they're more suspicious of management. Employees are less willing to participate in employee surveys, even though they're anonymous. They feel they are coded in some way."

Recently, the business analyst has rooted for his deeper satisfactions elsewhere. His hobby being photography, he has settled on a quest to establish a local arts center in his New Jersey town. He now sees that as his driving focus. "The only way they could get rid of me is to terminate my position," he said of his Chase job. "And there are always gas stations to pump and there are always 7-Elevens, and I'd seriously be willing to do that. I guess the merger has directed me to pursue my passion of starting an arts center, no matter what that takes."

Burned out of corporate life. He is 43.

The Art of the Layoff

There is an actual Merger Office. Not a physical room per se, but a "virtual office" made up of some twenty people from the two banks. Chemical's chief administrative officer, a man named Joseph Sponholz, presides over its daily workings. It is this entity that concerns itself with the monumental arcana of stitching together the two huge companies, and to do so it relies on a tool it calls MOM—the Merger Overview Model—a piece of computer software that keeps track of everything that has been done and has to be done. On a minute-by-minute basis, it wrestles with an equation that is supposed to produce $1.5 billion in savings over three years and eliminate 12,000 people.

Mr. Sponholz, as MOM's daddy, gave a sense of the routine, which he likened to preparing for D-Day. First, "mapping" teams with representatives from both banks compiled facts about the Chase and Chemical departments that could be used to plan their integration. These were supposed to be stark facts, with no subjective judgments, the whole point being to get Chemical and Chase people doing things together without animosity. Other integration teams, then, did the harder stuff: Managers were put in place, starting from the top and moving down the pyramid, and business integration plans were hashed out. Among the most important early decisions had to do with technology. Branches, for instance, can't be merged until it is decided which check-clearing system to use.

When Chemical combined with Manufacturers Hanover, Mr. Sponholz said, things moved too slowly, exacerbating anxiety. Rather than go individual system by system, as it did last time, Chemical bunched related systems into forty-one groups it called "suites." That meant fewer decisions and fewer emotional spats. People became attached to their systems and felt wounded if they weren't picked. As Michael Urkowitz, who was in charge of integrating the consumer credit unit, put it, "It would be analogous to being told that your child is not the most gifted in the class."

As early suites were chosen, Chemical usually seemed to have the winning hand. Deposits systems: Chemical. Statements and ATMs: Chemical. Check processing: Chemical. It was decided that the trading floor would be consolidated at Chemical's headquarters. The final count, however, was sixteen Chemical suites, fifteen Chase, and ten joint.

Judging the human beings themselves was trickier going. Chase executives call eliminated people "saves," an affable-sounding notion resonant of the achievements of relief pitchers. In this case, it denotes savings to the company, thus positioning laid-off people as something of a corporate asset. Chase hopes to get a third of the saves from layoffs, a third from retirements, and a third from attrition. Companies have traditionally preferred to conceal their attrition, because the concept has a foul odor to it, but Chase said it experiences roughly 20 percent turnover a year. Of course, this occurs unevenly. Vice chairmen hang around; tellers in Manhattan turn over at a 50 percent clip. To weed out the people, managers have received a 26-page booklet titled "Companywide Guiding Principles for Selection." It stipulates criteria like employee performance, "value to the organization," and "skills important in a merger or rapidly changing environment." It frowns on seeking a balance of people from the two banks "for the sake of balancing alone."

On the delicate matter of affirmative action, Chase management says it knows that the Federal Equal Employment Opportunity Commission sees a red flag if the makeup of a downsized department deviates more than 3 to 4 percent from its original demographics. Hence Chase's wish is that the layoffs not breach that barrier.

 The New York Times POLL

Worried that their grip on their jobs is loosening, most workers say they are willing to make concessions to employers if it would help save their jobs. They are especially willing to get more training and work longer hours; a cut in pay or benefits would go down harder.

■ If it might increase your chances of keeping a job, would you...

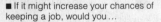

| ALL RESPONDENTS WHO ARE WORKING OR WANT TO BE | THOSE ALREADY HARD-HIT BY A LAYOFF | | ALL RESPONDENTS WHO ARE WORKING OR WANT TO BE | THOSE ALREADY HARD-HIT BY A LAYOFF |

...Get more training or education

Yes 93% Yes 95%

...Work longer hours

82% 87%

Managers readily admit, however, that there is no distilling human emotion from such an imprecise process, and that politics and long-term bonds will surely figure in the equation.

The selection booklet offers sample fill-in-the-name scripts for meetings with "nonselected" employees. Such as: "Today is your last day with the company. Please turn over your files on the ABC project to (name of employee) and spend a few minutes bringing him up to speed." Or: "The merger of Chase and Chemical will result in changes to the structure of many business units. As you know, our unit and the jobs in it are affected by these changes. Unfortunately, a. You were not selected for a position in . . . b. Your job has been eliminated from the new organization. Your last active day in the unit will be (date)."

The booklet suggests that the message be terse and unapologetic, and the whole nasty matter wrapped up within

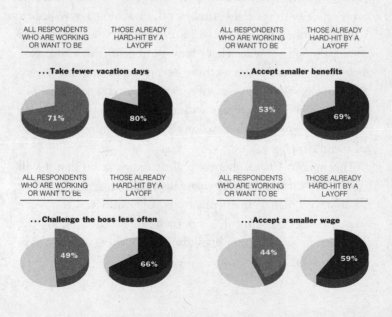

| ALL RESPONDENTS WHO ARE WORKING OR WANT TO BE | THOSE ALREADY HARD-HIT BY A LAYOFF | ALL RESPONDENTS WHO ARE WORKING OR WANT TO BE | THOSE ALREADY HARD-HIT BY A LAYOFF |

...Take fewer vacation days   **...Accept smaller benefits**

71%   80%   53%   69%

| ALL RESPONDENTS WHO ARE WORKING OR WANT TO BE | THOSE ALREADY HARD-HIT BY A LAYOFF | ALL RESPONDENTS WHO ARE WORKING OR WANT TO BE | THOSE ALREADY HARD-HIT BY A LAYOFF |

...Challenge the boss less often   **...Accept a smaller wage**

49%   66%   44%   59%

five to ten minutes. It offers some additional tips: "Don't provide extensive justification for the decision"; "don't engage in discussions about past performance"; "use silence to give the employee an opportunity to react to the news"; "you may need to restate the message to insure that the employee knows that the decision is final and has been made at the highest level." The booklet notes that employees will have four primary reactions: denial, anger, sadness, withdrawal. Precautions: Be sure to restrict access to confidential files and computer systems; if strong reactions are anticipated, alert Security and Medical. Still more tips: avoid terminating people on their birthday or anniversary date with the company (alas, managers confessed they have not bothered to research birthdays or anniversaries), and look for signs of anxiety among employees—i.e., withdrawal, unshaven appearance, weird habits. An employee relations counselor gave an example from another downsizing company: For weeks, a man sat in his office with the lights turned off, clutching a newspaper.

At the moment, most layoffs are still in the indefinable future, though some workers have gotten notice. The severance packages are sweet as these corporate arrangements go: three weeks salary per year of service, 26 extra weeks of pay for those who have 25 years with the company, plus a $2,500 grant that can be applied to any sort of training, including ballroom dancing.

Throughout Chase, there is a clear expectation that it will experience carnage heavier than Chemical. Time will tell. For the first 300 management positions, Chemical said the score was 53 percent Chemical, 47 percent Chase. But among the positions of power, the breakdown is closer to 60–40 in Chemical's favor.

Mr. Sponholz said he was cognizant of the current jitters and swarm of rumors. "We learned last time that employees get very anxious," he said. "So being as open and forthright as we can be is very important. We're doing a lot of communications."

Gallows Humor

The news comes right to every employee's desk, in a neat, multi-page newsletter titled Merger Update. They can have it on paper and by E-mail. The missives appear roughly every other week. Some contain an opening message signed "Walter" for Walter Shipley and "Tom" for Tom Labrecque. There are also town meetings. There is also a 24-hour hot line for merger questions. There are voice-mail messages from senior officers before key announcements. There are seminars. One subject: "What is a merger?"

To many workers, however, the material is saccharine and platitudinous, and it never tells them what they really want to know: Do I have a job? Employees, listening to the hollow sound of impermanence, have put their own mordantly black spin on things. They refer to the hot line as 1-800-PINK-SLIP. When Chemical and Manufacturers Hanover merged, employees referred to the combination as Comical Hangover. Around the office coolers at Chase and Chemical today, the workers are calling the new union Chasical or Chi-Chi's. And, feeling the need to amplify on the incomplete communiqués, they have distributed some sardonic Merger Updates of their own.

One mock memo, ostensibly from Mr. Labrecque, under "Frequently Asked Questions":

"Why did the merger happen?

"To bring into existence the best banking and financial services company in the world, bar none, without par, without equal, post no bills, void where prohibited."

And: "Why am I facing layoffs, why is my career in ruins, why can't I sleep at night?

"Your largely insignificant life is being sacrificed to bring into existence the best banking and financial services company in the world, bar none, without par, without equal, post no bills, void where prohibited."

And: "How has the Labrecque family been affected by the merger?

"People ask me this wherever I go. I am sad to report that the two weeks in Bimini scheduled for mid-September have, tragically, been rescheduled for early January because a few selfish 'bad apple' non-team players at both Chase and Chemical demanded that we finish the second-tier organizational chart before I left. Scuba lessons had to be rescheduled. Paolo, the massage boy, had to be paid despite the cancellation. Substantial penalties were paid on the Supersaver airfares due to cancellation less than three weeks prior to embarkation. My travel agent is seriously miffed and not speaking to my special assistant in charge of accommodations. In short, the merger has been an inconvenience for all of us, but it is a necessary inconvenience if we want to create the best banking and financial services company in the world, bar none, without par, without equal, post no bills, void where prohibited."

And: "When will I know if I'm being laid off?

"You, you, you, is that all you care about, you? Please understand that we need to think about 'us,' which probably doesn't include you. It's about time you started to think about the greater whole, buddy. It should be an honor to be laid off."

Advice on how everyone can help make the transition smoother: "If you're hired by 'Chasical,' get down on your knobby knees and thank your maker that you've been selected to join the best banking and financial services company in the world, bar none, without par, without equal, post no bills, void where prohibited by law. If you're fired, be a man about it (even if you're a woman). Don't complain, 'Boo hoo, I got fired.' 'Boo hoo, they're going to foreclose on my mortgage.' 'Boo hoo, my kids have no money for food and clothes.' This is counterproductive and may detract from the efficiency of the new worker we're trying to install at your desk."

Advice on how to insure a job at the new Chase: "Take your boss to lunch. Buy him/her a gift (under the $250 limit, please). Tell him/her over and over again that your only hope, dream and aspiration is to serve for little or no pay and work inhuman hours to make this place the best banking and financial services company in the world, bar none, without par, without equal, post no bills, void where prohibited."

Washed Up at Twenty-nine

Fast-food lunch at the South Street Seaport with a young, emphatically pragmatic woman with a rather short employment history as a second vice president with Chase. Eating pizza with a glazed look, she gave the crucial shape of her department, similar to the form many Chase departments were taking. The newly named boss was from Chemical. Of the ten people directly beneath him, six are from Chemical, four from Chase. Her odds, she reasoned, were not outstanding. "I'm fairly new," she said. "So if they do last in, first out, I'm dust."

Gripped by lassitude, she said her productivity had dropped. She felt implacable despair. With the secret speed of clock hands, a malaise had set in, a pervasive sense of spiritual sickness which undermined her normally buoyant nature. Mornings blended into afternoons into evenings. Until recently, she had two roommates, and she saw their lives as a modern corporate allegory. All three are 29, and all three graduated from college expecting long and prospering business careers. In the last few years, one roommate was downsized from Manufacturers Hanover. The other was downsized from Atlantic Records. And, after a reorganization, she had lost her job at a previous bank she wishes to remain unnamed. It took her two months to connect with Chase.

"Here we are, all having been in the same boat," the woman said of their abridged job paths. "We've all lost jobs, and we're not even thirty, an age when you're supposed to be highly desirable at corporations. I'll never forget the day my roommate came home with her boxes. The same day she was notified, she had to clear out. She was twenty-five. I don't get it. Is the world crazy or am I going crazy?" Everyone in her department, she said, was punchy and touchy. There was a tension and a fatalism that never really went away. "If you come in five minutes late from lunch, they start, 'Oh, were you out on an interview?' " Someone recently circulated a fictitious memo outlining the latest Chase early-retirement program. The age requirement had been lowered. Eligibility began at age 35. "A lot of people at Chase are fairly optimistic," she said. "They haven't gotten it yet. I'm pessimistic, because I've been through this. There are people from my previous job who are still at the outplacement office I used to be at. That was two years ago."

She finished her pizza, leaving the crust. She wanted to walk. "I think there is going to be a backlash. Maybe not this

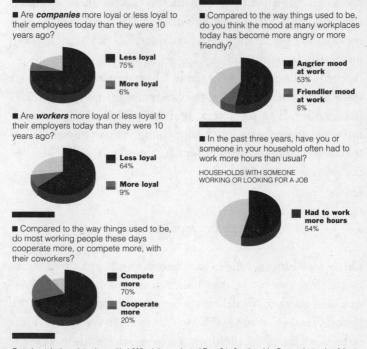

The New York Times POLL

Economic insecurity and fear of losing a job gnaw at workers still on the job. Poll respondents see the bonds of loyalty between employees and companies and the spirit of friendly cooperation among employees being eroded by anxiety and pressure to work harder for less.

■ Are **companies** more loyal or less loyal to their employees today than they were 10 years ago?

■ **Less loyal** 75%
■ **More loyal** 6%

■ Are **workers** more loyal or less loyal to their employers today than they were 10 years ago?

■ **Less loyal** 64%
■ **More loyal** 9%

■ Compared to the way things used to be, do most working people these days cooperate more, or compete more, with their coworkers?

■ **Compete more** 70%
■ **Cooperate more** 20%

■ Compared to the way things used to be, do you think the mood at many workplaces today has become more angry or more friendly?

■ **Angrier mood at work** 53%
■ **Friendlier mood at work** 8%

■ In the past three years, have you or someone in your household often had to work more hours than usual?

HOUSEHOLDS WITH SOMEONE WORKING OR LOOKING FOR A JOB

■ **Had to work more hours** 54%

Based on telephone interviews with 1,265 adults conducted Dec. 3 to 6 nationwide. Respondents who did not answer, did not know, or thought there had been no change are included in totals but not labeled separately. "Those already hard-hit by a layoff" means people who said they or someone in their households had been laid off at least once in the last 15 years, and that the layoffs had caused crises in their lives.

year, maybe not next year, but there's going to be one. People aren't going to give 100 percent anymore. I see this with a lot of my friends. I'm not going to be like my dad and work till ten o'clock at night and never see the kids. What for? So I'll be thanked with a pink slip?

"I think it all has to do with Wall Street. Every day, there's that stock price staring at you. If it's too low, managers say, 'Why, let's get rid of some more people and watch it rise.' I wish corporate executives could see all the faces of these people they're downsizing. I wish they could see them shopping for food and putting their kids to bed. All they seem to care about is the bottom line. And therefore all of us are nothing but Social Security numbers."

For months now, a good many Chase employees have been using their work phones quite openly and shamelessly to market themselves to recruiters, searching for escape hatches. A month after her pizza lunch, the young woman herself bailed out of her wobbly encampment to a new job with a smaller company in another state.

The View from the Top

On an easel in his office, Tom Labrecque keeps three stick-figure drawings of the sort children accomplish in art class. Actually, they are the dabblings of Chase workers. During the Vision Quest exercise, everyone was asked to sketch the "ideal state" for Chase. People drew Chase castles with merry figures dancing about them, Chase boats sailing to a future celebrated by dollar signs, people trooping across the "Vision Quest bridge." Mr. Labrecque chose three to keep on permanent display as reminders of the dream.

Mr. Labrecque said he appreciated the churning emotions of employees: the anxiety and despair, and even feelings that the dream had been abandoned. But he said that plenty of people shared his optimism, and that the uglier part was the unfortunate cost of a seismic transition to what he believed was an inevitable and healthier environment. "Since 1985, we've been going through a secular change as great as the Industrial Revolution. And we don't know how it will turn out. But I think the assumption that it will turn out to be a negative is a wrong bet. And yet that does not take one minute away from the micro-negatives that are going on."

He acknowledged the primal anger about the dimensions and frequency of layoffs, but said that this was an unnatural phase because companies had misguidedly deferred layoffs for so long: "If you've got fifteen years worth of backlog in downsizing, the downsizings will be more severe." And he recognized that there were generational divides: "The people under thirty-five are much more flexible than the people who are over forty-five." It was evident to him, he said, that workers who found the new world unpalatable would have to leave the company. There was a Chase person thinking of opening a plant store, someone pondering becoming a park ranger, someone else contemplating a new life as a missionary. Mr. Labrecque thought this was splendid. He said he had heard from severed people who were working for charities at half their banking pay. He said they were happy.

Mr. Labrecque is an imposing man who gives off a steely-cool, confident demeanor. When asked if he felt emotion over the forsaken jobs, he fell silent for a few moments. "I wouldn't be human if it didn't affect me. I've been working these issues for thirty-five years. I've faced a lot of crises. In the service, I was one of two people finishing the amputation of somebody's hand because no one else was there. Does that affect you? Sure it does. But if you're doing what you think is right for everyone involved, then you're fine. So I'm fine."

Thomas G. Labrecque, chief executive of Chase Manhattan, has cut 10,000 jobs with more to come. "If you're doing what you think is right for everyone involved, then you're fine. So I'm fine."

War Stories

One Chase worker related the experience of her downsized friend. The human-resources person who delivered the fatal decision accepted her corporate ID and told the woman she would have to cancel her free checking account. Then she handed her some paperwork. With a weak smile, she explained that it was an application to start an account of her own with the bank.

"Don't you dare," the woman said, shooting her a death look. She threw the application at the functionary and stomped out.

Not all human-resources people, of course, are so oafish. How, then, do the executioners live with themselves? A human-resources person who has given scores of employees their end-of-job news spoke to the issue succinctly: "Thank God for Budweiser." Another: "It's like a police officer or a fireman. You find a dead body in a building, you can't take it personally." Another, who had dismissed 500 employees and counting, was more expansive: "At first, it hurt in the stomach in the morning. It may seem callous, but after a while there's a sort of numbing. You go through the steps without getting too emotional. And you think to yourself, 'When will my day come to be on the other side of the desk?' That, in the end, is how you live with it. You realize that everyone's day will come on the other side of the desk."

As for his own future, he was reasonably sanguine. He knew his department would lose people. "I know what needs to be done to survive," he said. "Just be quick on your feet. I've laid the groundwork over the last three years in terms of networking. I've made sure I know the right people. I've made sure I was a generalist, not a specialist." But in the new world, he felt he had another important qualification on his résumé: He had eliminated hundreds of people with nary a complication. "We had only one lawsuit in the group I was responsible for. It was dismissed after one hearing. That record counts in my favor." A good man, in other words, in a corporate storm.

Many Chase employees have been through rounds of layoffs, but not a big merger, and they are entirely different beasts in the trauma they unleash. As Chase people have talked to more and more Chemical people, they have gleaned some sense of how this all goes. Chemical employees, after all, did the drill with Manufacturers Hanover.

To wit:

The head of one group at Chemical notified the employees beneath him that after the reorganization jobs would be eliminated. Right away, a secretary in the group began bringing to work issues of *Guns and Ammo* magazine. She would point out to her boss particular weapons being advertised and say offhandedly, "What do you think of this? Wouldn't it be a good gun to get?"

A bluff? Serious stuff? A few weeks later, the staffing decisions completed, the secretary was among those let go. A human-resources officer broke the news to her in a cold sweat, with an armed security guard posted outside the door. As it happened, there was no gun or violence. The secretary simply cried.

Elsewhere in Chemical, a group of fifteen people was downsized to one. The woman who was left felt incredible guilt. "I cried for two days," she said. "Some of these people were my dear friends. One was very bitter at me, because he had more tenure." For five months, until she was transferred, the woman attempted to tackle the work of the fifteen. She toiled through sixteen-hour days. She reported each morning to a work area designed for fifteen people. She sat alone, surrounded by fourteen empty desks, feeling as if she were in one of those creepy end-of-the-world movies.

A merger survivor described the pronounced post-merger change in workload: "In the old days, it was nine to five with room for lunch. Now it's nine to ten with time for lunch every now and then. People are carrying over more vacation days than ever before. They can't get the work done. A lot of people in this bank are saying to themselves, 'If I survive this new merger, do I even want the job?' I'm one of those people."

The Purge in Legal

The lawyers heard first. The news came December 13, two days after Chemical threw a Christmas party for the Chemical and Chase attorneys. How absurd the party seemed now. There were Chase and Chemical lawyers flagrantly fawning over the senior managers. Little did they know it was too late. The decisions had already been made. Of Chase's 126 lawyers, 38 were told that their Chase careers were over. Chemical dismissed 15 of its 150 lawyers. And so they became the first department to be fully downsized. Or almost fully downsized. It seemed evident to the lawyers that too many managers were kept, doubtlessly to smooth the transition, and that some of them would eventually vanish as well.

Being fired is always the same, but each person takes it in his own way. Some ego-bruised lawyers began to chatter in denial of the truth. Some left at once, banging doors behind them. There was a lot of anger. Many felt that a disproportionate number of women and workers with abbreviated hours were eliminated. (There were rumors that only the women were let go, which was not the case.) One woman spoke of a class-action suit. It was also noticed that youth seemed to carry weight. A group of eight lawyers was eliminated except for one man, the youngest of them. "We heard at the beginning that Chemical wanted a staff that would carry it into the twenty-first century, and that meant young people," one lawyer said. "It's depressing when people look at you askance because of your age—and your age is forty."

Chase said the statistical reality was this: Of the 53 eliminated lawyers, 30 were women and 30 were older than 40. The proportion of women fell by three percentage points, while the proportion of men increased by three percentage points. The proportion of lawyers over 40 actually rose by one percentage point. Only one minority lawyer was fired, but there were just 14 to begin with.

To the survivors, the place seemed suddenly cold. Time drifted by without touching them. People felt remorse for those who hadn't made it: a pregnant woman, a woman on maternity leave, a woman who had just adopted a child, a man with three children and a wife at home.

People carry a version of their lives with them, of who they are, and most of the time they think they know. Now some of the lawyers were unclear of even the most rudimentary script. It did not take much to get them to fulminate about their plight. "You get jaded," one of the lawyers remarked. "I'm jaded. They use deals like this to whip people to work harder. It's fear. And people burn out. But modern management thinks, okay, they burn out, they burn out. They'll bring in new people. We're all fungible. I think it's management that should be made to walk the plank. I don't think our management did the best for us people. I think it's a sickness in corporate America that the senior management thinks they own the corporation. And I don't know where this sickness ends." A biting joke made the rounds: "The good news is you have a job. The bad news is you have a job."

One of the fired lawyers, a woman with young children, said she felt beaten down by it all. She was trying not to dwell on her condition. She found it hard to imagine ever working for a big corporation again. Then again, she couldn't be sure what she would do. "You hear all this talk about how this strange new environment can be great for people; they get pushed to do things they always wanted to do, like open a flower shop or a pet store. Well, guess what? Most people would like a job. Most people aren't entrepreneurs. They would like a place to go each day and collect a paycheck and have someone at the desk next to them. We're pushing up against the possibilities for a lot of people. It's not like we can all load our goods into a covered wagon and go out West and farm some land with a hoe. And a lot of those people died. They died."

The lawyers found Career Vision and the Chase determination to be the "employer of choice" all so irrelevant now. "Yeah, employer of choice," one of the eliminated lawyers said. "Some choice. I assume they're not still holding those career workshops and all, are they? What's the point? Who would go?"

Modern Re-education

The Managing Your Career workshop was being held in downtown Brooklyn in the big Metro-Tech building where some 6,000 Chase employees work. Fourteen Chase vice presidents had assembled for one of the more basic offerings in the Career Vision program. The room was furnished with a cluster of a half-dozen office-drab tables, and had the aroma of institutional sterility and daily housekeeping. Lying on the tables before each of the participants was a glossy three-ring binder, and the previous inhabitants seemed to have left behind an air of exhausted potential.

The workshop extended over two days, and much of this beginning part dwelled on various self-administered psychological tests intended to afford the takers a sense of who they are and what work situations best suited them. In actuality, a number of the employees confided that the central reason they had signed up was to meet people, thereby broadening their network of contacts who may help them if they need a job. One man, though, called it his "40,000-mile checkup, to see if I ought to be working at a bank or playing the saxophone."

The facilitator gave a little spiel: "When we first started doing this course, people thought it would be to provide everyone with a new job. That really is not something you should expect. What you should expect is to learn something about yourself so you can go out there and do the right thing for yourself." There was some rustling and murmuring in the room. With a crisp cheerfulness, she went on to state that one of the objectives was to develop strategies for anticipating and adapting to change. "Nothing could be more relevant right now," she said. "Change is it. We're knee-deep in it."

There was more rustling.

The facilitator suggested a little experiment. "Take a piece of paper and sign your name," she said. When everyone had finished, she asked, "How was that?"

"Easy," someone said.

"Comfortable," replied another student.

"Like duck soup, like falling off a log," the facilitator said. "Okay, now put the pen in your other hand and sign your name."

Everyone struggled.

"How did that feel?" the facilitator asked.

"Terrible," a woman said.

"Imagine if you had to write with your left hand in your job all day," she said.

"I think I would type," someone said.

The facilitator explained in a declamatory voice that the exercise was intended as a metaphor for those who had not managed their careers well enough so that they did not fit their jobs. But in fact it was a metaphor for the work environment at Chase. The instability and pervasive paranoia in the air made all of them feel as if they were writing with the wrong hand.

Now people went over their scores on the Myers-Briggs Type Indicator, a test based on the typology of Carl Jung that intends to identify a person's style. The facilitator went around the room to hear the ratings. People spoke of being I's (introverts) and E's (extroverts). They were F's (feeling people) and T's (thinking people). They were also to rate their jobs to see if they possessed extroverted jobs or feeling jobs or whatever, and then determine if they matched.

"My test shows that I'm definitely an I, but I think my job is really for an E," one man said. "Or maybe it's for an I who's in-between being an E."

"Isn't that interesting?" the facilitator said.

There was something utterly surreal about it all. Upstairs and across town, people would soon be getting news they hoped never to face. Some of these very people could be among them. Yet they were being asked to assure themselves that they fit well in a job that might no longer be theirs.

One woman said, "I took the test several times and came out an F. That's the reason I kept taking it, because at work I definitely operate as a T."

The facilitator said, "How do you feel about that?"

A Chase vice president shared some entries from her diary.

Sept. 20. Things to work on:

1. Get drapes for bedroom (can I afford a rug, too?).
2. Lose 10 pounds.
3. Find a new job.

Nov. 12. Things to work on:

1. Think about hosting Thanksgiving or going to cousin Bob's (Life is too short!).
2. Lose 5 pounds.
3. Find a new job.

Jan. 4. Things to work on:

1. Find a new job.
2. Find a new job.
3. Find a new job.

Watch Your Back

One way employees at Chase have tried to hedge their bets is to establish their own informal networks throughout the bank and the larger world of work. They keep lists of people with whom they try to keep in touch. That way they have contacts if doomsday comes. One man showed his own collection. He kept it in a grade school-type composition book. It was alphabetized and included 107 names. He flipped to T. "I just got this one yesterday," he said. "Guy I met in the men's room."

Networks, though, have also been buckling under the strain. People are getting tired of fielding calls from colleagues in pursuit of work. Moreover, with companies constantly downsizing, it is colleague pitted against colleague in a Darwinian struggle. The person at the next desk may be your co-worker and teammate, but he is also your competitor if bodies must go in your department. A middle-aged man with wavy hair and a creased face told of how for years he has taken lunch practically every other day with a fellow worker in his department. They relished gossiping about the office, denigrating their boss, and complaining about the woeful state of the Jets and Giants. These lunches continued after the Chemical merger was announced, spiced now by hectoring. ("Heard from benefits lately?" "Checking out the trailer park?" "Get the five-year-old a job yet?") But then the man said he began to hear disturbing speculation. His department was likely to incur severe hits. He began to think of himself and his colleagues as the "walking dead."

He confided these developments to his wife. She told him to watch his back. The next morning, he noticed his friend in their boss's office, chuckling about something. His first thought was that he was politicking. Could it be possible he was badmouthing him? He quickly worked himself into a nervous lather. Later, he pleaded other commitments when the subject of lunch came up. The pair ate once a week for a while, and the conversations were more strained. Then they stopped having lunch altogether. The friend did not protest. Apparently, he, too, had consulted with his advisers and drawn similar conclusions.

Now they were both watching their backs.

This is what Chase's Employee Assistance Program had to say about the merger and its discontents: "Few people like change, especially a lot of it," the program's quarterly newsletter reported. "Change is hard for you to accept if you did not initiate it, do not understand it or do not approve of it. But once management decides to make a change, rarely does balking help. Your best bet is probably to work on modifying your attitude and accepting change."

The newsletter spelled out fourteen different steps workers could take if the stress was really gnawing at them. These included:

- Take control in those areas of your life where you can and let go of those things over which you have no control.
- Be sure to get adequate rest and eat nutritional meals regularly.
- Exercise regularly.
- Take time out to take deep breaths when feeling overwhelmed.
- Explore Career Vision offerings.
- Make time to enjoy yourself; use your On-the-Town card.
- Learn meditation, yoga, or some other form of relaxation.

For the employee assistance counselors, trouble is habitat, the very air they breathe. In the immediate aftermath of the merger announcement, far fewer people than usual presented themselves to speak with counselors. That was because workers were in shock. Almost everyone spent their days and evenings in a state of vague disbelief; if they talked about it, it would become real and the tension would graduate to actual fatalism. Once the shock wore off, however, people hit emotional trip wires, and considerably more than the normal quantity of stressed-out workers began showing up in quest of help. Through the chatter of simple observation and remarking that went on, evidence was discerned.

Hollis Evan works as the head of employee assistance; one of her jobs is to see her own caseload of patients. She is a small woman with short hair and empathic eyes. At times she was amazed to see the before- and after-effects of the merger.

"Most people pull in," she said. "They don't even talk to their family or their spouse. They don't want to worry them. They use other negative coping strategies. They drink. They eat more. They eat less. Some get angry and push people away. They explode. It's the whole kick-the-dog syndrome. They are the victims. 'This is happening to me! Why should this be happening to me? Who's out to get little old me?'

"The people in total denial, they won't show up saying they have a job-related problem. They come in mentioning other problems. Things are rough at home. The kid is acting up. They can't get along with the pets. What is really happening is they are projecting the stress onto others. The problem is them and their job.

"We have stress-support groups that meet once a week for six weeks. We do deep-breathing exercises. We concentrate on cognitive thinking, on developing a more realistic picture of what is going on. We talk about aerobic exercises."

Outside, the wind blew as if the world were empty. Ms. Evan stared out the window a moment, suppressed a yawn and then she said, "I have heard a lot of people talking about religion. About exploring their roots. About getting down to something basic, something that will say something to them. They want an answer. Trouble is, it's not an easy question."

The New Company Man

Is there a modern corporate employee, someone who accepts the new ways? What does he look like? How does he sound?

There are many paths into banking. Matt Hoffman came by piano. He is 35, grew up in Indiana, went to college in upstate New York to study music. For two years, he was a self-employed pianist in New York, doing gigs, playing at a restaurant in Rockland County, accompanying an elderly and abusive man who wanted to keep his voice in shape in his home.

The pace was too much. He decided to enter the business world. He began as a teller at a Westchester branch of Irving Trust. He was always a self-starter. On his lunch breaks, he didn't loiter with other tellers. He went and interrogated the mortgage people and the loan people, learning new things, and this led to swift promotions. Running out of challenges, he moved to Marine Midland as a business development officer and, five years ago, to Chase. He is a cluster manager overseeing several branches in Westchester. He never sought security in corporate work, and thus the merger doesn't especially throw him. He has embraced Chase's career assistance and felt he had sharpened his abilities, become a resilient worker. His background has given him an emphatically modern outlook on work. "I feel my job is to do the best that I possibly can, but my whole area could look totally different in five years through no fault of Chase," he said. "I can't imagine any corporate entity owes anyone a career."

By virtue of his background, Matt Hoffman is perhaps the archetypal corporate man of the future. His introduction to the world of work was a terrain where his paycheck depended on how well he sold himself each day. Nothing was guaranteed past tomorrow. No one could assure him that they would take care of him in declining years. He has imported that mindset into banking and, currently, into Chase, and he has found the fit to be all too perfect. For an odd reality of the new work environment is that the turbulent world of the freelance classical pianist is more alike than unlike the world of the corporate employee. He, too, has to sell himself every day, and he, too, doesn't know if the gig will be there tomorrow.

There are indeed other modern employees, usually young, who have seen this future and in some way accepted it for what it is. Look at Richard Fischer, a Chase customer repre-

Matt Hoffman may be a model of the new company man who does not see his job as an entitlement.

sentative in Bardonia, New York. He goes from work to school, pursuing his MBA with Chase paying the bills. He sincerely feels the merger will offer him more. "I feel I have a lot to offer Chase," he said. "If it came down to it, I'm not afraid of rolling up my sleeves and being a teller again." He has taken a self-assessment class at Chase, another in writing a résumé. "Even yesterday," he said, "I was in a class on how to interview." He was a business administration major in college, and learned about the future. "I remember we did a case study of workplace banking. It pointed out that before you turn thirty, you change jobs six times." He is 24.

A fair number of feisty, high-propane people at Chase relish the merger. They assume (not necessarily correctly) that they will retain their jobs and their roles will swell in importance. As one finance person put it, "There are a lot of people in their twenties who are saying to those who are unhappy, 'Don't screw up my opportunity to be somebody and make a lot of money in this bank.' There's a generational animosity." Throughout the bank, people are scrambling to position themselves. Donald Skelton, a safe deposit manager, is planning to go to college for the first time at night this summer, at the age of 46—assuming he is still employed. It was a rude awakening to him that, after twenty-five years at Chase, he makes less money than his daughter, who just graduated from college and began a computer programming job.

But the modern employee also has his own renegade scheme, with him, not any company, at the center. A 25-year-old business analyst explained his view: "Most people my age

Fred R. Conrad/*The New York Times*

Scrambling to improve his chances, Donald Skelton, a safe deposit manager at Chase, plans to go to night school this summer at age 46. He had a rude awakening after twenty-five years at the bank when he learned that his daughter, fresh out of college, earned more than he.

have come to work for a big company with the intention of getting the training and acquiring the skills they need to move on, and most people, myself included, really would like to either own their own company or work for a smaller company. People really don't have the loyalty they used to to a big company."

The crucial unanswered question is how far can you push these resilient people before they, too, break? How hard can you work them? How many times can they bounce from company to company and still smile?

The Last Hope

The end of the line is actually any of three floors—the fifth, eleventh, and twelfth—at 640 Fifth Avenue, near Rockefeller Center. These belong to the New York office of Right Associates, the nationwide outplacement firm. It is something of a human recycling bin, where downsized Chase workers take up temporary residence as they begin what Right counselors like to call their "marketing campaign." Right Associates offers elaborate services—career counseling, networking sessions (fliers were stacked up for a "senior human resources" networking meeting the next day for out-of-work human-resources executives looking for jobs paying in excess of $100,000), an office, abundant coffee, secretarial assistance, not to mention little fun events like periodic turkey raffles— at a cost to Chase of 16 to 20 percent of the employee's annual compensation. Receptionists fielding messages for the cast-off tenants make a point of answering the phone, "Executive offices," for outplacement itself is something of an industry of denial.

Unemployment may appear to be the great leveler, but there are hierarchies even among the jobless. The better your former job was, the more luxury accorded you while without it. With no outplacement operation of its own, Chase sends everyone—from tellers to what are known as the KEs, or key executives—to Right. What they get there, however, depends on rank. The lowest levels merit counseling and a cubicle for three months. The KEs get a private office on a separate floor and more elaborate nurturing for a year. Everyone, however, earns secretarial help. And while the KEs' lounge is posher, the lounge for the rank and file has a pool table. And it is probably true that people like tellers who are laid off from Chase will actually live better in their early days of unemployment than in employment. For the first time in their careers, they will have a desk and phone of their own, plus an underling to type letters.

People can come to outplacement as often as they like—once a day, once a week, or once a year. More often than not, attendance is arithmetically related to how desperately you need a new job and how disabled you are by lost confidence or straitened by fear. The large monetary settlements and years of stock options bestowed on the KEs tend to keep their attendance rather spotty. On balmy days, it was pointed out by Right counselors, the most likely place to find a KE is on the golf course.

Right Associates adjures its charges to stay highly visible. Dredge your memory and call everyone you are even faintly familiar with ("There's no telling who your vet knows," a counselor said. "Call the butcher. Maybe your plumber is a ditz, but he could be fixing the toilet of the executive vice president of Union Carbide.")

"You'd be amazed at the number of people who never bothered to network," said Nancy Geffner, the head of Right's New York office. "We had a person who for twenty years never once left the executive dining room. Did he even go to the bank? Not him. He had a staff person do it. People at the very high levels don't have a clue about how to find a job. They never had to. It's interesting, but these people don't do much of anything on their own. They can't use a computer. They can't type. They're fairly helpless. The truth is, the top group needs the most help."

Andrea Eisenberg, the account manager for eliminated Chase workers, said she had gleaned certain, somewhat different, traits about these people. They had strong networks. They were intelligent. And, despite the recurrent dire news about the shrinking banking world, almost to the person they wished to remain in banking. "That's unusual," she said. "A certain percentage in other places want to rethink what they're doing." Another characteristic, she said, was that they were in shock. "Even though there's all this going on, they're surprised it happened to them."

Walking through the floors and looking in on the cubicles and offices, Nancy Geffner nodded at the spartan furnishings—a desk, two chairs, and a plant. "We don't make them too fancy," she said, "because we don't want them to move in." It was a chill, gray day around the Christmas holidays. Ms. Geffner peeked in on a man with his chin propped up on his fist, staring out the window. She remarked, "This time of year, we have to watch people carefully. No job, other people happy—you know."

By now, one middle-aged woman had come close to spending as many days at Right Associates as she had at Chase. She was downsized early last year. She had passed through mourning and was well into acceptance. "If someone says, 'Gee, Chase was wonderful for setting up all those employee programs,' that gets me going," she said. "But after the initial detoxification period, you get over the anger. I wouldn't recommend Chase to anyone, but I'm over the anger." She cleared her throat. "I've changed. I used to think that having a stable job reflected on your moral integrity and your being a solid human being. Now when I see people doing flaky things to make money—say, opening a muffin stand—I say, 'Go for it.' We were talking about this in one of our groups here, of thinking outside the box. Someone said, 'Hey, there is no box.' "

She went on: "If companies keep having this constantly revolving workforce, the company has no memory. It's like it's continually giving itself a lobotomy. It's not a good thing to not have a memory." She had to leave, to go out into the gray, bone-cold dusk to her apartment and her cat. She mentioned that she keeps a collection of the Chase coffee cups inscribed with the Chase values in her kitchen as some sort of comical reminder of the day that catapulted her into outplacement. "I look at the cups and laugh," she said. "They're funny now."

Did she use them?

"Oh, no," she said. "I never drink out of them. They probably leak."

3

Where Dignity Used to Be

Rick Bragg

THE TWO MIDDLE-AGED men live only a few Southern California freeway miles apart, in different worlds. One man feels complete only when he is in a suit; the other feels strangled by even the idea of a tie. One managed people; the other worked with his hands. Yet if they ever chanced to meet, talk, to share the best and worst times of their lives, James Sharlow and Robert Muse would feel as if they were gazing into a mirror. Both men have been laid off from jobs that powered and defined their lives, jobs that ended with those lives yet unbuilt. In both, the experience left a hole that lets their pride leak through; so many months later, they still search for something substantial enough to patch it.

Mr. Sharlow was the operations manager for a plant in the San Fernando Valley, a boss with mutual funds and tropical dreams who worked so many nights and weekends in his gradual ascent that he missed big chunks of his daughters' childhoods. His plant was closed three years ago.

Mr. Muse was a machinist in Torrance, an aircraft worker who was so proud of his work and so enamored of jets that he scanned the quitting-time sky for vapor trails as he flew his car along Hawthorne Boulevard. The machine shop where he worked has been closed two years now.

Both men feel they failed their wives, failed their children. Failed. Both men feel that they were lulled into a false sense of security by corporations that assured them they were part of a broader company family. Yet both men still slip sometimes and refer to their old employers as "my" company, and if they had the chance they would go back in a heartbeat, all forgiven. They are alike the way millions of other laid-off workers are alike, cast aside in the name of corporate survival, marketplace advantage, irresistible pressure from Wall Street. The difference in James Sharlow and Robert Muse is in the depth of the fall, and the force of the landing.

Mr. Muse ended up as a maintenance man, making enough money, barely, to keep his family's modest house, to keep them just this side of a growing population of new poor. His new job is just a job, but he holds to it tight, like a drowning man catching a trailing rope from a passing ship, grateful.

Mr. Sharlow had money in the bank, and he continues to prop up his family's old lifestyle with dwindling savings. Yet in some ways his descent was much more drastic, and so it has been harder to accept, to check. He goes to sleep wondering if he and his wife, Gayle, can salvage their retirement dreams, and their hard-earned image of themselves, with an executive position before they drain the future dry. For three years he held out for a job that would put them back into their old lives before finally making a decision that he dreaded, hated.

While Mr. Muse's fall was shorter in some ways, there is a sickening realization that it might not be over. He goes to sleep wondering if his new, low-paying work will last long enough to pay off the mortgage, and if he and his wife, Nancy, will live out their days on Social Security, waiting at the mailbox every first of the month for the government check, scheduling their lives around it.

Both men worry that their wives and children think less of them, but although both families have been tugged, twisted, and strained by the missing money and the pressure it caused, they remain intact. They are held together by love, however corny that sounds, and by the simple fact that they need each other now more than ever. One man firmly believes he will rejoin his old life. Mr. Sharlow has sent out thousands of résumés. He studies business and trade journals, so he can keep his knowledge fresh. Mr. Muse knows that he can probably never work again in an industry altered forever by the rise of the global economy and the fall of the Iron Curtain. Yet he keeps up with developments and reads trade magazines, on the slimmest chance, or a tiny miracle, that the shutdown factories will whir to life again.

For Mr. Muse and Mr. Sharlow, the past is like an antique car parked in the garage. It may no longer run, but you still like to sit in it, now and then, to smell the leather.

The Good Life Lost

To the beggars downtown that autumn day, every wing-tipped stride of James E. Sharlow seemed to resonate with prosperity. His suit was boardroom gray, his tie was red silk, his creases as crisp as fresh money. One ragged man sidled up to him with a sad story and an outstretched palm. "Excuse me, sir," he said, "but could you spare five dollars? I've got a family to feed. I haven't worked for a long time."

"Me either, fella," Mr. Sharlow said, and kept walking. In the 1990s, he has learned through bitter experience, discarded workers come in rags and Ralph Lauren.

He met some friends for lunch—laid-off, white-collar, middle-aged men like himself—and paid his tab with money drawn from his retirement accounts. Then he slid into his shiny black Mercedes, the one with the badly slipping transmission, and followed the Ronald Reagan Expressway home to the house and life in the San Fernando Valley that he can no longer afford.

The 51-year-old Mr. Sharlow lost his $130,000-a-year job in January 1993 when the plant he managed was shut down, permanently. After giving twenty-six years of his life and loyalty to one big corporation, Eastman Kodak, he found himself chasing white-collar jobs in a market already glutted with unemployed manufacturing executives. For Mr. Sharlow, his wife and two grown daughters, it is not only a matter of temporarily doing without new cars, nice vacations, and unbridled trips to the mall, but a steadily creeping unease that their downsized existence could be permanent. More than anything, they all want the layoff to be only a ripple in their old life, not the beginning of a new one. "I believe in the American dream," he said, with a resistance that is part pride, part hope, part denial. "I feel it fading. I still believe."

So while the layoff has eroded his dreams of retirement and stolen his family's long-range security, it has not, on the surface at least, greatly changed the look of their lives. Mr. Sharlow always saved, and over the years put away about $300,000. Now every three months he dips into the money for about $10,000 to pay bills and the mortgage on their roomy, ranch-style house, with a small pool out back, on a street of small but manicured lawns and Lyndon Johnson—era

Jim Wilson / The New York Times

James Sharlow

architecture in Northridge, northwest of downtown Los Angeles.

Gayle, his wife, calls it: "Keeping up the front." Every withdrawal from their savings costs them money in penalties and interest, but what she takes home from the $30,000 annual salary she earns as a secretary will not even cover the house payment of $1,800 a month. So they sacrifice their future to pay for the here and now, and at night she takes long walks so her husband and daughters cannot see her cry. "I just want to pretend things are like they used to be," said Mrs. Sharlow, a slim, gracious blond woman who, lately, always looks a little tired. She spent years finding the perfect curtains. Now she hoards paper towels and soap.

Gayle Sharlow, who is 51, grew up in a household where money was short, precious. Sometimes now, when she forces herself out of bed at five-thirty in the morning, she looks down at her still-sleeping husband and feels a flash of anger: He can hold out for a good job. She just goes to work. Sometimes, she feels like begging him to take a job, any kind of job, instead of holding out for one that fits his dreams. She fears they will lose their house, their retirement, all of it. But she never wakes him those mornings, never does speak up. His work was not merely part of him. It was the defining part.

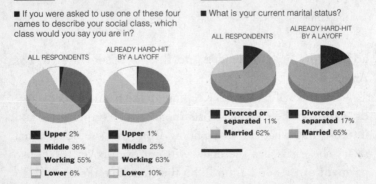

The New York Times POLL

Job insecurity affects families emotionally as well as financially. A life crisis caused by job loss turns lives and households upside down, leaving people scarred, scared and embittered about their prospects and their place in life, even after they have found another job.

■ If you were asked to use one of these four names to describe your social class, which class would you say you are in?

ALL RESPONDENTS

ALREADY HARD-HIT BY A LAYOFF

■ **Upper** 2%   ■ **Upper** 1%
■ **Middle** 36%   ■ **Middle** 25%
▨ **Working** 55%   ▨ **Working** 63%
▢ **Lower** 6%   ▢ **Lower** 10%

■ What is your current marital status?

ALL RESPONDENTS

ALREADY HARD-HIT BY A LAYOFF

■ **Divorced or separated** 11%   ■ **Divorced or separated** 17%
▨ **Married** 62%   ▨ **Married** 65%

"How could my family not think less of me now?" asked Mr. Sharlow, a large, tall, balding, bearded man who looks like a boss. Once he was a husband and father with a great job, and now he is just a man chasing one. "I thought it would take a few weeks, a few months, and then I would be working again," he said. "I want to tell companies, 'Take me on for a month. Don't pay me. I'm sure I can outwork most people if you'll give me a chance.' " His guilt over not working, over not bringing home even a small paycheck to help pay the bills, has done battle with his fear that a low-paying, stopgap job will be the end of the line. "I'm afraid it might be it, the best I could do."

How long can he hold on? He does not know.

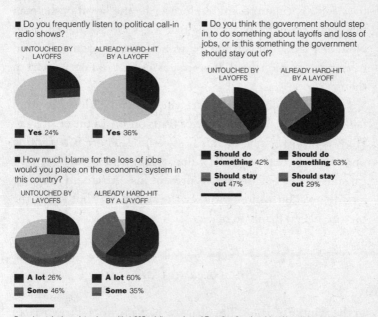

■ Do you frequently listen to political call-in radio shows?

UNTOUCHED BY LAYOFFS   ALREADY HARD-HIT BY A LAYOFF

■ Yes 24%   ■ Yes 36%

■ How much blame for the loss of jobs would you place on the economic system in this country?

UNTOUCHED BY LAYOFFS   ALREADY HARD-HIT BY A LAYOFF

■ A lot 26%   ■ A lot 60%
■ Some 46%   ■ Some 35%

■ Do you think the government should step in to do something about layoffs and loss of jobs, or is this something the government should stay out of?

UNTOUCHED BY LAYOFFS   ALREADY HARD-HIT BY A LAYOFF

■ Should do something 42%   ■ Should do something 63%
■ Should stay out 47%   ■ Should stay out 29%

Based on telephone interviews with 1,265 adults conducted Dec. 3 to 6 nationwide. "Already hard-hit by a layoff" means people who said they or someone in their households had been laid off at least once in the last 15 years, and that the layoffs had caused major crises in their lives (10 percent of all respondents). "Untouched by layoffs" means people who said they have neither been laid off themselves nor know anyone well who has been laid off in the last 15 years (28 percent of all respondents).

Gayle Sharlow does not blame her husband for what has happened to them. She blames the company he was once part of, they were all part of, body and soul.

The layoff of a senior manager is hardly a new phenomenon in modern America; Jim Sharlow saw it happening all around him. But when his turn came, it shocked him. Mr. Sharlow, who missed watching his daughters grow up because he routinely put in twelve- and fourteen-hour days, believed that he was part of a company family. The company discarded him six months short of the date he needed for a decent pension.

"He gave them twenty-six years, and it meant nothing," said his older daughter, Karen, who is 26. She and her 21-year-old sister, Laurie, still live at home, and both have seen their own lives and expectations altered forever by the layoff of the man who once stood for everything that was solid and dependable. Neither makes enough money to help their parents, beyond paying an occasional bill. It embarrasses him to take help from them.

"I know I'll never feel safe again," he said. "I lost my job, I failed my family. I . . ." His voice trails off into a bitter silence. He was fifty when he did his first résumé. There is a painting on his living room wall of a sailboat disappearing into a tropical sunset. The boat used to represent his retirement. Now he uses that sailboat money to pay the water bill, but keeps the picture nailed firmly in place.

She Loved to Dance

In the winter of 1968, Jim Sharlow had a primer-brown 1947 hot-rod Chevrolet convertible, and most of his hair. He was in serious love with a good-looking woman who loved to dance.

When the gray snow did not pile up too high, Batavia, New York, outside of Rochester, was a lot like paradise.

James and Gayle ate fried dough rolled in powdered sugar at a joint called Pontillo's and planned a life. "He got a tax refund for $110," she said. "He was going to buy some pistons, but he got me a ring." The only thing that could have made it better was a real job. His father had been a tool-and-die man who worked his whole life for one company, and his son, against his wishes, trained to do the same. "He wanted me to do better, to wear a tie," he said.

But when he was 23, Eastman Kodak recruited him, trained him to be a machinist, promised him a long and happy future. Everyone in Batavia knew that when you got on with Kodak, you were set for life. His father forgave his choice of careers—it was Kodak. But his time as a blue-collar worker would be short.

Almost immediately, he started climbing. Unlike the college boys—his bachelor of science degree in engineering management came much later—Mr. Sharlow could use his head and hands. For the next several years, he was used in mechanical, engineering, assembly, electrical, and fabricating areas, in increasingly managerial roles. "It just seemed like overnight he went from a closet full of work shirts to a closet full of white shirts," Mrs. Sharlow said. He remembers the first day he wore a tie. An ornery machinist cut it off with a pair of scissors, and stuck it on the wall. (He is not sure, but it might have been a clip-on.)

Each promotion improved his family's quality of life. It made college a certainty for his children. And after a while, he felt comfortable being a boss. He had worked up from the bottom and there was a pride in that. If a machinist could not make a part work, Mr. Sharlow would tuck his tie in his shirt

James Sharlow, right, during his early years as a machinist at Eastman Kodak.

and make it himself. He felt he had earned his white shirts, his growing power.

"Kodak was everything," Mr. Sharlow said. "How far I could go seemed to depend on my own ambition." He worked late nights, weekends, holidays. "I remember going to a dance recital and saying to Gayle, 'That girl on the end is really good.' And she said, 'Jim, that's your daughter.' "

He did dirty work for them. Years ago, back in Rochester, it was his job to find fat in some departments, then trim it. He laid off several people, some who cried, others who begged.

One man killed himself. "He was a young guy, just got married, just bought a house. A Vietnam vet. He saw the pink slip in my hand and asked, 'That for me?' I told him, 'I am afraid so.' He asked if there was anything I could do. He pleaded with me. Two months later he committed suicide. The name is gone, but I can still see the face."

In 1987, the company offered Mr. Sharlow his own small plant, making highly technical aerospace parts on military contracts, in a land where it never snowed. His job history backs up his assertion that he is a good manager. At the Northridge plant, a subsidiary of Kodak, he increased net profit by 10 percent in his first year and by 19 percent his second. A lot of people got rich in the Reagan era, and the Sharlows, while far from rich, got their share. "We did all right," Mr. Sharlow said. He started to play a little golf. His daughters became cheerleaders and sorority women. His wife became a power shopper.

They thought it would last forever.

"What Did I Do Today?"

The days inch along, like 9 A.M. traffic on the San Diego Freeway. It has been three years since that first morning-after, when he opened his eyes and thought, "I don't have a job today." But still he shaves and showers and dresses in neatly pressed khakis and sport shirts: the executive on his day off. "It helps with my self-esteem," he said.

The plant was shut down as a cost-cutting measure, part of an industry-wide slowdown caused by the melting Cold War. Mr. Sharlow said that other California managers with the company found jobs back in New York. He asked to be transferred back, too, but he was a little too late. He might have pushed harder and faster for a return to Rochester, but even after the plant's closing was announced, he trusted the company to hold a place for him. "I knew there were hundreds and even thousands being laid off. I guess I thought I was special. Then the day came when they made a business decision to let me go. It was, ''Bye, and don't let the door hit you.' "

His last day he went home and had four manhattans and wondered how to start over. It was the saddest day of his life. "My dream was to retire down in St. Petersburg to a little place on the Intracoastal Waterway, with a sailboat tied up to a little dock in back. I measured the money over a lifetime to try and get there."

At noon one Thursday afternoon, his mailbox is jammed with outgoing envelopes, all résumés, follow-up letters, hopes. By afternoon it will be filled with bills and junk mail and what he has come to call "Dear John" letters: "Dear Mr. Sharlow," they say, "Thank you for your interest, but . . ." And then they promise to keep his résumé on file.

In the last three years, he has sent out 2,205 résumés—by his own, precise count. For his efforts, he has landed ten interviews; once he was one of two finalists for a job managing a manufacturing plant in Southern California. That job had drawn 3,000 applicants. He scours *The New York Times, The Wall Street Journal*, the *Los Angeles Times*, the *St. Petersburg Times* (his mother lives in Florida and he would like to be near her), as well as trade magazines and newsletters, searching for openings for a plant manager, department head, anything that fits his experience. He will not say what he expects to be paid, but has come to realize that it will not approach his old salary.

One potential employer told Mr. Sharlow that he could not hire him because his company could not give the kind of pay and benefits he had come to expect. As the months tumble by, he wonders how many jobs he lost because, once in a fat period in his life, he had it too good. He shrugged off the rejections at first. Now, his wife says, "You see him sitting there, and you can feel the disappointment coming off him."

Mr. Sharlow has always been a Republican, and he still is. His troubles, he believes, do not have a lot to do with politics. A big corporation decided it would make more money without him than with him or his plant, and that desire for a slightly wider profit margin cost him his job. He does not see that kind of thinking as singularly Republican.

He has refused to become a couch potato, could care less about *General Hospital*. He does chores. He runs errands for a shut-in elderly neighbor. He wishes his dog, Scooter, had not died. Scooter was good company. The evenings are the worst for him, when his wife comes home tense and tired from a lousy day. He sits on his couch and thinks: "What did I do today? What did I do?"

Bigger Than All of Them

The meeting room is wall to wall with well-dressed men and women like Mr. Sharlow, cloaked in double-breasted armor, shielding a rumpled reality. It is one of the rules here at 40-Plus, a self-help organization of laid-off, white-collar workers in Los Angeles: Continue to dress like someone important, stay in character. Fortune 500 companies seldom hire managers who spend six days a week in their bathrobes, watching reruns of *Ironside*.

There is a woman who lost her sales job and then her husband, because he valued her less without the paycheck. There is a graying former supervisor who believes he was laid off because he was too old, and a younger man angry that the Japanese owners who took over his insurance company let him go with no warning. They pore over want ads, talk job-hunting strategy, train to re-enter the modern, meaner corporate reality, and try not to be bitter about the fact that they have enough discarded brain power here to run many companies. They drink coffee, but have to get it themselves. "It's not hopeless," said the president, Ben Cate, but it is bleak. One of their number had just found a good job, and the others grilled him about his résumé, negotiations, salary, searching for the secret.

For Mr. Sharlow, this group is important in another way. When he sees the other tossed-aside executives, it proves he is not alone, that something bigger than him is to blame. When he walks into this place, his whole manner changes. He is back in an office, he has a purpose. His step quickens, his confidence seems to swell. He is like a hooked fish let loose again in a stream.

A Reminder of Poverty

The hardships of other families that have lost a regular paycheck are still only an echo for them. Gayle Sharlow hears it clearest. She has heard it before. Her daughters have never been close to poor; neither has her husband. Her father was a hard-working carpenter who did his best to provide, but they often lived from paycheck to paycheck, and luxuries were scarce. For her, the threat of poverty is too familiar, like a ripped dress she thought she had thrown away for good, but may have to wear again.

Listen to her:

"I grew up with nothing, absolutely nothing. This layoff gnaws at my guts. It's a fear. I stock up on soap and paper towels because I'm afraid we might run out and not be able to afford any more. I try not to lose hope, but I'm afraid we will lose the house, everything. Gone. It's not silly to think about. It happens to people, people we know. I get mad and want to say, 'You'll just have to get a job at McDonald's.' But we keep up the front. I still go to the mall, but I do a lot more looking than buying. We still go to dinner. And at night I go for my walks so they can't see me cry."

Behind the front, there have been difficult choices. When her father was ill recently, she agonized over whether to pay $1,300 for the last-minute plane ticket to go see him. She chose not to go. There are times when she wishes they had never left Batavia, that the house was smaller, their dreams more modest. There would be less to lose then.

Mr. Sharlow got a year's severance pay when he was laid off, so only in the last two years has he had to peel from their original savings of about $300,000. The withdrawals, countered by profits on his investments, have left him with about $250,000. The bulk of their nest egg is in a 401(k)—an ever-changing mix of mutual funds, stocks and bonds. He juggles them now and then, trying to squeeze out every penny. That means he sometimes is more aggressive—they now have no money in CDs because interest is low—and sometimes less. He only gambles in the stock market when he is almost sure he will win. Two winters ago, when the market dropped sharply, he sold and put the money elsewhere. He knows the key to the market is long-term investment, but he could not afford to watch their savings vanish. He has not borrowed; he does not even use his credit card. He makes sure that he meets his life insurance premium. To drop it would be unthinkable, selfish.

The Sharlows have come to like California, but the cost of living is sucking up their money. They would sell the house, move to a less expensive neighborhood, but the market is bad and the 1994 earthquake did damage still unrepaired. And besides, the house has come to represent roots, stability. Giving it up would be admitting they have lost. The living room has cracks in the ceiling, but for now the house and family are intact. Mr. Sharlow says his wife is supportive, that they do not have the ugly yelling fights—and worse—that have ripped other families apart in the wake of a layoff. The Sharlows rarely talk about Gayle's fears for the same reason she does her crying out of sight: She believes he has enough to worry about. "Everyone should know. He has always been a very good provider for his family," she said. "I want to make sure everyone understands that."

They hear of others, many others, who did come apart under the pressure. One man had a nervous breakdown, left his family, and moved to New Jersey to live with his mother. They know men barely clinging to marriages and self-respect. Another laid-off executive and acquaintance of Mr. Sharlow killed himself over Christmas. Mr. Sharlow thinks that maybe he lost hope.

"Don't think Jim Sharlow and his family are typical," said Mr. Cate, the 40-Plus president. "They're not. They're doing good."

Life Lessons

Their childhoods were as carefree as love and money could make them. "When it happened, what bothered me was, I couldn't get a new car," said Laurie Sharlow, who was in her teens then. "I know that sounds really bäd, but that's the way it was then." This is the way it is now: "When I ask Dad for twenty dollars, I'm ashamed."

The layoff that shocked and hurt their father and chilled their mother did all these things to Laurie and Karen. It also made them angry. "We've been taught our whole lives that if you give your loyalty to someone or something, it gives you something back," Karen said. "In our house, we didn't even use anything that wasn't Kodak, Kodak film, Kodak cameras." The loyalty was all one-sided. To them, the corporate family is no more real than any other fairy tale their father told in their childhoods, a fairy tale now replaced with a harsh sensibility that seems out of place on the young women, who pledged Tri Delta.

"No one will take care of you," Karen said. "We know."

"I know I don't cry much anymore," said Laurie, who studies television and filmmaking at California State University at Northridge, and works part time as a secretary. All the things that seemed so important, boyfriends, parties, have been shoved into perspective, cheating her out of a period in her life that should have been carefree. "I missed a lot," she said.

Karen works in the international retail department of Warner Brothers, part of the new growth industry in Southern California. Although she makes only about $30,000 a year, she saves as much as she can, preparing for a repeat of what happened to her father, knowing it might never come, unwilling to take a chance. In better times, she would have probably moved into her own place, because her father would have been able to help. Now she saves the rent money, and, like her sister, lives in her old room, its walls covered with

Jim Wilson / The New York Times

James Sharlow fears that a stopgap job may be the best he can find. "How could my family not think less of me now?" he asked. "I believe in the American dream. I feel it fading."

pictures of fresh-faced girls in cheerleader outfits and prom dresses. Everyone is smiling. The layoff came too late to take everything, but it took their peace of mind.

"I feel guilty," Mr. Sharlow said. "One of the girls will see something they'd like to have and I'll say, 'When Daddy gets a job.' " He would like to promise his daughters, his wife, and the man in the mirror that everything will be fine again, but the "Dear John" letters keep coming, the phone still does not ring. Even now, three years later, he is still vaguely disbelieving that all this has happened, that the company—he still refers to it as "my" company—is no longer part of his life. "It's like you're standing outside the castle," he said, "watching the drawbridge go up."

In December, the Sharlows took a Florida vacation they could not afford. They walked along St. Petersburg Beach, the executive and his family on holiday. He caught himself scanning the real estate, looking for a house with a dock in back, with room for a boat.

Epilogue: Winter

The guilt won its battle over pride. Jim Sharlow went to work. He wakes up early again, but does not put on a suit and no one notices if his shoes are shined. He took a temporary job at the college where his wife works. Technically, he is a consultant in its electronics department, but most days he works with his hands again, repairing televisions, video cameras, VCRs, and other broken equipment. He makes less money than Gayle.

"I don't manage people now," he said. He carries a screwdriver. It was supposed to last just three months, but he got a one-month extension. Now and then he sees things on the job he would do differently, he would do better, if it were up to him, "but no one is interested in what I have to say now."

It all came down to the simple fact that he could no longer stand to wait: for the good job, for his tired wife to get home. Now the two ride to work together some days. The transmission in the Mercedes slips so badly that sometimes he has to beg it to roll.

He will not say how much he earns now, only that if the job lasted all year, he would still earn a little less than Gayle's $30,000 salary, which they used to consider "a nice little extra." They make enough money to pay their mortgage, as well as some, but not all, of their bills. But they still have to borrow from savings. "It just won't be as much. In that, it's a blessing," he said.

For Gayle, it did not bring the relief she expected, only what they had really known all along, that "you can't build a life on this."

In some ways he is back where he started, with tools in his hands. But instead of a young man looking toward his future, he is middle-aged, and dreaming backwards. "I was an operations manager for a plant, and I was a damn good one," he said. "The thing I hate about this is the fear—no, fear isn't a strong enough word, it's terror—that I'd just better forget my dreams and do this, and do it for the rest of my life. Maybe this is it.

"Maybe this is the best I can get."

Pride and its Discontents

The wedge-shaped B-2 Stealth bomber sliced through the brownish-blue California haze. Robert Muse lay back on the hood of the pickup and watched it fly, like a boy gauging the progress of his paper airplane. "Some of me may be in that plane," he said. "My parts. I helped make it fly."

The jet was executing what aircraft workers call a flyover, a low-altitude pass, staged so employees at the Northrop Aircraft Division could view their creation against a canvas of clouds. Mr. Muse was laid off from his job as a machinist two years ago, but he came to the flyover anyway, to be part of it. Even now, so long after his job disappeared, he thinks of himself as an aircraft builder. The emptiness of that image of himself has been the hardest thing to accept, harder than the loss of the good money and benefits, harder than the fact that he now rides around town in a 16-year-old Datsun with no spare tire in the trunk.

For 28 of his 47 years, Mr. Muse was one of the most skilled and exacting blue-collar workers in America. Now he is a maintenance technician at half the $20 an hour he used to get. The hands that once sculpted complex components out of exotic metals now feel their way through air-conditioning ducts, trim tree branches, unclog toilets. "I do what needs doing," he said. He is grateful for the new job because the paycheck allows his family to hold on to a three-bedroom home on a still-safe street in Torrance, just south of Los Angeles, and pays the bills, as long as they eat a lot of hot dogs and buy nothing they can do without. But the take-home pay, less than $350 a week, is more like the kind of money he made when he was a young man with no responsibilities, when the only thing he had to worry about was the gas in his car and drive-in cheeseburgers on the weekends.

Robert Muse earns half what he did before losing his job as a machinist two years ago. "You don't plan for the future anymore," said his wife, Nancy. "You live day to day."

He has been laid off before. But like other blue-collar workers who would lose their jobs when business was bad, he always knew there would be a call-back. What is different now, what is different for so many millions like him, is that this layoff is forever. He is left to adjust to his whittled-down dignity or live in the past. He does a little of both. "I know nothing is for sure in this life," he said. "But I spent thirty years at it. That should count for something. Now there's just a void."

Much of that empty space is filled with bitterness, anger. In March 1994, his company decided it could buy some parts cheaper than its own people could make them, and closed the machine shop. One moment in the last, desperate months sticks like a fishhook in his memory. "A vice president walked into the meeting hall and said, 'Even if you work for nothing, you're still too expensive,' " Mr. Muse recalled. Now, instead of company medical benefits and enough of a pension to pay for a dignified retirement, he has plaques for excellent work, certificates for perfect attendance, and a transistor radio.

In California in the last eight years, about one in three aerospace workers has been declared too expensive. In 1988, there were 707,000 aerospace and high-technology workers in the state; in 1995, the workforce had slipped to 473,000, a loss of 234,000 jobs. Up and down the streets of Torrance and Long Beach and other places where these workers made their homes, FOR SALE signs stick up like weeds. Through the trickle of laid-off workers still coming and going, the blank windows of union halls stare out on the rubble of what used to be manufacturing plants. Middle-aged men who used to set rivets can now can recite the daytime TV schedule by heart.

Mr. Muse's older brother, 50-year-old Roy, was laid off by McDonnell Douglas in June 1993. He's watched so much

Oprah, he told his brother, "I began to hate men." Another brother, 46-year-old Larry, still works in the industry but has been told his job will be history, too, someday soon. When he and his brothers congregate, drinking beer and talking airplanes, he only has to look across the kitchen table to see his future. "It's a little like the plague," Robert Muse said.

For as long as they have been a family, he and his wife, Nancy, and their daughters, Vicky, 23, and Carrie, 17, have lived comfortably, neither rich nor poor. The layoff has created economic hardships they have never known. But beyond even that, there is an uncertainty, a dread that if it happened once it can happen again, and drive their standard of living ever lower. "You get scared to spend a penny," Mrs. Muse said. "Even though he has a job, you get scared he won't. You don't plan for the future anymore. You live day to day."

The layoff, one Northrop manager assured the workers in those last days, was purely business, nothing personal. Mr. Muse has tried to see it that way, too, to try to lay it to rest.

He cannot.

For nearly a year, he and his family went without health insurance because they could not afford the $600 monthly premiums. He gambled no one would get sick or be hurt, and he won. But he hated it, because of the constant worry, because it was degrading, a poor man's tactic to cheat a basic working man's responsibility. His older daughter lives with her baby and boyfriend in a dangerous neighborhood, because it is the best they can afford on their own low-paying jobs. He wants to help them move to a better and safer place, but there is no money for it now. His worries, and his guilt, pile higher and higher.

It is personal, he says. "It's like the company telling you that you're no damn good."

The Boneyard

Northrop Grumman's modest flight museum occupies a corner of the company's plant in nearby Hawthorne, monument to the soaring—and dubious—achievements of the industry. There is a lean fighter jet, which never flew a mission, and the stubby, radio-controlled flying bomb, which looks as if it was designed for Porky Pig. Robert Muse walked through the boneyard of rejected, abandoned planes, pointing to a strut here or a panel there, reciting little facts about stress tolerances or heat resistance, information that used to be so vital, now just useless numbers rattling around in his head.

Across the parking lot, now mostly deserted, is the machine shop where he used to work. He used to have security passes, but the company took them away on his last day. He would have liked to have kept them, as souvenirs. It is hard not to live in the past if that is where so much of your happiness resides. "It'll just eat you up, if you let it," he said.

He is a tall, lanky man who likes to wear cowboy boots and western shirts, to sip slow on a cold beer and flick through the channels while scratching his dog's ears. But he loved to work, because while anyone can handle the remote control, not everyone can take it apart, add a little bit of wire and a piece of tinfoil and use it to open garage doors and dim the lights in the hall.

Unlike many other blue-collar workers, Mr. Muse did not simply inherit his father's place on the assembly line. His father was a straight man for magicians, the one who would volunteer from the audience to be sawed in half. Robert Muse had no showmanship in him, but he could have told you how the tricks worked. After high school he went to work in the aircraft industry. In 1966, Douglas Aircraft hired and trained him to run a turret lathe. He was laid off in 1971, but back then a lay-off was only an inconvenience. "If one company laid you off, you were sure someone else would pick you up quick," he said, "We called it the merry-go-round." Four months later, he was making precision parts for Northrop. The job lasted twenty-two years.

The work, to a layman, sounds impossibly precise. "The cellophane on a cigarette pack is four times thicker than the margin for error on some parts," he said. It was natural that the people who did the work would be proud of it, he said. They were the blue-collar elite. Not just anyone could do the work. The math alone left some people dumbfounded. "There was a feeling of, 'I'm doing my job, and I'm doing a good job. So why should it ever go away?' " he said.

On a blind date, he met Nancy, who had grown up around planes herself: her father was a pilot, her mother, a stewardess. They got married, bought a house and then, sixteen years ago, moved up to a nicer one. They had two children along the way. He volunteered for the company fire department and was the safety monitor, environmental monitor, and secretary for the employee involvement group. In his spare time he souped up a 1964 Chevelle and outran Corvettes from light to light on Hawthorne Boulevard. He voted Republican, in part because Republicans were usually hawks and hawks voted for the mili-tary contracts that allowed him to be an aircraft worker.

As the Soviet Union splintered, and the implications for the defense industry became clear, the relationship between man-agement and workers at the plant became colder, more con-frontational. But even then, management assured him that his job was safe, that he would be able to retire with a company pension and health plan. "They said, 'Don't worry. Your jobs are fine.' Go out and buy your houses,' " he recalled. "They lied to us," he said, to keep the skilled workforce intact and producing, "dangling that lollipop in front of us."

But in the months before his layoff in March 1994, with their jobs clearly on the chopping block, the machinists took it on themselves to try to save the machine shop. Through harder work, less waste, and rising desperation, they sliced costs, increased production, even volunteered for pay cuts. "We told them, 'Look, we did it. We saved you money,' " Mr. Muse said. "Then they took it all away from us."

The last weeks, after the layoff was announced, were the worst, because so many workers refused to believe it was over. "He made the comment to us several times that we shouldn't give up hope, that people are saved at the last minute," Mrs. Muse said. "He told us that sometimes, on your last day, people walk up and say, 'We found you a job.' "

The Chevelle sits in the garage now, gathering dust. "I can't afford the insurance," he said. "But I keep the registration up. I'll bring it back to life. Someday." He is still a Republican. He is not much stirred by social issues—he is a "live and let live" kind of man—but he still believes in a strong defense, in building planes. Even though he is coming to terms with his life, there is still a glimmer of hope that, someday, the plants will come to life again, and that they will need him.

What Money Can Buy

The graffiti signal a change from Robert Muse's quiet neighborhood to the one his daughter Vicky comes home to after her part-time job at Sears. Mr. Muse looked out from his car window on treeless streets and boxlike apartment buildings, at the sidewalk where a young man traded little packets of

Jim Wilson / The New York Times

For 28 of his 47 years, Robert Muse was one of the most skilled blue-collar workers in America, helping build jets for Northrop. Sometimes it is hard for him not to live in the past, his happiest time. "It'll just eat you up, if you let it," he said.

fleeting happiness for crumpled cash. "She lives here," Mr. Muse said. "Can you believe it?"

Over the days, as he talked about the layoff and what it had cost, he fluctuated between sadness, bitterness, and anger, usually short-lived, beaten back by natural cheerfulness. Before his layoff, he was an infectiously happy man, said his friends and family, and the ghost of that is still here. But as he stared out on the street, he was disgusted, helpless: "I don't want to cry about it. But I feel like I've been stabbed in the back."

No, the heart.

Brothers

It takes a lot of Old Milwaukee to take the edge off three big men's fears. The Muse brothers, all large, middle-aged men with beers in their fists, sat at Robert's kitchen table and talked about the future as if it were a box that they were afraid to open. Together the men represent three stages of a journey now common throughout blue-collar America.

Robert has come the farthest: After his layoff, there was never any question that he would have to find work immediately. He took a job crawling under houses to install wiring for security alarms. It was hard, dirty work, and one day he had to share the crawl space with an unidentified, long-dead animal that had elected to tunnel under the house to die. The stench gagged him. "I thought, surely I can find something better than this," he said.

A year ago, after training in computer and electronics repair, he was hired as a maintenance technician at a company that builds solar panels. Some days he works on electronics and computers, some days he cuts weeds. He does the work with a smile, but it is all teeth, no heart. "It's work, man," he said. He cannot even afford to stay true to a particular brand of beer. "Now, I just drink what's on sale."

Roy Muse worked for McDonnell Douglas for twenty-nine years and was laid off six years short of qualifying for full pension and benefits, including health insurance, which he regrets more than anything. He has kidney problems, and has had to spend thousands of dollars to continue his old health insurance. Now his savings are down to nothing. At 50, he is training to be a medical technician, in the hope of landing his own low-paying job in a growing industry. Nowadays, the Muse brothers said, it seems like all growing industries are built with the labor of low-paid and desperate people. Even so, Roy says, the competition with other retrained people is so tight that he is not sure of finding a job when his program is done.

He and his wife have three sons. Their house, their future, hang on his finding work soon. His wife has a low-paying, part-time job to help them survive, but some bills go unpaid. His unemployment insurance ran out a long time ago. "You know you've always heard about bills piling up?" he said. "Well, they do. They do pile."

Their baby brother, 45-year-old Larry, already has a layoff notice in hand from his company, also an aircraft manufacturer. "They keep stringing me along," he said, but quickly adds that he is not complaining, that he prays the company will find a place for him. "I'm still dedicated," he said, "I'm still loyal." Unlike his brothers, whose families and nostalgia tie them down to Southern California, he is willing to move. He has been married four times, and has learned not to get attached to one particular house. He will chase work wherever it takes him. Most recently, he has been assigned to a four-month tryout with a branch plant in Lake Charles, Louisiana. "I kind of like Louisiana," he said.

Larry Muse did some quick arithmetic to calculate how much of their collective lives they had devoted to the industry. "Seventy years," he said. "Right here."

"It was a good ride," Roy said, "wasn't it?"

Robert nodded. "Till they don't want you anymore," he said.

Wife and Mother

The Muse house would disappoint a thief: the one obvious treasure, a big-screen television the size of a refrigerator, is too heavy to steal conveniently. Yet this modest house, so neat and clean without so much as a cushion out of place, is a museum of irreplaceable things. There is a sculpture of a child's handprint preserved in clay, and an engraved plaque with a jet plane covered in fake gold. Over their kitchen table someone has pinned a yellowed slip of paper with a priceless poem from third grade, or was it second?

"What we had was wealth," Nancy Muse said, as she stood with one foot on the immaculate beige carpet of the den and one on the gleaming linoleum of the kitchen. This is as much her world as the factory was his, and the change brought into her life by the layoff has been as painful and demeaning as what her husband endures. "There ought to be a law against it, against taking it all away," she said. "Don't they have any conscience? Don't they care?"

The New York Times POLL

Many Americans feel they are losing ground financially and are worried about what the future holds, for themselves and their children. These worries are sharply magnified for those who have been through a layoff.

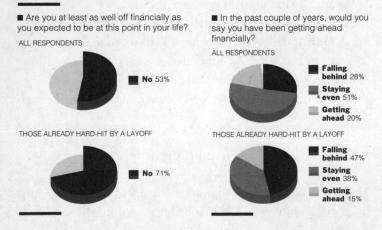

■ Are you at least as well off financially as you expected to be at this point in your life?

ALL RESPONDENTS

No 53%

■ In the past couple of years, would you say you have been getting ahead financially?

ALL RESPONDENTS

Falling behind 28%
Staying even 51%
Getting ahead 20%

THOSE ALREADY HARD-HIT BY A LAYOFF

No 71%

THOSE ALREADY HARD-HIT BY A LAYOFF

Falling behind 47%
Staying even 38%
Getting ahead 15%

She has been the backstop for the deprivations and disappointment her family endures, because she runs the house. Mrs. Muse has had to look her 17-year-old daughter in the face and tell her that promises made over a lifetime about college had been turned to lies by the layoff. "We always told her, 'You have to go to college,' and we always told her we would help," said Mrs. Muse, a tiny, quiet woman who tends to let her husband do the talking until the conversation curves into an area where she is the expert. "Now she's a senior and it's time for us to make good on it, but all we can do is say, 'Well, uh, well . . .' "

Over the years, the Muses put away about $60,000 for their retirement. They had planned to use some of that money for Carrie's college. The plan was, as their children eventually left home, they would not only restore any missing savings but add to the nest egg, maybe even have $100,000 by age 65. It is the stuff motor homes are made of.

Now they try to hoard the $60,000 for their old age. But they fear emergencies will peel away the little they have, and they can add nothing to it because this new job pays so little.

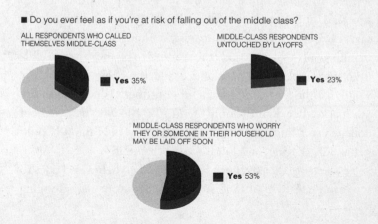

■ Do you ever feel as if you're at risk of falling out of the middle class?

ALL RESPONDENTS WHO CALLED
THEMSELVES MIDDLE-CLASS

■ Yes 35%

MIDDLE-CLASS RESPONDENTS
UNTOUCHED BY LAYOFFS

■ Yes 23%

MIDDLE-CLASS RESPONDENTS WHO WORRY
THEY OR SOMEONE IN THEIR HOUSEHOLD
MAY BE LAID OFF SOON

■ Yes 53%

When he is 65, he will draw a tiny pension from Northrop, but it won't even pay the electric bill, Mrs. Muse said. They are afraid of growing old with nothing to live on except Social Security, and are aware that, barring some miracle, it is precisely what will happen.

"I'm not sure what's going to happen to us in the future," she said. Every time she thinks of it, she added, "It's like a kick in the stomach." Carrie, she says, is working hard to try and win a scholarship, and while it makes her proud it also breaks her heart. For Carrie and her generation here in Southern California, there is little choice. The option of the well-paying blue-collar job is an anachronism. It is either college, which cannot guarantee a good job anymore, or minimum wage.

In her high school, Carrie said, the layoff of a parent is so common that there is little sympathy left. "It's like, 'So your dad was laid off. Big deal. Mine's been laid off a year,' " she said. Still, she suspects but does not know how deeply it hurts her friends; behind the dismissive bravado, she says, "We just keep it to ourselves."

Mrs. Muse accepted her role as wife and mother a long time ago, not because she did not want to work—after all, she says, raising children and managing a home can be a hard and thankless job—but because she wanted to be there as her children grew up. She is nearing 50 and is willing to work for wages for the first time in her life, but there is nothing in the job market her dignity could stand. "People who had years of college can't find anything," she said. "The only thing I could get is Burger King, and I don't need that crap."

So she takes the paycheck her husband gives her and tries to work miracles with it. She walks grocery store aisles looking for the cheapest brand. If a store has a sale on turkey, they will eat turkey four times a week. Dixie, their dog, used to eat what the family ate. Now sometimes there is nothing left, so she eats dog food. "The food prices increase, the utilities go up, but we have so much less to work with," she said. Their house payment is $550 a month and their utilities run $250 a month. They spend about $400 a month for groceries and other basic needs. Then there are the big expenses they have to make sure they put aside for, like $1,400 a year in property taxes and $740 for car insurance. What is left from their income of $1,500 a month is pocket change.

The family across the street is in the same bad shape, as are two or three families down the block. One family just packed up in the dead of night and left, abandoning their house to the bank and leaving their friends to wonder whatever happened to them. Other families just split apart. She hears about them at the supermarket. That will never happen to them, she said. He is not going to give up the one part of his life that is still good; she depends on him more than ever to provide, to keep them in a house, in a warm and safe place. You could not pry them apart with a tire iron. Like the plague, as Mr. Muse said, the layoff affects each family differently, ripping some apart as it cleaves others tightly together.

The whole family, along with uncles Roy and Larry, went out for dinner one night last fall at a neighborhood restaurant, a place where a steak and shrimp go for $6.95. They talked about the changes in life, how Robert only gets a haircut now when he badly needs one, and how Roy is going to have to work for several months as an unpaid intern when he finds work, if he does. Carrie talked about how bad Christmas had been, how "we used to get lots and lots of presents," and never knew it was a luxury. As she talked, her father dipped his head toward his plate, as if to say, I'm sorry.

Then the three Muse brothers—a maintenance man, an aspiring X-ray technician, and one last aircraft worker desperately trying to hold on to a fading way of life—started to talk about planes.

4

The Fraying of Community

Sara Rimer

To WALL STREET and the world, it was the National Cash Register Company. Then, it was modernized, computerized, streamlined down to NCR. But in Dayton, Ohio, the company was always just "the Cash." The Cash got rich selling its cash registers to the world, and it rewarded its workers with good livings and unrivaled benefits, and its hometown with a firm hand of civic guidance and millions of dollars of good works. They were all bound together—the company, the workers, and the town. To a lot of people here, Dayton was the Cash, and the Cash was Dayton.

"NCR was part of Dayton's soul," George Bayless, a 58-year-old banker, said as he drove past the vacant swath of Main Street where thirty yellow-brick NCR factory buildings once stood. As a boy, Mr. Bayless learned to swim in the big pool in the park that NCR's founding patriarch, John Patterson, built. He played French horn in the NCR band. And when he graduated from high school in 1955, he marched down the aisle of NCR Auditorium, just as generations of high school graduates had before him, and would for two decades more. Nearly all of it has vanished in the steep decline and takeover of NCR: the buildings, 20,000 jobs, even the NCR name; the security, the middle-class aspirations, the way of life. And today, as its

With jobs less permanent, and with making a living harder, Dayton residents are too stretched for activities that made the city a community. A sense of common identity is lost.

faraway corporate parent, AT&T, prepares to break into three pieces, the future of Dayton's hometown company is profoundly unsure.

The same could be said of the future, and the present, of the entire town. For Dayton was always much more than just the Cash. Daytonians invented and manufactured many of the staples (and a few of the quirky incidentals) of American prosperity, and companies like Frigidaire, Delco, Dayton Tire, Huffy Bicycle, and Esther Price Chocolates joined with the community in an unwritten social contract crafted on a foundation of profits and jobs, plenty of jobs. Now, this test marketer's vision of average America is deep in midpassage between two economic eras: the old era of making things and of job security, and the new one of service and technology, takeovers, layoffs, and job insecurity. And the entire cloth of society, which most people in Dayton once wore so comfortably, feels as if it is out of style and could just wear out.

Everything, seemingly, is in upheaval: not just the jobs and lives of tens of thousands of people, but also the big corporations, the banks, the schools, the religious and cultural institutions, the old relationships of politics and power, and, especially, people's expectations of security, stability, and a shared civic life. "Now that there are only a few big hometown companies left, people are less certain about the community, too," said Brad Tillson, publisher of *The Dayton Daily News*, which itself is owned by an out-of-town company these days. "It creates tremendous uncertainty in people's lives. The tie between individuals and the community is less certain, and more fragile. It's scary for everybody."

All workers may be replaceable. Not so volunteers. When one man, Vinnie Russo, left NCR in the turmoil after the takeover—he felt he had little choice, he said—and found a new job in Louisville, the eighty-five boys of Pack 530 lost their cubmaster; a new one has yet to sign on. With so many women working, it is harder to find people to help in the schools and libraries. Churches are losing members. So are service organizations; people say they cannot leave work for meetings, even if they last only an hour. In a town with a tradition of charity, the United Way has missed its $20 million goal by $1 million in each of the last two years.

It can be confusing, living in Dayton in 1996. Like much of the Rust Belt, this sprawling region of nearly a million people is not as rusty as it was fifteen or twenty years ago. Many of the economic indicators are, if not exactly dazzling, at least promising. Unemployment is low. There is plenty of work available, even if many of the jobs do not pay what the old ones

EBB AND FLOW

"Dayton was a work town," said the Rev. Raleigh Trammell, a local minister. But the nature of the work is profoundly changed. A look at job losses and gains in the Dayton area over the last few years:

Most of the jobs created around Dayton in recent years have been low-paying ones in service or retail businesses, like the Victoria's Secret telemarketing center.

30 Years of Change: Employment in the Four-County Metropolitan Area

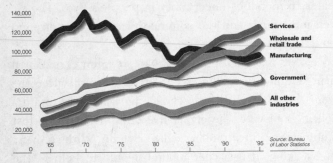

Source: Bureau of Labor Statistics

July 1992 NCR lays off 200 workers as it closes the Brown Street plant, which once employed 20,000 people.

March 1993 The Defense Electronics Supply Center will move, costing 2,800 civilian jobs.

May 1993 The Energy Department says it will scale back work at Mound Applied Technologies in Miamisburg, wiping out 600 to 800 jobs.

August 1993 Mead Data Central says it will cut 400 jobs.

October 1993 NCR eliminates nearly 500 jobs.

May 1994 General Motors says it will add a third shift and 1,000 to 1,200 jobs at its assembly plant in Moraine.

July 1994 Victoria's Secret says it will hire 1,000 workers for a new telemarketing center in Kettering.

March 1995 Matsushita says it will build a second Panasonic electronics plant in Troy and create 350 jobs.

Spring 1995 ABF Freight System begins construction on a new office and warehouse that will employ 400 people.

April 1995 A new service center in Dayton for the U.S. Postal Service that will employ 600 people is announced.

September 1995 AT&T G.I.S. (formerly NCR) says it will lay off 1,300 people.

paid. Dayton has not, of late, undergone the staggering layoffs of, say, the aerospace industry in Southern California. "By most of the traditional criteria, Dayton is doing pretty well," said Mr. Tillson, who sits on the board of the Miami Valley Economic Development Coalition, which was formed in 1994 to help guide Dayton into the new economic era. "But people just don't feel that way."

They know that thousands of jobs—middle-management, government, blue-collar—have disappeared, and that more could go at any time. The anxiety is everywhere. From the mostly white East Side to the mostly black West Side; over coffee in the new $300,000 homes of suburban Centerville, in the classrooms at John Patterson High School downtown: the conversation inevitably returns to the loss of jobs, the fear of losing jobs, the decline of the middle class, the rise of the global economy, the end of the American dream. "Downsizing—I hate that word," Chuck McElligott said one evening, recalling the feelings of all the people he knew who had lost their jobs. " 'You just blew my life away, and you're telling me I was downsized.' "

Here in Dayton, with its dwindling Democratic core city and increasingly Republican suburbs, people do not tend to blame government for what is happening. Nor do they expect government to fix things. Government hardly comes up in the conversation at all, except once in a while when someone like George Bayless will throw up his hands and declare: "And they can't even balance the budget in Washington."

And yet Dayton is *not* falling apart. People here talk a lot about their communal ability to work things out, and the civic physics of Dayton today is indeed a constant push and pull. Dayton's arts organizations may be getting less corporate money, but with that threat as inspiration, the Dayton Art

Institute has raised a record $18 million in two years, including $11 million from individuals. The city's public schools may be struggling to prepare their students for the needs of the new economy, but Sinclair Community College is confidently busy—virtually twenty-four hours a day, seven days a week—training, or retraining, 65,000 Daytonians for these post-industrial times.

Chuck McElligott and his family are also working hard to cope. Mr. McElligott, 55, a one-time University of Dayton football star, lost his job five years ago when the graphic-design company where he had spent twenty-three years shut down, partly because of the problems at NCR. He considers himself lucky to have found another job, even if it is for longer hours and less pay. His wife, Armonde, gave up her volunteer work at the library and got a paying job, teaching school. "We are not," she explained, "a family of whiners." Still, college for Charlie, the youngest of their three children, was going to be tough to afford.

But last fall the future seemed full of possibility for Charlie, a senior and the best player on the football team at suburban Oakwood High School. He had cardboard boxes stuffed with letters from interested Big Ten schools. In the second game of the season, he broke his pelvis in two places. Football was out for the rest of the year. And so, it became quickly apparent, was the football scholarship.

Mrs. McElligott recalled her son's reaction at the hospital, when the doctor described the seriousness of the injury. "His eyes welled up, but he didn't cry," she said. "Then he looked at us, and said, 'Okay, we've got to think of Plan B.' "

This is what Dayton feels like right now: All the people, and all the institutions, are groping for Plan B.

"The City of a Thousand Factories"

History, local history, is also part of the conversation here. People may sometimes feel as if their community is in danger of splitting apart, but history is still what they own together.

George Bayless and his friends were talking local history one day at a weekly lunch meeting of the Sertoma Club, a volunteer service organization. "Dayton is known for its inventions," said Bill Ganger, who sells real estate. The other men started rattling off the list that, in one form or another, Daytonians always seem to invoke when they are asked about their hometown: the Wright Brothers' flying machine, of course, and the cash register (invented in 1879 by a Dayton restaurant owner named James Ritty, as everyone at the table had learned in grade school), but also the automobile self-starter, carbonless paper, the step ladder, the mood ring, the pop top, S & H trading stamps. "Don't forget the Yellow Pages," Mr. Ganger said.

What Dayton has always been is a practical town. After all, Erma Bombeck is from Dayton, and who is more practical than Erma Bombeck? And so while out-of-town journalists dismissed Dayton as an unlikely backwater setting for the recent Bosnia peace talks, people here thought it was the perfect place. "We're good at working things out," said Steve Sidlo, managing editor of *The Dayton Daily News*. "People and insitutions have always worked well together here."

Never, according to the common history, did Dayton's people and institutions pull together more fiercely than during the flood of 1913. With record rains and surging rivers, the flood killed three hundred people and left tens of thousands more homeless (including George Bayless's mother,

Elsie, who was a little girl at the time). Dayton's biggest industry, the Smith & Barney maker of railroad cars, was ruined, along with scores of other businesses. Luckily (or was it destiny?), the National Cash Register Company was planted on high ground. The company and its founder, John Patterson, became the unifying forces in the city's recovery. Factories that built cash registers now built rescue boats—assembly-line style, one every eight minutes. Overnight, the company was transformed into an emergency shelter, hospital, and printing plant for *The Dayton Daily News*. Patterson led the citizens of Dayton in a huge clean-up—and in a drive to raise $2.15 million for a series of dams that have held to this day. From this vast common effort, the town rebuilt, and modern Dayton was born.

In the decades that followed, the Cash boomed, and so did Dayton. While Detroit made cars, Akron made tires, and Pittsburgh made steel, Dayton made all that and more. They called it "the city of a thousand factories." There were not just NCR, General Motors and Chrysler, but Dayton Press, Dayton Tire, Dayton Malleable. All over town today, people talk about how their parents came up from Appalachia, or from Alabama and Georgia, and went to work. Their stories, too, are part of the common history: stories of a town where a poor man or woman without a high school education could earn a decent wage and catapult almost overnight into the middle class.

"My father came here from a hollow in Kentucky when he was fifteen," said Mike Turner, who at the age of 35 is the mayor of Dayton. "His high school had closed for lack of funds. He worked on the railroad to get here." Raymond Turner got a job as a busboy in a cafeteria. At 18, he was hired at General Motors, and there he stayed for forty-four years, making washers and dryers at the Frigidaire plant, then oper-

Keith Meyers/*The New York Times*

Kathleen Stewart felt lucky to grow up in a prosperous city like Dayton. "There was money everywhere." Now she's paid so little, she can't replace her refrigerator and stores food in a cooler in the snow. Her son is considering leaving town.

ating a machine that made automobile compressors. The job sent Mike Turner to college and on to law school.

Kathleen Stewart, who is 53 now, was one of a family of eight children raised in a Dayton housing project. Her father, Alexander Tackas, had arrived on a boat from Hungary and gone to work as a machinist in a toy factory. "How did I feel about my future?" Ms. Stewart asked. "I felt lucky. I was from Dayton. All you had to do was grow up. There was money everywhere. You didn't worry about an education, especially if you were a girl. They told you not to go to college." And so Ms. Stewart, who was a promising artist, turned down offers of art school scholarships and went straight from high school to the NCR plant. "I was making $3.50 an hour," she said.

NCR helped give Dayton an identity, with institutions like a school and auditorium, which were razed when hard times came.

"That was big money in those days." After scarcely a year on the job, Ms. Stewart was seriously injured in a car accident. "I was hospitalized for several weeks," she said. "NCR took care of everything. They paid for every penny. They treated you like you were family." It was a different era, she said. "The microchip hadn't been invented."

By the 1970s, though, it had, and this city that had thrived on its mastery of technology was in danger of being done in by it. In deep financial trouble, NCR belatedly embraced the electronic age. "Who wanted a mechanical cash register?" Mr. Bayless said. "It was obsolete." The company began carving out a niche selling automated teller machines and computer systems linking department stores. It also moved its manufacturing south, and abroad, where labor was cheap. A wrecking ball demolished the factory buildings, and NCR Auditorium.

Twenty thousand NCR jobs were lost, and soon the layoffs were echoed all over town: General Motors, 10,000 jobs, half of them at the Frigidaire plant, which closed; Chrysler, 5,000 jobs; Wright-Patterson Air Force Base, 3,000. Dayton Press, 3,000 more. By the mid-1980s, a third of Dayton's manufacturing jobs had been lost, about 50,000 in all. The city, and the society, that rose from the flood were effectively gone.

And a new Dayton began to emerge. In the churning of businesses opened, downsized and taken over, thousands of jobs have disappeared; many, many more have been created. But that is only part of the story. Most of the new jobs, or at least the ones that do not require a college education, have been in lower-paying retail and service work. Indeed, median family income in Montgomery County, which includes Dayton, rose only about $1,000 between the 1980 and 1990 Censuses, from $34,903 to $36,069. And the unions, which once helped keep wages high, have lost much of their membership, and more of their power. The local AFL-CIO, for example, had about 70,000 members in 1975 and fewer than 50,000 today.

Then in 1991, the Cash was no more. AT&T acquired the company in a hostile takeover. It was a disastrous marriage. The company lost a half-billion dollars in the first nine months of 1995 alone. "You knew things were changing, but when AT&T took over NCR, that was the landmark that proved it," Ms. Stewart said. "People can't depend on anything for the future. Anything can change in a New York minute."

Around Dayton, nothing so symbolized the unease over NCR's new identity as the name change, to the futuristic AT&T Global Information Solutions, or GIS. It felt as if some outsider had summarily renamed the town. The depth of that unease showed what a hard time a lot of people here were having with the new language of global economics, power, and information. Everyone had always known what cash registers were, and how they worked. But hardly anyone outside the company seemed to know what Global Information Solutions meant, or what it did. Whatever the solutions were, they couldn't *see* them. When a reporter requested a tour of GIS headquarters in December, a company spokesman, Bob Farkas, seemed puzzled. "I'm not sure what there is to see," he said politely. "We don't manufacture anything here anymore. It's just five floors of cubes."

All of which is not to say that Dayton has stopped making things. General Motors is still the largest private employer here. But if the local GM strike in the winter of 1996 was most simply about the company's efforts to farm out parts production to nonunion companies, it was also about workers' fears for what remains of the well-paying manufacturing life. And so today, Dayton is trying to re-create itself yet again. A new wave of small high-tech companies dot the fringes of town, working on computer projects with Wright-Patterson. And everyone here is asking the chronic question: Can this cradle of invention reinvent itself well enough to make up for the losses of the past?

When Ms. Stewart returned to work after getting divorced, the best job she could find was at an electronic engraving company, where she took home $14,000 last year. When her refrigerator broke in early January and she could not afford a new one, she made do with a cooler and garbage bags buried in the snow outside her back door. "Right now I have a great freezer," she said the week after a blizzard buried Dayton. "It encompasses the whole city."

Her three grown children all live in the area. So do her four sisters and three brothers. She stays in close touch with all of them. Security used to be a job at NCR. Now, she said, "Security is my family." Her 25-year-old son, David, is trying to negotiate the new world as best he can. He makes about $8.50 an hour, including commissions, working nights at one of the big new service businesses, the Victoria's Secret Catalog company. There, hooked up to a telephone and a computer and surrounded by blow-ups of celebrity models, he sells Savoy robes and Miracle bras made abroad to customers from all over the world.

Mr. Stewart, who was initially hired as temporary help, considers himself lucky to have a permanent job at Victoria's Secret. It is a step up from his last job, running a label press in a factory for $6 an hour. Still, he says he is thinking about enrolling at Sinclair. What does he want to study? "Something with a guaranteed job." His other plan is to leave Dayton and go south.

"We Are the New Homeless"

Karen Myers is 40 years old, a lawyer, and the mother of three. Her husband, Robert, is a pediatrician. Her father-in-law worked for the old NCR. They live in a new neighborhood of custom-built homes in Centerville. Some 100 houses in the area were on the market last fall, after GIS announced its latest round of 1,300 layoffs. Family by family, she says, her community is being taken apart. "Many of these kids I see are on their fifth or sixth move because the company keeps saying, 'We're not making enough money; we need to downsize more,' " she said recently. "It used to be military families. Now it's modern life. It really hurts the child's ability to develop those long-term commitments. It's devastating to the sense of community."

Mrs. Myers is on the board of the Centerville United Methodist Church, a medium-size church. "I see people moving to the mega-, super-sized churches," she said. "I don't see them moving because the churches offer more services. They're able to attend without commitment. You can go and be one of the many and be invisible." Mrs. Myers was talking over coffee and muffins with her neighbor, Mary Ellen Knecht. Mrs. Knecht and her husband, Mark, who quit his job at GIS last fall for more satisfying and lucrative work, have four children.

"We are the new homeless," said Mrs. Knecht. NCR had moved her family from Indianapolis to Wichita, Kansas, to Dayton to South Carolina and, four years ago, back to Dayton. Each time they bought a house with a thirty-year mortgage. In South Carolina, Mrs. Knecht was president of her Methodist church women's group. She sang in the choir. She helped set up computer labs in the schools. Now, she said, "I'm not building anything here. I attend church. I haven't joined. When they pass around the attendance card on Sundays, I want to write down: 'I'm moving.' " Now the family was planning a move to Virginia. Mr. Knecht has been living there since October, when he took a job with a software company called DataFocus.

Sipping her coffee, Mrs. Myers said: "My husband has been clipping articles out of *Pediatric Journal* on the effects of moving on kids."

Mrs. Knecht asked: "What do they say?"

Mrs. Myers: "You don't want to know."

"The Safety Net Was Us"

Monday mornings, Cinda Woodward rises early, very early, so she can send her husband, Jeff, off at five-thirty on the first leg of his weekly commute—the ninety-minute drive to the Cincinnati airport. By noon, he arrives in Gainesville, Florida, where he goes to work as the chief financial officer for Gold Standard Multimedia, an electronic health-care publishing company. He rents a small apartment where he eats, sleeps, and exercises on a NordicTrack. Thursday night he is back at the Gainesville airport. "Assuming everything works, I'll be home by half past midnight, sometimes two-thirty," he said

Keith Meyers / The New York Times

With opportunities slim in Dayton, Jeff Woodward has become a nomad. On Monday mornings he bids farewell to his wife, Cinda, and children, Leslie and Paul, and flies to Gainesville, Florida, where he is an executive. He returns on Thursday nights.

cheerfully. "I've rationalized it to myself that I'm gone three nights and home four nights."

Home is suburban, white, Republican Oakwood. The Woodwards, who have two children, chose the neighborhood for its schools, and this year their 18-year-old daughter, Leslie, is at the top of the senior class at Oakwood High, considered one of the best in Ohio. The school is a Tudor knock-off ivory tower, with a working fireplace in the library and only 440 students. They call it the Dome. But now even the Dome has cracks. Leslie knows students whose parents have lost their jobs in corporate downsizings. The way she sees it, "My dad was lucky to get a job. The only problem is it's in Gainesville."

Mr. Woodward—who left his Dayton job at Mead Data Central in May of 1995 after it was acquired by Reed Elsevier PLC, a Dutch-British conglomerate—is one of the new nomad dads. They have been laid off, transferred or, like Mr. Woodward, they have simply decided to leave, dissatisfied with what their corporate lives have become. Now they commute by plane to new jobs that they consider no more permanent than the old ones. Three of Mr. Woodward's former Mead co-workers have become nomad dads, too. One commutes to Manhattan, another to New Jersey, the third to Chicago. "I'd rather be the one to be the nomad than drag the whole family around the country," Mr. Woodward said, adding that at 48, he considers himself fortunate to have the education and the financial flexibility to adapt to the new world. (That financial flexibility made the mechanics of adaptation a good bit easier in the spring, when he began flying his own plane to Gainesville.)

Against his commuting grind, Mr. Woodward is trying hard to hold on to the family life and community that he says anchor him in the world. And so at ten-thirty on a Saturday morning in early January, after a week made even more grueling than usual by the blizzard, he was at choir practice at the Oakwood United Methodist Church. The sun was streaming through the stained-glass windows. Cinda and Leslie were in front, raising their voices in strains of "Agnus Dei." Leslie's 14-year-old brother, Paul, would have been there, too, but he had a saxophone lesson. Mr. Woodward was at the lectern. He is not just a member of the choir, he directs it. He never considered giving up the choir, he said later. Neither, apparently, would any of the other twenty regulars. They all showed up that Saturday. "The choir is like an extended family," Mr. Woodward said. "This is how you keep in touch."

Choir rehearsal is followed by another ritual: Mr. Woodward takes Leslie to lunch at a Chinese restaurant. Sunday afternoons after church, he shoots baskets with Paul. The family then visits Mr. Woodward's 83-year-old mother, Bess Woodward, who lives with his brother, Steve, in the town of Springboro. They all have dinner together.

But across Dayton, scores of other people are too exhausted, or frustrated, or just too plain busy, to keep in touch. "No one," said Kathleen Stewart, "has time to eat dinner together anymore." Everywhere you go, you meet working mothers who used to stay home, people with two jobs who used to have one, high school students who have taken jobs to help out their families and prepare themselves for the future.

Monday through Friday, Eva Brodie is a $6.50-an-hour teacher at the YMCA day-care center. Friday nights and weekends, she earns $5.50 an hour at a United Dairy Farms convenience store. Ms. Brodie is 34 and raising one son alone. Fortunately, her mother, Eunice Jackson, who is retired from Wright-Patterson, helps out with child care.

Mike Sampson, a 32-year-old army veteran, works days as a county inspector. Nights, he makes $5.65 an hour selling washing machines at a Best Buy mega-discount store. Still, these two jobs are a big improvement over his last two: He used to work 11 P.M. to 5 A.M. at the Dayton Airport, unloading planes for Emery Air Freight. His second job, at a welding equipment factory in Troy, started at 8 A.M. That left him about two hours to sleep between jobs—in the front seat of his car in the factory parking lot, with a blanket pulled around himself and his alarm clock, on the dashboard, set for 7:45.

Charlie McElligott also has a job—cleaning a dentist's office once a week. Last summer he worked construction, too. He is saving for an essential tool—his first computer.

Mr. Woodward said he became concerned about what all of this was doing to Dayton's community life in the early 1990s when, as Mead's representative, he headed the planning and allocations committee for the Dayton United Way. "It has gotten harder to recruit people as volunteers," said Mr. Woodward, who had to give up his United Way position after he left Mead. "A lot of the women have gone back to work, and because of that a lot of the guys have picked up bigger child-care responsibilities. It spreads around, and makes everyone less available."

Business leaders and politicians used to clamor for invitations to lunch at the Sertoma Club, which helps the poor. Today the club is down to fifty members, its influence is at an ebb, and speakers are hard to find. The Rotary Club is having membership troubles, too, and so has eased its rules: Rotarians no longer must attend 60 percent of meetings or face expulsion.

George Bayless would never consider missing one of the weekly Sertoma lunches, or the annual Christmas party for inner-city children, or the annual charity basketball game that

Keith Meyers / *The New York Times*

State Representative Lloyd Lewis Jr., right, said that blacks rarely got good jobs, but always got laid off. Now downsizing is hitting the white middle class, "where no one ever thought it would go," he said.

he helps run. His 84-year-old father, Harold, a retired minister and a member of the club since 1948, leads the group each week in the opening prayer. "Did you ever read de Tocqueville?" asked the younger Mr. Bayless. "One of his points was that Americans in 1831, they associated together. There were all these associations. It was one of the things that made America work, that made it unique. The safety net was not just government. It was us."

The View from the West Side

Job losses and economic uncertainty are hardly news to blacks in Dayton. Few blacks ever got on at NCR, and the jobs they did find, usually in Dayton's hot, dirty, and dangerous foundries, were never guaranteed. "We were always the last hired, first fired," said Lloyd Lewis, Jr., a black state representative. "We'd do it every five, six years. They'd lay off the bottom of the workforce, then hire them back. The wife always worked—day work, laundry work. We always had two incomes to make up."

Dayton, which is 40 percent black, has long been racially segregated. Blacks live on the West Side, whites on the East. When Mr. Lewis, who is 69, graduated from the University of Dayton with a business degree in 1948, NCR offered jobs to all his white classmates, but not to him. He was fortunate. He escaped the foundries by going to work in his family's Goodyear tire franchise, and today he lives in a middle-class West Side neighborhood.

A lot of Dayton's black foundry workers ultimately made it out, too. But no one ever talked about downsizing factory and foundry workers. "Downsizing—that's a middle-class term," said Mr. Lewis, who two years ago retired as an assistant vice president of the Dayton Power & Light Company. "Now it's affected the white middle-class middle management, where no one ever thought it would go." And while plenty of middle-class blacks are also being hurt, they do not feel betrayed the way so many whites do, Mr. Lewis said. "We never had it to be betrayed. It's just like the Depression. People jumped off the top of skyscrapers. Black people didn't commit suicide. You couldn't commit suicide jumping out of a basement."

The Reverend Raleigh Trammell made the great migration north from Georgia in the 1950s and created his own job, making sandwiches for factory workers. For rich and for poor, he said, "Dayton was a work town." Today, though, black inner-city Dayton is not the work town it used to be. With little to replace the foundries, unemployment is around 15 percent, compared with 4.8 percent in the county. To people there, who have little mobility, the new jobs, in the suburbs and outlying areas, might as well be four states away.

The day before Christmas, Fred Sampson, 49, and Joseph Atkinson, 20, were earning a few dollars at Mr. Trammell's church, loading crates of oranges for poor families.

"What happened to all those places?" Mr. Atkinson asked, referring to the shut-down foundries.

"Cheap labor," Mr. Sampson said.

Power Leaves Town, Too

"It was a white boys' club," said Mr. Tillson, the publisher, describing how power and politics used to work in Dayton. The white boys were the corporate executives. They ran the town through its city manager, mayor, and city commission. These days, though, the white boys' club is mostly gone. "Power is distributed now," said John Moore, who went to work at Wright-Patterson as a clerk in 1946, and eventually became the first black personnel director there. "There are more people at the table." Mr. Moore, who is retired, is chairman of Sinclair Community College.

The waning of the white boys' club made it easy for Willie F. Walker, president of the Dayton Urban League, to introduce himself to John Granzau, chairman of Standard Register, at a 1991 reception for a new banker in town. At lunch a week later, Mr. Walker made his pitch. He needed two community workers for an inner-city neighborhood. The price: $60,000 over three years. After another lunch, this time with the chief executive, Mr. Walker had his workers.

But today, stories like that are less common. The entire community, black and white, has less access to corporate power and money. More of Dayton's top executives are accountable to headquarters somewhere else, and what with global economics, a lot of them aren't even in Dayton half the time; they're on airplanes. David H. Ponitz, the president of Sinclair, told of one local executive who had been trying for six months to get $50,000 from his company's out-of-town headquarters for a community project. "There used to be more CEOs who could make immediate decisions on community issues," Mr. Ponitz said. "Now there is more checking with corporate offices outside of Dayton to get those same decisions. And they usually come at a lower level of interest, and a lower dollar level."

Frederick C. Smith, the retired chief executive of Huffy Bicycle, recalled a 1993 luncheon with Jerre Stead, then the chief executive of AT&T's new acquisition. Mr. Smith, along with five other local business and community leaders, had been summoned to the old NCR private dining room. "Jerre Stead walked in at precisely twelve o'clock," Mr. Smith said. "We were all in coats and ties. He came in a cardigan sweater. He let us know he was sandwiching us in between meetings with *Business Week* and Morgan Stanley. He talked for one hour almost nonstop, and left at precisely one o'clock.

"I went home later and told my wife, 'I didn't understand a word he said.' It was all about the information highway and globalization and 'It's a new world.' " Dayton scarcely came up in the conversation, Mr. Smith said. "Jerre Stead didn't know a thing about Dayton."

In June of 1995, Mr. Stead left to head a software company in Virginia. He was replaced by Lars Nyberg, a Swede who had never lived in America.

Given the changes at GIS, it is not surprising that the United Way missed its goal the last two years. In 1995, with a $400,000 corporate contribution, the company remained the fund's biggest corporate giver. But as its workforce fell to 3,500, from 4,500 in 1992, employee contributions fell to about $840,000, from about $2 million, according to Jim Keeney, the regional AFL-CIO's liaison to the United Way.

Now, as the company prepares to be cut loose from AT&T, it is planning a rescue strategy based on a return to its business roots: computer systems for stores, banks, and big companies. And, said the chief financial officer, John Giering, it remains committed to Dayton. "We are still very supportive of the community," he said. Mr. Nyberg has begun to be more visible around town. He attended a Rotary lunch in December, and held a community reception in January. "I think as time moves on, and we become a public company," Mr. Giering said, "Lars will be spending more time in Dayton."

Where Have the Banks Gone?

George Bayless was alone in his office in Dayton's fading downtown. Nobody was in the adjoining offices. After yet another "consolidation" last fall, Mr. Bayless was the only person left in his department at National City Bank. "Is it a permanent job?" he asked. "As permanent as any job is nowadays."

Mr. Bayless has had an intimate association with Dayton's banks over the years. In the last decade, he has had to get used to a lot of changes. Gem Savings & Loan Association, where he started out as a teller thirty-six years ago, was merged into the Cleveland-based National City Bank. Mr. Bayless, who was then a purchasing officer with his two daughters just barely through college, says he was lucky to keep his job. (With the bills mounting, his wife, Charlene, stopped volunteering at a public television station and went to work as an administrator at a cellular phone company.)

Mr. Bayless ticked off the other changes: "Winters Bank became Bank One. Third National became Society, which became Key Society, which is headquartered in Cleveland." Third National was where he opened his first savings account, when he was 10 years old and a paper boy. Today, there is only one locally owned financial institution in town, Citizens Federal, a savings bank. With the loss of the hometown banks, small-business owners say it can be harder to get a loan. But more than that, out-of-town ownership is another blow to the sense of Dayton as a distinct hometown. Kathleen Stewart is not looking for a loan, and she has no money to invest. For her, it comes down to trust. "I've dropped banks," she said. "They all changed names so many times." Now she uses a credit union.

Looking out the window of his third-floor office, Mr. Bayless sees empty space where once there were buildings, and not many people. "The city just doesn't seem to be as neat as it used to be," he said. The crowds are at the suburban malls. "I'm not a mall person," he said. The one department store left downtown, the landmark Elder Beerman, is clinging to life. Before Christmas, local merchants and businesspeople mounted a "Shop at Elder Beerman" campaign to save the store. Several landlords even offered their tenants rent rebates. Photographs of old steam engines decorate Mr. Bayless's walls. He is a train buff. "People talk to each other on trains," he said. "You discuss the world, the scenery. You don't do that on an airplane."

Mr. Bayless, a Republican who votes in every election, claims that economic change has turned him into a cynic.

"It's not my nature to be cynical," he said. "But I'm cynical when people say, 'We're going to acquire you, but we're not going to lay anyone off.' " He no longer believes the experts, either, he said. "On the bus the other morning, I was reading an article in a magazine about how good employment figures look," he said. "Do you know what happened? These people have dropped out. They're off the rolls. All the middle-class professionals aren't counted anymore. They collect unemployment for six months, then they don't have a job, then they run out of benefits, and all of a sudden they become nonpersons."

Mr. Bayless is still a person. He has a new title at the bank these days. He is the business recovery coordinator. In the event of a disaster—"a fire, say, or something like the Oklahoma City bombing"—it would be his job to come up with Plan B. In that sort of disaster, he said, he would know how to help people—"whereas, the economy, people's attitudes, you can't repair those disasters."

Studying for an Edge

At John Patterson High School downtown, Gary Cooper, who teaches marketing, was telling his students for the umpteenth time why they must—not should, but must—go to college. "Look at the future," he said. "Manufacturing's downsizing. It's an international market now. It's an international world. You're in competition with people you don't even know." Mr. Cooper's students can look at what's left of the past every day from their fourth-floor classroom window. The view: the shutdown General Motors Harrison Radiators plant and its enormous, empty parking lot. The plant has moved south of town, to Moraine, but all that the students know is that the high-paying manufacturing jobs are no longer just outside the high school doors.

One of Mr. Cooper's most determined students is 17-year-old LaShanna Martin. Her mother works at a soap factory. Her stepfather works on the assembly line at Chrysler. "It's a lot different now," LaShanna said. "You can't just get out of high school and go to work." Even if she could get hired at General Motors or Chrysler through connections and luck, she would not start at $14 an hour, the old pay scale, but at about $7.50. LaShanna intends to go to college and become a marketing executive.

At the nearby John Patterson Career Center, also a public high school, the principal, Tim Nealon, says he worries that too many of his students lack even the basic math and reading skills that are essential in today's economy.

If there is one institution that is trying to prepare Daytonians for the future, it is Sinclair Community College. Sometimes it seems as if every other person in Dayton is either enrolled at Sinclair, taking a class there or planning to do so. They are studying everything from computer graphics to medical data processing to advanced manufacturing. Eva Brodie, the day-care teacher who moonlights at the convenience store, takes an early childhood education course on her lunch hour. LaTonya Harris, a single mother of two who earns $11 an hour as a senior data controller at Lexis Nexis, gave up her second job—as a $5.35-an-hour Wal Mart cashier—so she could study information processing at night. She will graduate with an associate degree this spring.

Sinclair's nine downtown blocks of modern, rectangular buildings—with numbers instead of names, and no ivy anywhere—are a pure statement of utilitarian purpose. "This is everyone's hope, right here," 35-year-old Tommy Weems, a business major, said as he walked to his car after classes.

Mr. Ponitz, the college president, is considered one of the most important people in town. When he arrived twenty years ago, Sinclair had 7,000 students. Today there are 65,000. Their average age is 32. More than 20 percent of them have undergraduate degrees and are back to learn new job skills; many have been laid off. At $31 per credit hour—one-third the cost of tuition at Ohio State—Sinclair is the least expensive college in the state. "You have to understand what the new reality is," Mr. Ponitz said. "The new reality is that you have to know something that somebody else doesn't know, but that is not enough. You have to keep growing dramatically if you're really going to keep a job."

At ten o'clock one night, Rob Lind and eleven other men who are trying very hard to adjust to the new reality were gathered around a computer in a classroom in Building No. 11. They are learning to be machine-tool operators, and today that means they have to know computers. Class meets Monday through Friday, 10 P.M. to 7 A.M.—yes, 10 P.M. to 7 A.M. Mr. Lind, who is 32, had already put in his usual nine and a half hours at the garage where he has been a mechanic for fourteen years, making $11 an hour without benefits. "I can go anywhere from here and make fifteen dollars an hour," he said. Eventually, he added, he'll be able to earn $20 an hour. Last semester, Mr. Lind, who gets by on about three hours of sleep, earned a 4.0 average. "I didn't want to crawl around under cars my whole life," he explained.

Ron Hutchins, the director of the machine-tool program, promises his students that the trade they are learning will not become obsolete, at least not in their lifetime. "There is no machine yet that can build a car," he said.

In Search of an Identity

When a man loses his job, his identity is shaken. The same could be said for a town when it loses its old way of work.

"What is Dayton's identity now?" Mr. Bayless asked as he drove by the vacant, snowy expanse that once was the Cash. He paused a long moment, then shook his head. "I don't know."

As it gropes for a new identity, and with the centennial of powered flight just seven years away, Dayton is getting ready to celebrate its own hometown heroes—the Wright brothers. The old West Side bicycle shop where they began to develop the first airplane will become the centerpiece of the Dayton Aviation Heritage National Historical Park. "We're trying to gather around this flight thing," Mr. Bayless said. "We're trying to work out an identity based on that."

Speaking of history and identity, in January 1996, GIS had news that was received here as a small victory. "Drawing upon a 112-year history," Lars Nyberg announced, "we begin to build our exciting future by renaming our company—NCR."

5

Whatever Happened
to the Class of '70?

Kirk Johnson

THE FACES of the Bucknell University class of 1970 gaze out
from the yearbook with a wide-eyed hopefulness untarnished
by time. Though their hairstyles and clothes may look ever
more dated, the class members remain forever 22 years old
and unbowed, captured by the camera at a singular, ascendant
moment of their youth.

They came to this campus in Lewisburg in 1966 from farm
country Pennsylvania, from the suburbs of New York City and
from the shores of Chesapeake Bay, children of America's
middle class and of the great postwar economic boom. Born
mostly in 1948, they had known nothing but prosperity, and it
had imprinted upon them a pattern of belief and behavior as
profound as the one that the Great Depression had left upon
their parents. If anything, the tumult of the 1960s only deep-
ened their basic convictions about themselves and their
future. Many grew their hair and protested the Vietnam War,
but their campus never became violent, and the 1960s presented, in the end, another affirmation of hope: There were
shelters from life's storms. People were essentially civilized.

The great American promise still held, and if it ever faltered, they would be there to help set it right.

"Everything was on the upswing for us," said Mark S. Harris, a biology major in 1970, now a pediatrician in northern Vermont. "We were going to do a pretty good job by the world because the world was going to do a pretty good job by us. There was a confidence bred into us."

Twenty-five years on, a lot of those great expectations have been fulfilled. The 618 men and women of Bucknell 1970 have achieved and prospered. The vast majority are professionals, administrators, and managers. Many are at the heights of their careers, and some are millionaires. This is their lion phase. So what is most striking about these exemplars of middle-class success is what they have lost: their belief in the future and their faith in the rules of hard work rewarded. In the new economy of layoffs, limitation, and job insecurity, their expansive confidence has eroded, and many of them feel dated in their primes. The world that once seemed rich and ripe with potential has become, for many, a place full of fear—for their jobs, for their retirement and, especially, for their children. "There's an uncertainty at twenty-five years after," said Shirley A. Trauger, an English major who now runs a community arts center outside Philadelphia. "Just when we should be at the most stable time of our lives, we're not."

So here is their journey. One college class from one year: Bucknell 1970. It is not meant to be a microcosm of the nation, but a significant slice: one middle-class cohort on the cusp of change and what became of them. They left here on diverse paths, celebrating the sense of infinite possibility. But in middle age they have seen those paths converge. Some believed they could discover alternative ways to live, work, and prosper free of the lock-step compromises of corporate life, only to find that ideal corroded in a time of scarcity and cost-cutting. Others dedicated themselves to lives of social change, only to see economic change force the liberal political momentum of the 1960s into deep retreat. Many of the women, inspired by the nascent feminist movement, created new roles in the 1970s and '80s, only to find that they had to reinvent themselves all over again as their jobs, or their spouses' jobs, changed or simply disappeared.

But most of all, whatever life they chose, the men and women of the class of 1970 were believers—in the system and the old social contract binding companies and their workers. Now that system is being torn down, and if they are not victims, they feel like accomplices. They are the survivors, and often the executioners.

The way they were: the 1970 Bucknell University yearbook.

Richard A. Baumbusch, an electrical engineering major at Bucknell, was already a corporate veteran in 1985. He was working for CBS in New York, as a manager in a division that was going to be closed. The secret clock was ticking away to the surprise mass layoff. Then a co-worker approached. He was thinking of buying a house. Did Mr. Baumbusch think it was a good time to get into real estate? The man's job was doomed and Mr. Baumbusch knew it. But spilling the secret, he believed, would violate his integrity as a corporate officer and doom the company to a firestorm of fear and rumor. There was no way to win and no way out.

"I considered it my fiduciary responsibility to the business to keep my mouth shut, and yet here was this person coming for advice as a friend and a business acquaintance and I had material information that would affect him," Mr. Baumbusch said. "For someone with a sense of empathy and sympathy, which I like to think I have some of, it was very, very hard." In the end, Mr. Baumbusch swallowed his anguish and kept silent about the layoff. The man bought the house and lost his job. The secret held. But ten years later, all you have to do is watch Mr. Baumbusch tell the story to see how many times he has relived it, and second-guessed what he did that day.

The school that produced Mr. Baumbusch helped build the old economic order. Founded in 1846 by Baptists on the west bank of the Susquehanna River in central Pennsylvania, between the great cities of the Midwest and Northeast, Bucknell is a place of hard-headed practicality and bucolic beauty, of Federalist brick buildings and rolling hills where violets creep to the roadside's edge in spring. This rural setting has always made Bucknell self-sufficient and insular, and so perhaps better able to mold students in its own image. To come here is to absorb the old traditions and, for better or worse, become a Bucknellian.

The school's core strengths, the basis for much of its sense of heft and quiet competence, are the engineering and business schools. Bucknell has produced few truly famous names. The writer Philip Roth is one exception—he studied here in the 1950s and has become a sort of poster boy for the recruitment office. But it has produced many substantial ones. The Ivy League, from the Bucknell point of view, is where you go if you have arrived—Bucknell is for those on the way. "Hollywood would cast Bucknell as the vice presidents' school," said Scott G. Nichols, an economics major in 1970 who is now the dean for development at Harvard Law School, a kind of vice president himself. "They're going to be the quiet upper end. They really run the infrastructure."

But as that infrastructure has changed, so, too, have the school and its students. In their unrelenting focus on career goals and on the outsize efforts they believe are needed to achieve them, today's Bucknell seniors can seem like modernized re-creations of the Depression-era parents of the class of 1970. At Bucknell today, taking time off to find yourself feels dangerous. Caught between the pressure to commit to careers earlier than the class of 1970 ever imagined and the fear that those choices may turn out to be terribly, and joylessly, wrong, seniors say that pragmatism rules. The class of 1970 had dreams. The class of '96 has ambitions.

"The class of 1970 knew that great poetry would be written and great music composed and great novels written and it never occurred to them that they wouldn't be the people who might do it," said Douglas K. Candland, who has taught psychology here since 1960. "The current students know that these things will happen, but they don't have the faith that they might be the ones who accomplish those tasks—in short, we've cut out hope."

The men and women of 1970 knew they would win. It wasn't even something they could articulate, they said, it was just there, a given, like the air itself.

Gerald M. Brown got a half-dozen job offers after graduation and took the best, from Eastman Kodak, right in his hometown.

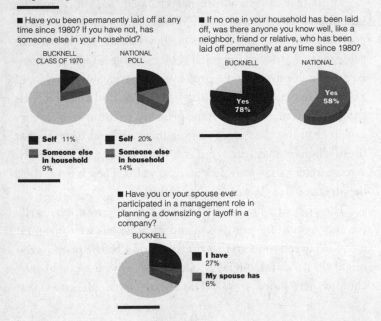

The New York Times POLL

The Bucknell class of 1970 has experienced the rise of widespread job displacement from three distinct perspectives. Only about one in nine have themselves been victims of layoffs. But the great majority have been witnesses, surviving in their own jobs while co-workers, relatives and neighbors lost theirs. And as middle-aged managers, many have helped to plan and carry out layoffs.

■ Have you been permanently laid off at any time since 1980? If you have not, has someone else in your household?

BUCKNELL CLASS OF 1970   NATIONAL POLL

■ Self 11%
■ Someone else in household 9%

■ Self 20%
■ Someone else in household 14%

■ If no one in your household has been laid off, was there anyone you know well, like a neighbor, friend or relative, who has been laid off permanently at any time since 1980?

BUCKNELL   NATIONAL

Yes 78%   Yes 58%

■ Have you or your spouse ever participated in a management role in planning a downsizing or layoff in a company?

BUCKNELL

■ I have 27%
■ My spouse has 6%

Peter Louthis and Robert P. Justman rejected everything about the mainstream and became carpenters in Aspen, Colorado, at a time when a carpenter's wage could still pay the rent.

Christine Dotterer invented herself. Shortly after graduation, she met a female physician for the first time in her life and realized in a flash what her own future could be. Shelby H. Diefenbach entered a corporate world that at last seemed promising for women.

College graduates in their 40's, like Bucknell's class of '70, are among the most politically engaged of people: they are much more likely than the average adult to register to vote, go to the polls and feel they have some say in government.

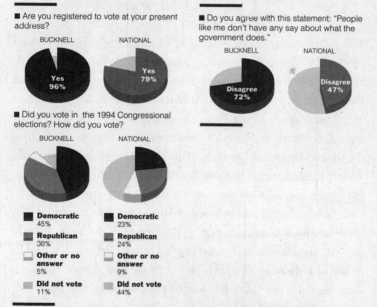

■ Are you registered to vote at your present address?

BUCKNELL — Yes 96%

NATIONAL — Yes 79%

■ Do you agree with this statement: "People like me don't have any say about what the government does."

BUCKNELL — Disagree 72%

NATIONAL — Disagree 47%

■ Did you vote in the 1994 Congressional elections? How did you vote?

BUCKNELL

NATIONAL

BUCKNELL
■ Democratic 45%
■ Republican 38%
□ Other or no answer 5%
▨ Did not vote 11%

NATIONAL
■ Democratic 23%
■ Republican 24%
□ Other or no answer 9%
▨ Did not vote 44%

Based on telephone interviews with 1,265 adults nationwide conducted Dec. 3 to 6, and with 503 people who graduated from Bucknell University in 1970 — 81 percent of all graduates that year — conducted Dec. 1 to 19.

They and their classmates came of age as a new economic order was taking shape, with its corrosive costs, its compromises, and yes, its new opportunities. Their experiences show how broadly and deeply America has been affected by that economic restructuring, and that while mass layoffs may be the most dramatic expression of the new era, little has been left untouched and unchanged.

"In 1970, I wanted to fight to change the world," said Gilbert L. Panitz, the 1970 class president, now an engineer for a major military contractor that has shed two-thirds of its employees in the last five years. "It's ironic that now I'm fighting to keep my job."

A Sense of Hollowness

The guarantee that once came with a Bucknell diploma, of a life insulated from economic instability, has been breached: about one in five households in the class of 1970 has lost a job permanently over the last fifteen years, according to a *New York Times* survey of the class. (See full survey, Chapter 11, for complete details.) Many of these people tell stories of emotional and financial hardship. But the damage has spread far wider, to those who have inflicted the pain and to those who have been forced to remain and watch. There are victims who look like winners, and winners with secret, silent wounds.

When he was growing up in Rochester, New York, Gerald Brown always wanted a house on Canandaigua Lake. His father, a bulldozer operator, would take the family there on summer days, but then they had to pack up and drive the thirty miles back home. For Mr. Brown, a lake house, and a Bucknell education, became symbols of the life his parents never had.

The Kodak job, begun in the summer after graduation, has taken him through more than twenty-five years now, and from his front window he can gaze out every day onto the shimmering jewel of Canandaigua. He is still in the department where he started out as a programmer, information services, and he has risen in the hierarchy, to senior systems analyst.

But he feels lost. The company that he grew to respect and even love is gone, transformed by downsizing into a place that he says he barely recognizes. Kodak has shrunk by a third, to about 96,000 employees, over the last five years. The last round of downsizing, in early 1994, wiped out 10 percent of Mr. Brown's department. "When I have lunch with my peers, we all have the same sense of hollowness," he said. "You're always left with the feeling, each time around, 'I'm dispensable, I'm not a vital cog in the machine.' Even though you're a survivor, even though you win, it's a hollow victory. It doesn't

Michael J. Okoniewski/*The New York Times*

GERALD M. BROWN
Senior systems analyst at Eastman Kodak, where he has worked since graduating from Bucknell. Lives near Rochester, New York

"When I have lunch with my peers, we all have the same sense of hollowness. You're always left with the feeling, each time around, 'I'm dispensable.'"

make you feel valuable when they say, 'I know you're doing three projects, Gerry, here's another one.' "

Mr. Brown once hoped his oldest son, David, who is 16, might someday become a Kodak man. Now he has no idea what advice to offer. "The paradigm I taught my son—work hard, take the AP courses, get into a good school and you will get a good job in corporate America like I did—that corporate America isn't there anymore," Mr. Brown said. "I can't steer him that way. What are the odds that anyone will ever again get twenty-five years at Kodak?"

Richard Baumbusch, the CBS manager, laughs at the idea of twenty-five years anywhere. Ultimately, he, too, was laid off by CBS, and he has been laid off yet again. But he shrugs those experiences off. Each time he got enough of a severance package to tide the family over. He bounced back. He learned to be adaptable and agile—hallmarks of the new corporate man. Indeed, one of the finer ironies of the new economic order, Mr. Baumbusch believes, is that his résumé is more attractive to employers precisely because it has so many jobs on it. Head-hunter friends tell him that companies these days are wary of hiring people with single-job résumés. The applicant might have absorbed too much of one company's culture; he or she might be rigid in outlook, unwilling to change. Perhaps, in looking forward, companies also want employees who have been around the block a time or two and won't fall apart when their new jobs prove temporary.

His last job loss, he acknowledges, was the toughest. Laid off from Citicorp in 1991, he moved his family to Colorado just as his oldest son, Andy, was hitting his stride at Mamaroneck High School in Westchester County, New York. Andy, now a senior economics major at Princeton, has vowed a life of self-employment after graduation—partly in response to his father's sometimes-jolting work experience.

Today, Mr. Baumbusch is an executive director at US West Communications, a unit of the telecommunications corporation US West. He lives in a walled enclave called The Preserve, just outside Denver, in a beautiful home of wood and plants. True, he never feels remotely secure in his job and never will again. But that's just the way it is, he says. Sometimes, having survived thus far, he even relaxes. "Sometimes I think I'm a little too relaxed," he said.

But he is not the man he was. He has seen too much. Like a third of the class members and their spouses from 1970, he has helped lay off people himself. He still remembers pretty much verbatim what he said to his home-buying colleague

Jim Wilson / The New York Times

RICHARD A. BAUMBUSCH
Laid off from two previous jobs, he is now an executive director at US West Communications, and lives outside Denver.

"I'm more aware of the pain involved in layoffs and relocations than I was. . . . It's an extremely lonely experience."

that day in 1985, the way he tried to convey a message of caution, a signal across a secret divide. "I said something like, 'Gee, if it was me, I'm not sure I would,' " he said. But the warning was vague, and the man's heart was set on the purchase. Mr. Baumbusch reached out, but not far enough. "I wanted to say, 'Can't you read the handwriting on the wall?' "

Mr. Baumbusch believes that the changing economy, in the end, has made him more compassionate in some ways, though he still probably would do the same thing and, if anything, feel even more torn. "I'm more aware of the pain involved in layoffs and relocations than I was," he said. "I'm more prone to spend more time helping people look for work than I was. It's easier for me to picture myself in that situation, losing self-confidence, sitting at home. It's an extremely lonely experience."

Every Man For Himself

Peter Louthis still remembers the opening line from the platoon leader's manual he was given in his Army Reserve Officer Training Corps class at Bucknell: The mission comes before the men. That one sentence, so loaded with implications about human expendability, became an obsession for him and eventually led him to change the course of his life. Two months short of graduation, the former American Legion Boy of the Year from Rhode Island, the Bucknell football captain and business major who had made all the right moves dropped out of school and failed to appear for his pre-induction draft physical. He went underground and ended up in Aspen, Colorado, living with no last name. He got work as a carpenter.

In 1970, Aspen symbolized escape—from the war, from parents, from the mainstream, from the middle class itself.

San Francisco had the Haight and the Summer of Love. Aspen was "Rocky Mountain High," its identity proclaimed pop-musically by John Denver, and even more emphatically by the self-described gonzo journalist Hunter S. Thompson, who in late 1970 had just run for Pitkin County Sheriff—and barely lost—on a platform promising to let the recently paved streets return to nature and arrest only "bad" drug dealers. But even without a Sheriff Thompson at the helm, Aspen was wide open and not inclined to ask a lot of questions.

And in 1970, the threat of being sent off to war also held—in the luck of the draw—the sweet sense that one *could* escape. If your draft-lottery number came out very high, beyond the reach of the remotest possible widening of the war, there was an explosive release of pressure that class members say is probably all but incomprehensible twenty-five years later. Most of the men from 1970 can still remember exactly where they were, who was there, and how drunk they got when their draft numbers were drawn for the first time during senior year. The unquestioned rule was that people with higher lottery numbers bought drinks for those with lower ones.

Donald L. Bird's number came up at 325. He would not go to war. His whole life, he said, suddenly opened up with an overwhelming sense of unlimited potential. Everything seemed possible, and with the pressure of Vietnam suddenly lifted, there was no rush to choose a path. He bought a used van, headed west, and arrived in Aspen in December of 1970. "I didn't take a single job interview," said Mr. Bird. "I hadn't made any plans, but I knew I did not want to join corporate America." Today he is the administrator of the Pitkin County Jail.

Robert P. Justman, an electrical engineer at Bucknell, also heard the call. With a lottery number that he remembers only as "over 300," he went to Aspen after graduation and, like Mr.

Louthis, took up carpentry, planning to stay perhaps a year. After his second day on the job, he knew he would never go to law school or business school or do anything requiring suits and ties and life indoors. He had found home. By early 1971, two dozen members of the class had arrived in town.

That old Aspen is mostly gone now. The new Aspen is about money. Range Rovers, known locally as Colorado Cadillacs, slink up to the curbs, and teenagers with just-so haircuts stalk the boutique-choked streets. With housing costs and demand soaring, the bargain-basement shared homes of 1970 are a thing of the past. The idea of Aspen as a kind of left-leaning, egalitarian alternate universe has been eclipsed.

Mr. Louthis, who ultimately got a draft deferment that allowed him to come out of hiding, is now a construction superintendent for a small company that specializes in multi-million-dollar mountainside mansions. The smallest home he has built since the late 1980s is 16,000 square feet, and some have been larger than 40,000 square feet. He and his workers wear white paper slippers over their shoes to protect the floors. And like business owners and managers all over the country, he has found that the mission, in the new economy, very often does come before the men. Two years ago, his company went through its first downsizing, cutting the staff of 110 by about 10 percent, using temporary workers and subcontractors instead. The old elements of his company's founding culture—the family-like feeling, the shared purpose and enthusiasm—are alive, he says, but they are struggling.

So is Mr. Louthis. He believes in his company, Hansen Construction, and wants it to prosper, but the impulse that brought him to Aspen is also still there, and sometimes the two are at war. Although he did not have to lay anyone off himself, he said, he is more acutely aware of being one of "them"

Jim Wilson/The New York Times

PETER LOUTHIS
He left school two months short of graduation, fled the draft, and found work as a carpenter in Aspen. He is now a construction superintendent for a small company that custombuilds multimillion-dollar mansions there.

"I know I've become part of the system I rejected . . . but I feel that I have still kept my individuality."

than he ever was before. "I know I've become part of the system I rejected, to an extent," he said. "But I feel that I have still kept my individuality." And so he encourages his employees to quit if they show even the smallest amount of initiative. Set yourself up as an independent subcontractor, then come back to me, he tells them. You'll keep more for yourself and you'll have a chance to build something. The company, Mr. Louthis tells his workers, "may not stand by you as long as you expect it to." He tries to hold out the same model for himself: draw a line beyond which the incursions and compromises of the business are too much, and be ready to walk away. Just as he did in 1970. "Right now we still have a family, we still do the raft trips and the picnic," Mr. Louthis said. "But the new world is more computer-like, and I can see us beginning to go that way, being cleaner and colder and more calculated—we have to stay competitive."

Mr. Justman also became a successful custom-home builder, and now lives and works in Austin, Texas, using what he earned from his first two Aspen houses as seed money. But his self-made success, in the new border economy of Texas, has also led to some struggles of conscience. Mr. Justman, who earned $4 an hour in the early 1970s in Aspen, now hires mostly Mexican immigrants at a starting wage of $6 an hour—though some men who have been with him for many years earn more, up to $13. He realizes that immigrant wages drive down the pay scale for native-born Americans, and some

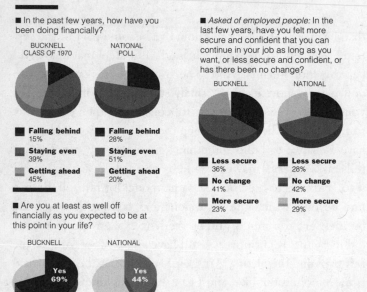

The New York Times POLL

Economically, the members of the class of '70 have prospered. But if anything, they express more worry about the future than the average adult.

■ In the past few years, how have you been doing financially?

BUCKNELL CLASS OF 1970

NATIONAL POLL

■ Falling behind 15%
■ Staying even 39%
■ Getting ahead 45%

■ Falling behind 28%
■ Staying even 51%
■ Getting ahead 20%

■ Asked of employed people: In the last few years, have you felt more secure and confident that you can continue in your job as long as you want, or less secure and confident, or has there been no change?

BUCKNELL

NATIONAL

■ Less secure 36%
■ No change 41%
■ More secure 23%

■ Less secure 28%
■ No change 42%
■ More secure 29%

■ Are you at least as well off financially as you expected to be at this point in your life?

BUCKNELL

NATIONAL

Yes 69%

Yes 44%

years ago, he began to worry that the practice might even be contributing to homelessness.

So he tried an experiment. He bought an abandoned apartment complex and tried to hire the squatters who had been living there, as well as some homeless people off the street.

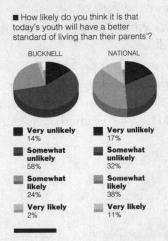

■ How likely do you think it is that today's youth will have a better standard of living than their parents'?

BUCKNELL   NATIONAL

BUCKNELL	NATIONAL
Very unlikely 14%	**Very unlikely** 17%
Somewhat unlikely 58%	**Somewhat unlikely** 32%
Somewhat likely 24%	**Somewhat likely** 38%
Very likely 2%	**Very likely** 11%

The 1970 graduates are much less inclined than other people to blame job insecurity on immigrants or foreign competition.

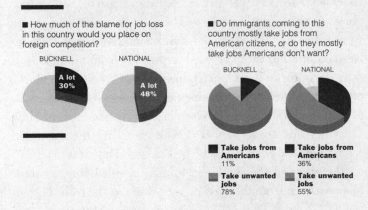

■ How much of the blame for job loss in this country would you place on foreign competition?

BUCKNELL   NATIONAL

A lot 30%   A lot 48%

■ Do immigrants coming to this country mostly take jobs from American citizens, or do they mostly take jobs Americans don't want?

BUCKNELL   NATIONAL

BUCKNELL	NATIONAL
Take jobs from Americans 11%	**Take jobs from Americans** 36%
Take unwanted jobs 78%	**Take unwanted jobs** 55%

It didn't work. The men would show up for a day or two and then quit, or come hours late for work. Although he still believes the self-made road is possible if you work hard and save, he's been led to the conclusion that many native-born Americans have lost the incentive to make those sacrifices. His Mexican workers, he said, still have the work ethic. "They're dream employees. At six dollars they're thrilled and honest and hard working," he said. "Where they come from you have to have the work ethic. Life is so much harder down there—there are no fallbacks."

And as international borders become more fluid, he argues that there is also a fundamental question of fairness. "Just because a guy didn't have the good fortune I did to be born north of the Rio Grande, I should punish him?" he said. "Is that fair?"

Feminism Compromised

When the class of 1970 arrived at Bucknell in 1966, the ideal model of female behavior was still a mythical being called the "Bucknell Lady." She had perfect poise and charm, wore white gloves to the football games to cheer on her men, and always wore a skirt to go downtown—never pants. Women in the class were required to eat their meals separately from the men, and their dormitories were locked down earlier, at eleven o'clock, even though the library was open until midnight. But by 1970, as the women's movement was being born, the student body had voted for coeducational dormitories, and the other old restrictions had been trashed. The Bucknell Lady was dead.

The story of the Bucknell woman is still being written. Many women from the class of 1970 were at the front lines in shattering the dichotomy between home lives and work lives, asserting themselves in professions and institutions once all but closed to them. Now economic forces have compromised those ambitions in ways the women never expected.

Shelby H. Diefenbach never remotely imagined that in her late forties she would be a self-employed businesswoman, mother, and the primary breadwinner for her family. An English literature major in 1970, she took the corporate road soon after graduation, intent on going where no woman had gone before. She went into marketing research, first for Campbell's, then R.J. Reynolds, then Apple Computer in California. In 1992, it all unraveled. Her husband's export business went soft in the recession. She had two small children, and the rising financial burden and ever-longer hours at the office filled her with stress and guilt. Then she got laid off.

It was a turning point. Feeling alienated by the grind, then burned because the opportunities that had been promised were ripped away, Ms. Diefenbach refused even to look for a new job. Instead, she set up shop as an independent marketing research consultant and found herself, to her surprise, on the winning end of a downsizing trend: companies were eliminating their research departments and contracting out the work. She gets no benefits, and her husband is now working as a consultant, too, but she says she is happy in a way she never was before. She is more confident of herself and her abilities, but more relaxed, too. She laughs more now. "We're struggling basically, when we should have a nice retirement stashed away," she said. "But we'd have to be in a homeless shelter before I'd go back. I have a great personality now. I never had a personality before."

Ann M. Morrison, a psychology major in 1970 and co-author of *Breaking the Glass Ceiling*, a how-to book for rising female executives, said that in many ways, Ms. Diefenbach's story had become a new model. Companies that were flush in the 1970s and '80s have retrenched, she said, making the nineties a decade of disappointment for many of their women. Advancement has been blocked and workloads have increased, even as many women need their jobs more than ever because of family pressures. In companies where everyone is watching out for their own jobs, she added, risk-taking has been thrown out the window: Despite the leaner, meaner, charge-the-barricades rhetoric of today's chief executives, no one wants to go out on a limb by hiring women or minorities when "safer" choices are available. But, she said, "More women are also going and making it on their own. That's a very encouraging factor."

Still, independence by itself has provided no immunity either.

Jim Wilson/ The New York Times

SHELBY H. DIEFENBACH
After working for four corporations, she works from home as an independent marketing research consultant.

"We're struggling . . . but we'd have to be in a homeless shelter before I'd go back. I have a great personality now. I never had a personality before."

Christine Dotterer's graduation from Bucknell marked the continuation of a tradition: she represented the third generation of women in her family to be educated here, beginning with her grandmother in the class of 1916. She also broke with family tradition, by taking a career after graduation. She stumbled on it, actually. She went to New York in November 1970 to be a social worker and met, for the first time in her life, a female physician. A new world suddenly opened for her. This was something she could be, something she could make all her own.

She has done that, achieving a detailed, layered vision. She wanted the autonomy of a small-town family practice, in Selinsgrove near her family's roots in central Pennsylvania, and she wanted to run the practice with a woman's sensibility. "It's not hierarchical," she said. "It's a female-oriented office, just me and two nurses, and we're all soft touches. If somebody is in financial trouble, we charge for a brief office visit even though it wasn't." There's a mix of old and new in Dr. Dotterer's little medical office on Selinsgrove's main drag, North Market Street. The small-town family doctor in a solo practice hearkens back to all the old notions of medicine in America. There's even a hitching post for horses out back of the office, and occasionally, Dr. Dotterer said, it gets used.

But a consciously feminist-minded practice, forged in the sea change of the early 1970s, was pretty much a new thing in rural central Pennsylvania when she created it. Although she makes a comfortable living, about $60,000 a year, there was always a larger agenda, she said. And as she tended to her patients and her staff on a day in late 1995, her stethoscope tossed over the shoulder of a bright purple sweater—forget the authority-figure white coat—she made her creation look warm and eminently successful.

In the last few years, though, Dr. Dotterer has seen her work transformed by the same forces of cost-cutting that are behind the layoff phenomenon, as more and more of her patients get their medical coverage through managed-care companies. The increased paperwork, she says, has forced her to computerize her practice and raise her rates. Worse still, she points out, her autonomy as a physician is being whittled down as insurers second-guess her treatment decisions. "The system can't pay attention to the needs of people, and paying attention to the physical and emotional needs of people was the feminist vision of my practice," she said. "It's being a mother hen, for lack of a better word, to my patients and to my employees, but the more I see the iron stamp of managed care on the practice of medicine, the more those wonderful things are being lost.

"I used to think I would be one of these people wandering around practicing medicine at eighty-five and having a good

Keith Meyers / *The New York Times*

CHRISTINE DOTTERER
A small-town family doctor in central Pennsylvania, she feels that managed-care insurance programs are threatening her livelihood.

"I used to think I would be one of these people wandering around practicing medicine at 85 and having a good time. I can't imagine that anymore."

time. I can't imagine that anymore. I can't imagine working to sixty-five."

Changing the World, Then and Now

Just before the class of 1970 was about to march out onto the quad for commencement, someone—Scott Nichols doesn't remember who—started tearing up a bed sheet and passing out the strips to use as armbands. People asked what the point was, what statement they were supposed to be making. "The answer from all quarters was a resounding, 'Who cares? What does it matter?' " he said. The armbands went on, and out they marched.

There was an ethos of engagement, protest, and social idealism in the class of 1970, and even if some of it was at times silly or mindlessly conformist, it led many people in the class to believe they really could change the world, or at least make it better. Many of those people have carried that sense of liberal commitment with them to this day. In a reunion survey of the class conducted by the university in 1990, for example, the class of 1970 had a higher proportion of people who identified themselves as Democrats than any Bucknell class for twenty years in either direction. But the 1960s candle of social action has been hard pressed by the economy of the 1990s, not to mention the advance of middle age.

Suzanne Murphy went to Portland, Maine, sight unseen in the early 1970s, and after bouncing around a few waitressing jobs, plunged back into the political and social goals that had gripped her at Bucknell. She managed a food cooperative, and helped organize a local group to protest United States involvement in Central America. All-day or all-night political discussion meetings became her social life. She found she could get by on very little money; something would always turn up. "The whole economy allowed me to do that," she said. "I could get a job and quit it and know I could get something else."

But the stress and difficulty of that lifestyle started to build in the late 1980s, and in 1989, just as Maine's economy was hit by a recession, she came in from the cold and took a job as an academic counselor in a local college. For the first time in her life, she got health insurance and even a credit card. Ms. Murphy said she realized that, in the '90s, she needed job security in a way she never had before. "I'm single, I don't come from wealthy parents and I felt like I had no safety net," she said. Of course, she added, "Some of it, as much as the economy changing, was simply getting older and wanting a little more structure. I feel like I lived out my youthful impulses, now I want the straight job. There are pressures to be practical."

For Gilbert Panitz, the class president, the feeling of social obligation—the belief that he and his generation somehow had the responsibility to fix everything that was wrong or broken—simply collapsed under its own weight. He went off with Mr. Nichols to Morocco for the Peace Corps, but upon returning, he struggled for years to find a path and a purpose. A newfound faith in God helped ease the load. "It made me realize that the world is really in God's hands, and that I needed to stop worrying about how to make a dent in the world and figure out how I best fit in," he said. "A burden was taken from my shoulders."

But now, with the deep downsizings at his company, Mr. Panitz believes he is being tested again. He fears so much for his job that he doesn't want his employer, or even the state he lives in, to be identified. Several years ago, he organized a prayer group at work—ten men who would gather at lunch to share their faith, maybe collectively raise their sights a little beyond their jobs and the constant, grinding stress of whether they could hold on to them. He's the last member of the group left at the company.

Independence Is Everything

Glen B. Maynard still has the 1969 Datsun 2000 two-seater convertible that he drove West in 1975 after graduating from Boston University Law School. He just had it repainted last fall. His law office, right above the Silverheels Grill in downtown Golden, Colorado, has a view of Table Mountain and the exuberant "Howdy Folks!" banner that stretches across the main drag, Washington Avenue. He walks eight blocks to work. He can live on $2,000 a month if need be. He has one associate, and never went in much for possessions or family commitments. "I never acquired a wife," he said.

In the last few years, more Americans have been "downshifting" their lives, discovering new tracks out of the consumer culture, and away from the complexity, stress, and anxiety of modern life. Mr. Maynard simplified his life long before it became trendy, and in an economy that rewards the self-reliant, that has been a formula for victory, or at least a way to fight to a draw.

Mr. Maynard had always had an independent streak. But his college years, overshadowed by a war that, to him, symbolized all the forces of life over which he had no control, pushed him even further toward autonomy as an end in itself. "I don't know what trade-offs have been made to stay independent," he said. "I'm sure some are economic. My choice is that I don't like to take direction from other people, I like to do things my way."

He could have taken many different, more conventionally successful roads. He was in the top 20 percent of his law school class, a National Merit Scholar and a member of the law review, and he watched as others with lesser credentials landed big jobs on the partner track. But Mr. Maynard looked at the people in those big firms and concluded that in ways perhaps so subtle they couldn't see, they were being molded and shaped to fit in a particular hole. They had given over their self-definition to a group definition, an idea that simply held no allure for him. The promise of perks and power were not enough.

In Golden, he has become something of a local figure, and a politically enigmatic one to boot. Several years ago, for example, he represented a citizens group in a land development battle against the town's biggest economic and political power, the Coors Brewery, which belches steam around the

Jim Wilson / The New York Times

GLEN B. MAYNARD
*A lawyer with his
own practice in
Golden, Colo. he
embraces a simplified
lifestyle to maintain
his independence
from others.*

"I don't know what trade-offs have been made to stay independent—I'm sure some are economic."

clock just down the street from Mr. Maynard's office. Then, just when he'd been pegged as a liberal environmentalist, he took a case representing a major developer who was being sued by the town. "It would be difficult to pigeonhole me," he said. "It's not so much that I want it like that—it just is."

Janice E. Thomas also left the beaten path. It just took her longer to realize what she wanted and how to get there. A conservative math major at Bucknell, the daughter of a career navy officer, she worked as a computer programmer at AT&T for eighteen years before deciding to throw it all over about seven years ago. "When I went into the business world, I thought there would be rewards," she said. "But it's like you're making widgets—you're a programmer and you sit at a desk and this is what you're supposed to do. I began to get the feeling that the work I was doing wasn't making a difference—for me or the world."

Asked to explain just what it is she does now, she struggles, settling finally on a label she invented herself: a mind-, body-, spirit-healing facilitator. She works from her modest home in Norwalk, Connecticut, helping people through a combination of nerve-muscle relaxation, meditation, psychology, and spiritual counseling. Her basic premise is that every person has a mostly untapped interior reservoir of regenerative power, a kind of will to heal that mainly needs encouragement and training.

She's a woman of the New Age, pursuing her dream the old-fashioned American entrepreneurial way. Her house is filled with candles, and she asks visitors to leave their shoes at the doorway. She grants that many people in spiritually conservative Fairfield County, Connecticut, are not quite ready for the service she offers. So she watches her tax deductions and her expenses, and though there are good months and bad, in the end she says she's no worse off materially than she was at AT&T—if indeed she would still have a job there at all. And she believes everyone is living on the verge of something else. All the old systems are breaking down, she says; the changing relationships between people and their jobs are simply one manifestation. In the voice of undying optimism, she believes that a new era is dawning that will be more open to self-fulfillment than any before. What we are experiencing, she says, with all its thrashing and turmoil, is the death rattle of what we knew.

"The world," she says, "is being destroyed so that it can be rebuilt."

Now, as the members of the class of 1970 approach the precipice of their fifties, there is a sense of mortality in many of their voices. Losing a job in your fifties is easier in the new economy, and finding a new one that is just as good is harder. "As you go forward and more and more people will have lived through this, you get more resilient and not so scared," said David L. Hall, a career bank executive who has been laid off and who has laid off others. "But the most dangerous fifteen years for our class is now approaching—the fifteen years to retirement."

Postscript: The Class of '96

Every generation has its pressure cooker. For the Bucknell class of 1970, it was Vietnam and the draft. But while many in the class of 1970 had a hard time even thinking about plans and goals in those chaotic times, the class of 1996 faces the opposite problem: how to avoid being swallowed alive by premature certainty. At Bucknell today, corporate recruiters connect with sophomores and even freshmen, encouraging students—or pushing them—to identify goals earlier than the class of 1970 ever imagined. Anxious parents preach practicality. "Focus," as a noun and a verb, sprinkles conversation after conversation, like an early line on one's state of grace, a mark of success or failure to come.

It may not really be necessary to scope out a life by the age of 21—it may even be counterproductive—but that hasn't made things any easier for Priscilla Stack. Ms. Stack is a bright, articulate psychology major from Mendham, New Jersey, who is distinctly lacking in focus. She doesn't know yet what she wants to do with her life, and in 1996, it would seem, that is a serious problem. There is pressure all around her, she complains, to choose and commit. It comes from friends, from parents, from potential employers, all of them beating the same maddening drum: competition is everywhere. You must dive in and start swimming. Stragglers lose. But, she wonders, what if you just don't know? And what if you choose wrong, plunging into a career only to find yourself trapped later in something you're really not very good at, or worse, that you hate? What if you wake up one morning in middle age and realize you messed up your life because of a decision you made in haste in your early twenties?

"Everyone has a direction," Ms. Stack said. "My dad is pounding on my head every time I talk to him. I feel like I have to make some kind of decision and pounce into it, but I just don't know." Even taking time off to grow up a little more—one of the great escape hatches for the class of 1970—seems closed to her. Future employers, she said, might think her a slacker. "I know it's not good if you take time off after graduation," she said. "It doesn't look like you're very motivated."

Keith Meyers / *The New York Times*

"My dad is pounding on my head every time I talk to him. I feel like I have to make some kind of decision and pounce into it."
PRISCILLA STACK, *psychology major from Mendham, New Jersey*

For many students, pressures like that have profoundly changed the college experience. The old model of college as a heady intellectual adventure, they say, just does not make as much sense as it did a generation or two before. The sylvan images remain—studying under the broadleaf trees, stretching the boundaries of independence from parents—but the old view of college as a sheltered place to come of age, question assumptions, and find your own truth before embarking on real life is getting seriously squeezed.

"From what I see of the world in general, and especially for people my age, we're a little more realistic about our goals than our parents were," said Karim Abdul-Matin, a biology major from Brooklyn who is planning on a medical career in New York City. "We can't become anything we want anymore.

We have a set number of options." Mr. Abdul-Matin has his own career track pointedly mapped out. He's intent on New York partly because that's where his family is, but also because he has connections there. Starting over in a new place is riskier now than it used to be, he believes, and any extra edge you can find must be used. He even knows where and how he wants to live: in a brownstone in the Park Slope section of Brooklyn. "The world is more established," he said. "There's not a sense of expansion the way there once was."

Professors who have seen the shift of generations say the pressure to be practical or safe is so overwhelming that for many students, even choosing a major has become an identity crisis: more than one in five members of the class of 1996 is

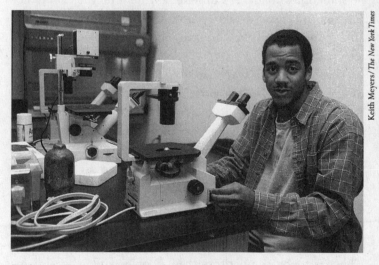

"We're a little more realistic about our goals than our parents were. We can't become anything we want anymore."
KARIM ABDUL-MATIN, *biology major from Brooklyn*

pursuing two degrees at once. "English because they love it, economics to get a job," said Marilyn R. Mumford, who has taught English at Bucknell since the late 1950s. This double-major trend, she said, is hardly a sign of confusion. "Students today are much more self-conscious," she explained. "They have to ask themselves more questions than the class of 1970 ever did, and I think they have a better total picture of the role of education in their lives. They have to keep their eye on the future." Professor Mumford worries, however, that by looking ahead so much, calculating the angles of getting from point A to point B, the students are losing their appreciation of the here and now.

The changes in the economy have also altered political perspectives. Douglas Candland, the psychology professor, says he sometimes conducts a little experiment on the children of the 1990s: He starts talking about the Peace Corps. It sparks an argument every time, he said, about the world and America's place in it.

The Peace Corps was one of the least complicated symbols of the 1960s. It spoke about youth and idealism, and the notion of improving the collective condition of humanity. Today, Professor Candland said, there are students in almost any class who will immediately attack the Peace Corps as an agent of cultural imperialism. Who are we to say to villagers in Africa or South America, the argument invariably goes, that our way is better and that they should be like us?

To the class of 1996, America is just another player. Seniors are more likely to talk about workers in, say, Singapore or China as tough competitors than as objects worthy of compassion—never mind that nations like China and Singapore aren't really the issue here. "It's not a selfish generation, it's a scared generation," Professor Candland said. "When you're worried about your own job or your parents' job, you're just far less likely to be altruistic."

Corporate recruiters are helping to sharpen the focus on the here and now. Over the last five years, career placement officials say, companies have dramatically stepped up their efforts, competing for the loyalties of students long before graduation. An executive at Andersen Consulting, which has become one of the most aggressive of the new-style recruiters, said the change in approach arose from the same cost-cutting and efficiency pressures that drive the downsizing trend. According to Warren J. Dodge, a partner in the firm's New York office, Andersen recruits at fewer colleges than it used to, but focuses on its chosen schools with a new intensity —grooming and developing potential employees beginning in their sophomore and freshman years, and, for promising minority candidates, even in high school. Mr. Dodge said Andersen tries not to pressure students. Other companies, he said, are the offenders. "We want to be recognized not as a recruiter, but as a partner," he said.

One senior who is ready to be a partner is Mike Wickerham, a 22-year-old management major from Pittsburgh with a giant American flag on his wall and a firm belief that capitalism is a struggle in which he will prevail. "I don't know where the country is going as a whole," he said. "But if there are only so many places, I'll have one of them."

Still, though, there are some rebels.

Alison Zampino would probably have more in common with the 1970 counterculture than with her own class. A psychology major from Belleville, New Jersey, with a pierced nose and a rough-edged style of dressing that owes nothing to J. Crew, Ms. Zampino said she would be going to San Francisco after graduation with no job and no particular goal

Keith Meyers/*The New York Times*

"I don't know where the country is going as a whole, but if there are only so many places, I'll have one of them."
MIKE WICKERHAM, *management major from Pittsburgh*

except to live in a place that she has heard is nice. She will worry about making a living when she gets there. She has no commitments at this point in her life, and she likes the feeling.

But this is not 1970, and Ms. Zampino is constantly on the defensive about her decision. Some of her classmates suggest that she is lazy, or too rich to care, or cluck that she is wasting her life, throwing away her main chance. "They get this look," she said, "like, 'You just want to live?' "

6

The Politics of Layoffs

Elizabeth Kolbert and Adam Clymer

IN THE FALL OF 1995, Senator Christopher J. Dodd, chairman of the Democratic National Committee, convened a meeting of about a dozen of the party's top political consultants to get some advice. Polls showed increasing disillusionment with the Republican Congress, but little evidence of increased support for Democrats. What positive message, Mr. Dodd wanted to know, could the party use to win over the growing numbers of disgruntled Americans?

On one side was a group of strategists in favor of appealing to middle-class voters by openly taking on corporate America, demanding to know why in a time of rising profits workers were being laid off and wages were flat. Such a message "gets the Democrats back home," said Carter Eskew, one of those who argued in its favor. Others worried, however, that the appeal of the message was precisely what was wrong with it: it sounded too much like the voice of "old Democrats." It would, they warned, invite charges that the party was inciting class warfare, and could ultimately end up alienating important constituencies, not to mention some of the party's major contributors.

This difference of opinion reflects a continuing debate among Democratic officeholders, and one of the central conflicts inside the Clinton reelection effort. Indeed, it illustrates the challenge both parties confront as they look to the November election and, indeed, to elections beyond: how to offer what one prominent Democratic pollster calls a "narrative" that would allow voters to make sense of a new, and often alarming, economic reality.

Even more contentiously, and certainly more publicly than the Democrats, the Republicans have been battling over what message to send to increasingly edgy voters. Until the last weeks before the 1996 primaries, most party leaders believed the Republican campaign would be fought over more abstract issues like balancing the budget and cutting the federal bureaucracy. But that expectation changed when Pat Buchanan, who had been advocating steep tariffs and stiff curbs on immigration to protect American jobs, won the New Hampshire primary. Suddenly, more gut-level issues like layoffs and the impact of foreign trade began to dominate the discussion. Mr. Buchanan's rivals found themselves scrambling for an alternative economic message, all the while denouncing his. And while in the end, it was Bob Dole, candidate of the party establishment, who won the nomination, the divisions exposed along the bruising way have hardly disappeared.

These forces of economic anxiety have been building for more than twenty years—in times of recovery as well as deep recession—as millions of Americans have lost their jobs and begun to slide, some slowly, others rapidly, down the economic ladder. So commonplace has the news of corporate downsizing become that the notion of lifetime employment has come to seem as dated as soda jerks, or tail fins. And a growing number of Americans have come to doubt one of the basic precepts of the national faith: that their children will have a higher standard of living than they did.

UPBEAT ECONOMY, DOWNCAST VOTERS

By many measures, the economy is in the best shape of recent years. Inflation and unemployment are low and corporate profits are strong, fueling a booming stock market. But many Americans are not sharing in the prosperity. Median family income has stagnated, and only the top earners have come out ahead in recent years.

The New York Times

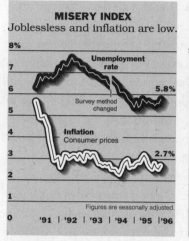

MISERY INDEX
Joblessless and inflation are low.

Unemployment rate — 5.8%

Survey method changed

Inflation
Consumer prices — 2.7%

Figures are seasonally adjusted.

'91 | '92 | '93 | '94 | '95 | '96

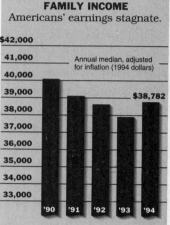

FAMILY INCOME
Americans' earnings stagnate.

$42,000
41,000
40,000   Annual median, adjusted for inflation (1994 dollars)
39,000
38,000 $38,782
37,000
36,000
35,000
34,000
33,000

'90 | '91 | '92 | '93 | '94

STOCK MARKET
The Dow climbs ever higher.

6,000
5,500   5,641.69
5,000   Dow Jones average of 30 industrial stocks; weekly closes except latest.
4,500
4,000
3,500
3,000

'91 | '92 | '93 | '94 | '95 | '96

INCOME DISPARITY
Only the top earners are gaining.

+20%

+15   Percentage change in real income from 1990 to 1994 for households in each quintile (one-fifth of the population, ranked by income)
+10

+5

0

−5

Top 5%

Low   Middle   High
Income quintiles

Sources: Department of Labor, Department of Commerce, Datastream

"You can't really depend on your job anymore," said Jay Lyons, general manager of Ridge Chevy Olds in Basking Ridge, New Jersey, just down the road from the headquarters of AT&T, which had recently announced 40,000 layoffs. "I just heard about another company laying people off. This is almost daily now." Within weeks, Mr. Lyons's dealership had itself gone out of business.

Both parties do have legislative proposals that their members argue would help dull the economic pain, from a middle-class tax cut to changes in the corporate tax code. But by and large, the political system has been slow to respond, at least in part because there are no easy solutions to the two parallel and interrelated economic problems behind that pain: layoffs and stagnant middle-class wages. Even Mr. Buchanan, who made fighting the loss of American jobs one of the central themes of his campaign, acknowledged that he did not know how, if he was elected president, he would respond to an announcement of more layoffs by a company like IBM or AT&T. "That's a very tough question, because I don't have the answer to it," he said on NBC's *Meet the Press*.

At the same time, there are many politicians, especially on the right but also on the left, who argue that the middle class is disillusioned not only because of economic change, but also because of social and political decline. And there are many in both parties who argue that their party's electoral prospects would best be served by focusing on these broad issues.

Months before an election, of course, it is impossible to predict the central focus of a campaign. Still, as they gear up for November, people in both parties say it would be impossible for candidates to ignore issues of economic change. "The core issue in '96 is there is a large chunk of the electorate that is very uneasy," said Bill McInturff, a Republican pollster who worked on Mr. Dole's presidential campaign until the senator shook up his campaign staff in late February. "All these major corporations are shedding workers. All around them people see their friends getting laid off. And the first question for any politician is, What can you say to these people that can convince them the political system can even deal with the issue?"

The Republicans: Unified No More

The day after the House passed a balanced-budget plan last November, Speaker Newt Gingrich called it "the first blueprint to give our children lower interest rates, lower taxes, and more freedom and more prosperity." As it turned out, this was a high-water mark for Republican unity. At that point, key Republicans were speaking with near-unanimity about the nation's economic problems. What ailed America, they said, was that economic growth in recent years had been too slow, and interest rates too high. They also agreed on the cause: a bloated and growing federal bureaucracy. This bureaucracy, they argued, was taking the hard-earned wages of middle-class taxpayers and giving them to others, be they welfare mothers or foreign investors clipping coupons on government bonds. The solution was to balance the budget and give middle-class Americans a $500-per-child tax credit. This would not only give families more money in their pockets, they argued, but also encourage job-producing investments. Before long, the economy would be growing fast enough to insure a rising standard of living for everyone.

Even heading into the primaries, all but one of the candidates seemed to agree that these were the key issues. But it was that one, Mr. Buchanan, who won the first primary, in

New Hampshire, and almost at once the Republican unanimity showed signs of stress. Mr. Buchanan has consistently—and directly—tried to appeal to workers displaced by economic change. In his speeches, he links middle-class anxieties to the rise of a global economy and trade deals like the North American Free Trade Agreement.

"I was not discomfited by the shutdown of the government," Mr. Buchanan said in Iowa, "but I was discomfited when I read that AT&T is laying off forty thousand workers just like that, and the fellow that did it makes $5 million a year, and AT&T stock soared as a consequence and his stock went up $5 million. I think our Republican Party better get back to worrying about working people losing their jobs from unfair trade deals that send those jobs overseas."

It is not clear to what extent Mr. Buchanan's economic message was the moving force behind his early success. A recent *New York Times*/CBS Poll suggested that it was his views on social issues, at least as much as economic ones, that attracted voters. But his message, which injected an unfamiliar note of economic populism into the primaries and led him to an awkward rapport with some lunch-bucket Democrats, forced layoffs and wage stagnation to the forefront of the Republican campaign.

In New Hampshire, Mr. Dole belatedly tried to respond to Mr. Buchanan. Speaking to the New Hampshire legislature, he declared: "Corporate profits are setting records, and so are corporate layoffs." In a speech a few days later, he offered anxious American workers what he called the "four freedoms of economic security," which included the "freedom from deficits" and the "freedom from unreasonable taxation." But the list failed to generate much interest, and on the eve of his loss in New Hampshire, Mr. Dole acknowledged that he had not expected jobs to be such a big issue in the primaries.

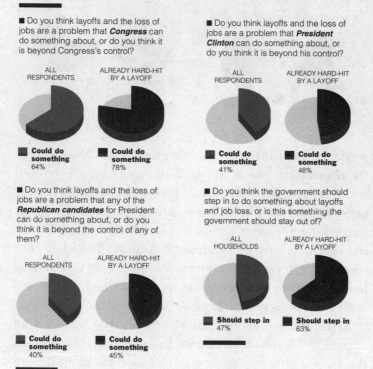

Who should be addressing the problems of layoffs and job dislocation? Most people think Congress could do something about it; fewer are sure about President Clinton or his Republican rivals. People who have been through a layoff crisis are more likely to feel that political leaders could do something, and are more apt to want government to act.

■ Do you think layoffs and the loss of jobs are a problem that **Congress** can do something about, or do you think it is beyond Congress's control?

ALL RESPONDENTS
ALREADY HARD-HIT BY A LAYOFF

■ Could do something 64%
■ Could do something 78%

■ Do you think layoffs and the loss of jobs are a problem that **President Clinton** can do something about, or do you think it is beyond his control?

ALL RESPONDENTS
ALREADY HARD-HIT BY A LAYOFF

■ Could do something 41%
■ Could do something 48%

■ Do you think layoffs and the loss of jobs are a problem that any of the **Republican candidates** for President can do something about, or do you think it is beyond the control of any of them?

ALL RESPONDENTS
ALREADY HARD-HIT BY A LAYOFF

■ Could do something 40%
■ Could do something 45%

■ Do you think the government should step in to do something about layoffs and job loss, or is this something the government should stay out of?

ALL HOUSEHOLDS
ALREADY HARD-HIT BY A LAYOFF

■ Should step in 47%
■ Should step in 63%

Even though Mr. Buchanan's candidacy faded into a protest campaign, the rifts he exposed in the Republican Party appear to be potentially lasting, and potentially even more profound than those between "old" and "new" Democrats. Ross Perot, the Texas billionaire, began once again to flirt with an inde-

People who have experienced a layoff crisis are more inclined to see immigrants as a competitive threat in the workplace than is the average adult, and to want the flow of immigrants curtailed.

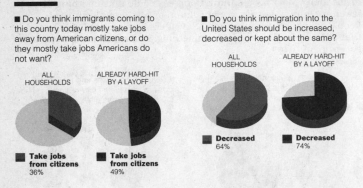

■ Do you think immigrants coming to this country today mostly take jobs away from American citizens, or do they mostly take jobs Americans do not want?

ALL HOUSEHOLDS   ALREADY HARD-HIT BY A LAYOFF

■ Take jobs from citizens 36%

■ Take jobs from citizens 49%

■ Do you think immigration into the United States should be increased, decreased or kept about the same?

ALL HOUSEHOLDS   ALREADY HARD-HIT BY A LAYOFF

■ Decreased 64%

■ Decreased 74%

pendent presidential bid just at the moment Mr. Dole secured the nomination, and as Mr. Dole's advisers are all too well aware, a Perot candidacy would further highlight these divisions. Where both Mr. Buchanan and Mr. Perot oppose recent free-trade agreements, for example, most Republican politicians are firmly on record in favor of them. And while both favor some form of protectionism to preserve American industries, many Republicans see no role at all for the government in securing private jobs.

Representative John Linder of Atlanta, who is faced with major AT&T layoffs in his district, told a reporter not long ago that his question was the first he had received about the job losses. "The good news to me, as one who doesn't think the government has a solution for everything, is that people aren't running to their government and saying, 'Fix this,' " he said. "They understand it is an entirely private matter."

Many conservatives go so far as to maintain that politicians like Mr. Buchanan are misguided when they say middle-class workers have got a raw deal. They make several counterarguments, all of them vigorously disputed by many economists, who say the conservatives are basing their claims on a highly selective use of economic statistics. One argument is that when fringe benefits are taken into account, middle-class wage growth has kept up with the growth of the economy as a whole. A second argument rebuts the existence of a "middle-class squeeze" by insisting that Americans on the top and bottom are constantly trading places. And yet another argument is that while income disparities grew under Jimmy Carter, they shrank under Ronald Reagan only to expand again under Bill Clinton. "The disparities in incomes were worse in the 1970s; we had real stagnation," said Steve Forbes, the publisher and unsuccessful Republican presidential candidate. "They started to really reappear with a vengeance again in the 1990s."

Yet even before Mr. Buchanan's successes, there were some prominent Republican strategists who wondered if the party was vulnerable to just the sort of appeal he has voiced. Although they all agreed with the party's economic prescription of cutting taxes and balancing the budget, they said they were worried that the rhetoric was inadequate, too disconnected from the frustrated lives of real voters. In an interview back in November, Mr. McInturff, the former Dole pollster, said he was concerned that Republicans were not communicating the party's economic agenda in terms that made sense of voters' everyday experiences. "As a party," he said, "we haven't connected the dots yet."

Similarly, Bill Kristol, a leading Republican tactician and the editor of the conservative *Weekly Standard*, argued that the party needed to refine its economic message to connect with voters who felt themselves being left behind by changing times. "It's to the Democrats' advantage to frame this as an economic issue," he said. "To some degree it's an evasion; they want to translate the cultural issues into economic issues. But I think it would be a mistake for the Republicans to just ignore it. I think a Republican economic agenda has to self-consciously explain how it will help the middle class." It will not be sufficient, he warned, for Republicans to say that " 'a rising tide lifts all boats,' because fairly or unfairly, a lot of Americans are dubious about that."

Democrats: An Awkward Position

The question of how to address the nation's growing economic anxiety is a particularly awkward one for a president who won election in 1992 by appealing to middle-class voters who were, in his words, "working harder for less." Many of these voters perceived President Bush to be out of touch with the economic difficulties they were facing.

Mr. Clinton has presided over a steady economic recovery, for which he would obviously like credit. Yet even as the recovery has produced rising profits for many corporations and their shareholders, it has produced only pink slips and falling wages for many of the voters who supported him four years ago. Mr. Clinton tried to embrace both of these competing realities in his State of the Union Message in January. The economy, he said at the outset, "is the healthiest it's been in three decades." But just a few sentences later, he acknowledged the underside of that same economy. "While more Americans are living better, too many of our fellow citizens are working harder just to keep up, and they are rightly concerned about the security of their families."

For Mr. Clinton and for Democrats in general, one of the central challenges is to come up with a convincing "narrative" that explains why Americans are feeling so insecure in the first place. It was just such an explanation, many Democrats maintain, that allowed the Republicans to succeed so spectacularly two years ago. "Part of the problem on our side," said Geoffrey Garin, a Democratic pollster, "is that the only coherent explanation that is out there is the Republican explanation"—that so many Americans feel hard pressed because Washington is taking too much of their money.

On factual grounds, Democrats dispute this explanation—and many economists agree with them—because federal tax receipts as a proportion of the overall economy have actually remained steady in recent decades. Moreover, the Republican account does not address the widening disparity between the incomes of middle-class and wealthy Americans: middle-class incomes, Democrats point out, have been flat even on a pretax basis, even as the incomes of the wealthy have grown dramatically. Politics being a visceral business, though, Democrats are not enthusiastic about engaging in a debate over economic statistics. Instead, they see their task as answering the Republicans' "narrative" with a better one. The difficulty, says Stanley Greenberg, the Democratic pollster who uses the term *narrative*, is that there are too many competing explanations for what has happened to the American economy. "The problem is there are many narratives, and they are complicated narratives. There's a trade narrative about the role of foreign competition and unfair trade barriers. There's a narrative about skills. There's a narrative about rising productivity and that in the long run people will see increasing gains."

Each of these narratives also suggests a different set of policy solutions. If the problem is unfair trade, then the answer, increasingly advocated by House Democrats, might be to adopt a tougher stance with America's trading partners. If the problem is corporations passing on the profits from increased productivity to shareholders but not to workers, then a possible answer might be incentives to change corporate behavior. This is an approach that has been proposed by such prominent Democrats as Richard A. Gephardt, the House minority leader, Senator Edward M. Kennedy of Massachusetts, and, perhaps most vociferously, Labor Secretary Robert Reich.

Finally, if the problem is skills, then the obvious answer would be to improve educational opportunities. There is in fact widespread and even bipartisan agreement that American workers would be better off if they were better educated, and polls suggest that voters, too, are overwhelmingly in favor of making it easier to obtain education and training. But the consensus breaks down once the discussion turns to how to do this.

Even as they continue to disagree, or at least leave unresolved, the question of what the problem is, congressional Democrats have started to produce a flurry of legislation to solve it. Mr. Kennedy, for example, is drafting legislation that would set a lower corporate tax rate for companies that have what he calls above-average records in areas like creating jobs, avoiding layoffs "simply to maximize profits," paying adequate wages and providing training. Senator Jeff Bingaman of New Mexico is preparing legislation that would provide favorable tax, regulatory, and government contracting treatment for corporations that invest in the United States rather than off-shore and devote a certain proportion of their payrolls to pensions and employee education. Congressional Democrats also plan to continue to try to force votes on parallel issues like a higher minimum wage, as Senate Democrats did in late March 1996. The fate of all these proposals in the Republican-controlled Congress is certain doom. But these issues may well play a central role in the congressional races this fall: Both Mr. Gephardt and Tom Daschle, the Senate minority leader, are hoping to make issues of economic security the focus of their conferences' reelection strategies.

Meanwhile, over at the White House, the question of what approach Mr. Clinton should take has been a matter of intense debate among his advisers. On one side are those who argue that to win back the high-school-educated white men who abandoned the Democrats in 1994, the president needs to lay out an economic agenda that speaks directly to middle-class anxieties. This group includes Mr. Clinton's top advisers from 1992, like Mr. Greenberg and James Carville. "If the Democratic Party can't talk about stagnating wages in a time of rising prosperity, why have one?" Mr. Carville said.

In the fall of 1995, in a research project financed by the Service Employees International Union and the AFL-CIO, Mr. Greenberg tested white, non-college-educated voters' reactions to various economic messages and found them unimpressed with the president's. The report warned that the president in particular and Democrats in general would not get a hearing from these voters unless they showed a strong populist identification with "the personal struggle of non-college voters trying to raise their living standards in a stagnant economy."

On the other side, though, are those who argue that an economic populist appeal is too divisive, and that the Democrats can forge a majority coalition only by emphasizing broad, unifying issues like Medicare and education that appeal to more affluent voters as well. This group, which includes most of the members of Mr. Clinton's new campaign team led by Dick Morris, also argues that the economic growth of his first three years in office is an accomplishment the president should boast about, not undermine.

From his recent speeches, Mr. Clinton seems to be trying to fuse these two messages, acknowledging voters' anxieties but rejecting a populist appeal. Speaking at a public-works garage outside Detroit in March, the president said: "The last time your country changed this much was a hundred years ago, when most people moved from living in the country to the city and town, when most people moved from working on the farm to working in the factory. And many of the same things happened a hundred years ago. There were people who made lots of money. There were people who found opportunities that they could not have dreamed of. And there were people who were severely dislocated and disturbed, and whose pattern of life was unsettled."

The president called on the federal government to do more "to create jobs and raise incomes and give these people who are being downsized a chance to go right with their lives." And he reiterated his calls for an increased minimum wage, tax deductions for college tuition, and federal vouchers for worker retraining. But he pointedly avoided mention of the kind of corporate tax changes his own labor secretary is advocating. "We are not a people who object to others being successful," he said. "We do not resent people amassing their own wealth fairly won in a free-enterprise system."

The Old Rules Fail

The bipartisan groping for a message to connect with economic discontent comes at a time of fundamental political uncertainty. Just as factory and middle-management jobs have become more insecure, so, too, have elected officials', and many politicians argue that the two developments are related. For years—though political scientists constantly recalculated their formulas—it was a simple truth that if the economy was good, the party in power won re-election. If it was bad, the opposition prevailed. An ailing economy in 1976 and 1980 was a critical factor in those elections, and congressional seats have regularly been won and lost over unemployment and inflation. One has to go back to 1968—in the middle of the Vietnam War—to find an exception.

But in 1992, the old rules failed. The country was at peace, the economy was in a recovery, and yet George Bush was badly defeated. Two years later, the rules performed no better. Once again the country was at peace and the economy was expanding. The models could not account for the devastating defeats that cost the Democrats control of both the House and Senate.

There are undoubtedly other factors at work besides changing economics. Innumerable polls suggest that voter volatility is a product not just of economic trends, but also of social trends, like concern over moral decline and a loss of confidence in government. But increasingly, politicians of both parties argue that there is a profound connection between what is happening in the voting booth and what is happening at corporate headquarters and on factory floors. The old models of voter behavior no longer work, these politicians argue, because they were fashioned at a time when economic growth translated directly into increased wages and job security. Yet for many middle- and lower-income workers, this is no longer the case. A low unemployment rate means little when a factory worker loses a $15-an-hour job and has to settle for one paying half as much. "The people who have seen their wages and benefits erode and their job security vanish, they are politically up for grabs," Mr. Reich said. "They're not liberal, they're not conservative, they're anti-establishment. They blame whoever's in power."

But they have not given up on government. The *New York Times* poll showed that 10 percent of the public had gone through a "major crisis" in their lives because of a layoff, either their own or a family member's. And 15 percent said they were "very worried" that they or someone in their family would be laid off in the next year. But while people in both of these groups were hostile to the economic system and to both political parties, they were also more likely than other Americans to say that government could and should do something about the layoff problem. In all, 64 percent of all Americans said they believed that "layoffs and job loss are something Congress can do something about." But among those who were very worried about a layoff, that figure jumped to 75 percent, and among those for whom a layoff had caused a major crisis, to 78 percent.

The poll also found that the public has yet to settle on a coherent explanation for the loss of jobs in this country, and so remains potentially open to either party's narrative. Three-quarters of the public put "a lot" or "some" blame on "automation, computers and technology," 84 percent a lot or some blame on "the economic system," and 81 percent put a lot or some blame on "business corporations." Eighty-six percent said foreign competition should get at least some blame, and

79 percent said the same thing about the federal government. Seventy-five percent placed at least some blame on American workers themselves, but only 50 percent blamed Wall Street.

Looking back, economists now say that the roots of today's economic insecurity can be traced back to the early 1970s. That is when the growth that had followed the Second World War began a twenty-year slowdown, and when middle-class incomes began to lag. Similarly, political analysts now go back to the early 1970s in an effort to understand today's uncertain environment. One of the defining traits of American politics over the last twenty-five years has been the defection of working-class, white voters, especially men, from the Democratic Party. These voters, who had been drawn into the party with the New Deal, left it for largely social reasons. But some of those reasons had an economic undertone; many saw their party as too concerned about blacks and the poor, ignoring the struggles of other working families. Repeatedly Republicans have defined their success with this group as the prelude to an emerging political realignment, only to see their gains wash away in harder times, like 1982 and 1992.

One of the lingering—and central—questions about the 1994 election is: Was this the portent, finally, of a permanent realignment or will the coalition once again fragment under economic stress? The group that swung most dramatically in 1994 was white males, or "angry white males" as they were quickly dubbed—particularly white men without college degrees. Exit polls showed their support for the Democrats dropped in two years from 59 to 40 percent.

It is no coincidence, some analysts argue, that this is the same group that has fared worst economically over the last two decades. According to Lawrence Mishel, research director of the Economic Policy Institute, a liberal think tank, real wages of white men with only a high-school education have dropped by 17 percent since 1979. In an article last fall in the liberal journal *The American Prospect*, Ruy Teixeira, the Economic Policy Institute's director of political science, and Joel Rogers, a professor of law, sociology, and political science at the University of Wisconsin, argued that the Democrats had lost control of Congress because these voters had embraced the theory that wasteful government spending and high taxes were responsible for their declining standard of living. To win working-class white men back, the two said, the Democrats had to offer "an alternative story that shifts the blame to other targets."

By some accounts, at least, this is precisely what Mr. Buchanan did with his campaign against foreign trade agreements and immigration. And notably, Mr. Buchanan's support was highest among working-class white men. In the New Hampshire primary, according to exit polls, about a third of his votes came from white men without college educations, and among this group he was far more popular than any of his rivals.

The View from the Ground

The politics of economic anxiety, of course, is not only being played out in the war rooms and on the hustings of presidential politics. The story is also unfolding in congressional districts around the country, in places as diverse and far-flung as Houston, Texas, and Erie, Pennsylvania. What emerges from conversations with voters and candidates in both cities is a sense that the debate could favor either—or neither—party in the fall.

Houston's Twenty-fifth Congressional District, which stretches east and south around downtown, takes in blue-collar neighborhoods around the Houston Ship Channel and more-affluent areas around the Texas Medical Center and Rice University. Voters interviewed there said they were doubtful that either party was even in touch with their anxieties. Many also said they wondered if the government could do much anyway, beyond getting out of the way.

Cliff Fehr was laid off a few years ago from his job as a sales manager at Tenneco Inc., and, after struggling, found a new sales and marketing job that paid about $30,000 less in annual wages and benefits. "Politically, it changed me a little bit," Mr. Fehr said of his layoff experience. "I've always been on the conservative side anyway, but now I'm probably more conservative. I'm very concerned about jobs leaving the United States and going overseas, more so than I was before." Mr. Fehr said he was more inclined to vote for Republicans because he felt the party was more sympathetic to business. "What the Democrats do is they'll tax the hell out of the corporation and really inhibit the money that's available to put back into growth."

Even some lifelong Democrats say they don't have much faith in what they perceive as the party's more activist stance on jobs. "I know the Democrats do talk a lot more about retraining and things like that, but I doubt it will accomplish a lot, frankly," said David Swig, a retired construction engineer. "We'd probably be better off if we saved the money."

Still, there are many people who have had job problems who credit the government—and more specifically, Democratic policies—with helping them get back on their feet. One is Sergio Garcia, a former oil-production analyst who was laid off from Chevron when his entire division was eliminated three years ago. A government-financed retraining program allowed Mr. Garcia to get a new degree in occupational technology and industrial studies; he is now a training coordinator for a consulting company. "At this point, the whole issue of retraining is at least being addressed by the Democrats," Mr. Garcia said. "I retrained myself, but I got some help—and that's the kind of thing this country needs."

The Twenty-fifth District, which voted comfortably for Bill Clinton in 1992 and narrowly for George Bush in 1988, leans Democratic. The Democratic incumbent, Ken Bentsen, a nephew of former Senator Lloyd M. Bentsen, said he believed that he could seize the economic upper hand by emphasizing that he had voted against several Republican proposals to cut funds for education and job training. "There's not much you can do to tell a guy that he can get his job back at AT&T," said George Strong, a political strategist who works for Mr. Bentsen. "But what you can tell him is what he and other people in a similar situation can do to get employed again, and there are a number of things the federal government can do to help."

In the early stages of the campaign, the two Republican hopefuls—Brent Perry, a lawyer, and Bill Brock, an engineer—are emphasizing conservative policies such as a balanced federal budget, which they say are most likely to prime the economy and create jobs.

Halfway across the country in Erie, where strip malls and vast factories, many of them shuttered, dominate the downtown landscape, the incumbent congressman, Phil English, is part of the freshman Republican class that swept Newt Gingrich to power. Enough of his constituents in the Twenty-first District have been voting Republican to keep the seat out of Democratic hands for eighteen years, even though the district voted for Mr. Clinton in 1992 and Michael Dukakis in 1988. But Mr. English, who won with only 49 percent of the vote in a three-way race two years ago, is himself performing a delicate balancing act as he fights to hold on in a district both parties see as a battleground.

General Electric is in the process of laying off 1,400 workers at its big locomotive plant in Erie, and both General Electric and the United Electrical Workers local acknowledge that Mr. English has worked hard to insure continued financing for Amtrak and other federal programs that help boost sales. And he has also worked, against many of his Republican colleagues, to preserve strands of the safety net, like assistance for people who lose their jobs due to trade agreements and extended unemployment benefits. Mr. English, who served in Republican state administrations in Harrisburg before heading to Washington, contends that he is a moderating force on the Gingrich revolution, who explains to his Sun Belt colleagues what life is like in the Rust Belt and gets concessions. He seems comfortable with this role, and he argues that even though jobs are the issue his constituents most often raise, "most people recognize that the role of the federal government is necessarily limited."

But local labor leaders say they are unimpressed by this argument. Jim Nelson, who followed his father into the presidency of the union local after about fifteen years as a stockkeeper in the locomotive plant's steel yard, argues that Mr. English's ultimate votes for the Republican budget and its cuts in social programs show that his allegiance was to Speaker Gingrich, not to "the guy that carries a lunch box going through the gate of this plant."

Mr. English's Democratic opponent is Ron DiNicola, a local boy who boxed, enlisted in the Marines, and went on to

Harvard and a California legal career before returning to lose a bid for the nomination two years ago. Recently, Mr. Di-Nicola wondered out loud how the government could encourage General Electric to weigh a responsibility to its workers and the community with its duties to its shareholders, its "obligation to the bottom line." He told the union that, if elected, he would work to lessen the pain of layoffs, by, for example, restoring unemployment compensation and training subsidies to their old non-taxable status. But, beyond that, he has generally steered clear of offering policy prescriptions.

When the General Electric workers look to the presidential race, many of them do so with concern. "The only candidate on the macro level who is talking about real-world economic issues, unfortunately, is Pat Buchanan," Mr. Nelson said. "Bill Clinton is going to have to start talking about the things Pat Buchanan is talking about."

7

Searching for Answers

David E. Sanger and Steve Lohr

GERALD GREENWALD SLIPPED into his limousine near O'Hare Airport in Chicago, leaned back and pondered a daring deal. It was the fall of 1995, and Mr. Greenwald had joined United Airlines as chairman a year earlier as a seasoned practitioner of the management arts, including layoffs. He had been an architect of Chrysler's recovery, shedding 60,000 workers. Buy struggling USAir, he figured, and United would add valuable routes, creating the nation's largest airline by far. "I wouldn't want to be on the other side of this," an aide recalled Mr. Greenwald as saying, referring to the problems he could create for rivals.

There was just one hitch. A year earlier most of United's 75,000 employees—the pilots, mechanics, gate agents, and middle managers—had bought a majority stake in the airline, taking huge pay cuts in return for a commitment that none of United's employee-owners would be laid off for five years. Buying USAir would take United deeper into debt, threatening the no-layoff guarantee. It would also put United's employees in the agonizing position of ordering the downsizing of USAir, killing off the jobs of 8,000 union brothers and sisters.

As the US Air plan circulated in the company, union leaders like John Peterpaul, the gruff representative of the mechanics

Steve Kagan / The New York Times

Gerald Greenwald, chairman of United Airlines.

on United's board, raised objections. He and his union colleagues could imagine the headlines if they took jobs. And many United employees were questioning whether the strategic gain was worth the risk to their own job stability.

By the time United's board met on November 13, a formal vote was not even necessary. "This was something we just couldn't do," Mr. Peterpaul recalled. "Too much pain." Mr. Greenwald agreed, but even today he wonders whether his company made the right choice. "What is job security? It's working for a strong company. We made the only choice we could at the time. But in the long run will United be better off going it alone? I don't know. We still debate it."

Decisions like United's—rare exceptions, to be sure—are reminders that layoffs are not the only option for businesses trying to compete in today's economy. Across America, some companies are resisting downsizing, searching for less painful ways to survive and prosper. It isn't easy. The sacrifices made at such companies are often substantial. And even the companies that have avoided layoffs say they do not know how long they can hold out. They are beholden, they maintain, to powerful forces beyond their control. Among them are new technologies that undercut jobs and Wall Street investors who continue to reward layoff announcements. Yet another force, and one likely to become increasingly important, is pressure from foreign nations, notably China, for American companies to move jobs onto their soil in return for access to their growing markets.

Many executives and economists, and some historians as well, agree that while the results may seem Darwinian, layoffs are a necessary part of the bargain in an economy that continues to generate wealth and new jobs, even as old ones fall away. Their argument is that unless companies are free to shrink—or die altogether—the American economy will come to resemble those of European nations, where the social prohibition against layoffs has made many companies reluctant to expand or test new businesses. The result, they point out, is both inefficiency and high unemployment, in some cases twice as high as the rate in the United States.

In recent years, though, others have wondered whether job-cutting has become too accepted as management's answer to problems. And when corporate executives pocket multi-million-dollar bonuses for driving up profits by slashing workers, some ask whether the pendulum has swung too far. "Capitalism swings to extremes," said Jeffrey E. Garten, a former investment banker and under secretary of commerce who is the dean of the Yale School of Management. "We are now deep into one of those extremes."

Recognizing the problem is one thing. It is another to frame a constructive debate about what steps might be taken to slow the downsizing or ease the difficulties of workers caught in the spiral. At bottom, many of the solutions being discussed involve a reordering of priorities to put more emphasis on protecting workers. This can mean concessions by both workers and executives to make sure a business remains strong enough to preserve jobs. It can mean a willingness by companies and even taxpayers to spend more to help workers through one of the most wrenching transitions in decades. It can mean taking a page from other cultures that lay off employees only as a last resort. And it can mean workers themselves trying to become more self-reliant.

Hits and Misses

Layoffs are sometimes a matter of corporate survival. Markets and technology change quickly, threatening to turn today's blue-chip powerhouse into tomorrow's basket case. Just a few years ago, three of America's biggest corporations—General Motors, Sears, and IBM—seemed to be sliding fast. In a 1993 cover article, *Fortune* magazine dubbed the three "corporate dinosaurs." Each had grown bloated and bureaucratic, and was being rocked by new forces: General Motors by leaner, quality-conscious car makers at home and in Japan, Sears by more efficient retailers like Wal-Mart, and IBM by a computing revolution led by the microchip and personal computers.

Three years later, after shifting strategies and shedding many thousands of workers, the companies are smaller, smarter, and more nimble. The out-of-control slide has stopped and, for the most part, so have the job cuts. Indeed, IBM recently announced that after cutting its payroll by 175,000 people since 1987, it is growing again, especially in its computer-services business, where it seeks to hire 10,000 workers this year. And it is awarding 8 percent pay raises to its surviving workers.

But some management experts argue that many companies downsize in a violent, overly hasty reaction to bad times. They cut without overhauling their strategy or the way they work. A survey of 1,000 companies by the American Management Association found that fewer than half the companies laying off people managed to increase their operating profits after workers were shed. "The question that too many companies ask is how can we get by with the minimum number of people," said Eric Greenberg, director of management studies at the association. "And you're not going to grow if you simply do the same work with fewer people. You end up with a demoralized work force and no new business."

Other studies have come to similar conclusions. Nitin Nohria, an associate professor at the Harvard Business School, recently studied layoffs over more than a decade at a hundred large American companies. Often, too many people are fired, he found, or the wrong ones, and those who survive aren't retrained to pick up the workload in a shrunken company. "Downsizing is typically viewed as a financial exercise," Mr. Nohria said. "Companies add up their costs per employee and say, 'If we have 10,000 fewer employees, that will save us that much in expenses and make us that much more profitable.' So they cut 10,000 people across the board." Yet that approach, Mr. Nohria said, rarely succeeds. Indeed, layoffs have failed to pay off at companies including retailers like Woolworth and Kmart and technology companies like Apple Computer and Unisys.

Layoffs often bring immediate rewards on Wall Street, as investors bid up the share prices of companies that announce cuts. But in the long term, there is scant evidence that downsizing helps investors. Wayne Cascio, a professor of management at the University of Colorado at Denver, studied twenty-five large companies that cut their payrolls by roughly 30 percent in any two-year period during the 1980s, then tracked their stock prices over the next three years and compared the cutters with similar companies in the same industries that did not make deep cuts.

Three years after they cut their payrolls sharply, the downsized companies had averaged a gain of 4 percent in the value of their shares. That group included Caterpillar, Clark Equipment, Halliburton, and Asarco. By contrast, the companies in the same industries that had not downsized registered average stock-price gains of 35 percent. "At the least, the research shows that downsizing is no magic bullet," Mr. Cascio said. "Often, there is no payoff."

The deep cuts can cripple product development, marketing, and customer service. As business evaporates, management is forced into further cuts. Sometimes, with angry customers clamoring, management recognizes its mistake and hires again. In rare cases, executives even admit their mistake. Consider the experience of Delta Air Lines, which last December and January watched its on-time performance plummet to the bottom of the list for major airlines. Complaints to the Department of Transportation soared. No one in Delta management had to look too hard to find the cause: In the last few years Delta had eliminated more than 10,000 positions, a mix of buyouts, multi-year leaves, and layoffs.

As air travel grew last year, the company failed to hire. And then the bad winter weather hit and schedules got thrown off. Delta found itself short of baggage handlers, maintenance workers, and customer-service agents. "Our customer service deteriorated," said Bill Berry, a Delta spokesman. "We found that we lost a lot of experience when we encouraged early retirements."

Now, Delta is hiring 600 workers.

A Popular Alternative

The United Airlines experiment in changing corporate priorities—putting job security on par with profits—is the largest and among the most visible cases of employees taking control of a company. It starts with people like Herb Hunter, who pilots 737s and makes well over $100,000 a year for it. A trim, laconic former Air Force pilot, he looks and sounds as if he stepped from the pages of *The Right Stuff*. But these days his confidence is confined to the flight deck. On the ground, Mr. Hunter muses about how he has "downsized my life" to meet the new realities of the airline world. He has given up 25 percent of his pay in return for more job security and a shareholder's stake in United, which he will receive at retirement.

Though many of his colleagues opposed the employee buyout, it was an easy decision for Mr. Hunter. He is still haunted by memories of the early 1980s, when United laid him off for two years during a severe downturn. "Suddenly I was sitting on a mortgage I couldn't pay," he recalled recently. "I got divorced, I worked in the Air National Guard just to put food on the table. Now I have one major interest: I want to work for an airline that will still be around when I retire."

Eighteen months ago, many doubted United's buyout would assure its survival. Today, while the airline still has plenty of problems, the signs are encouraging. In the last year, the company's stock price has doubled, easily outpacing the industry's average. United's share of the market is rising, along with the revenue generated by each employee.

As the priorities of United's employee-owners changed, so has the corporate culture. Sick time is down 20 percent. Grievances filed by the pilots are down 75 percent. So are worker's compensation claims. And the unions, with a greater stake in corporate profits, are suddenly far more flexible about work rules. When the airline wanted to renegotiate with the pilots to allow round-the-world service, the talks took just two days.

Another telling statistic is that the list of pilots seeking jobs at United has swelled to more than 10,000, even though the airline now pays less than some of its biggest rivals. "There were a lot of naysayers when this started," said Captain Hunter, noting that some form of the deal had been rejected

A computer-enhanced photograph of United's workers that was used in advertisements following the employee buyout of the company.

five times before. "The conflicts of interest seemed too big: How could the union negotiate when it was also serving on the board? But if you took the vote again today, I think it would be overwhelmingly positive."

The harmony at United may not last. Other employee-ownership experiments, as at Weirton Steel, have dissolved in bitter recriminations. And at United there are periodic rumblings of dissatisfaction. The company's new employees now work for lower starting pay and a somewhat smaller stake in the company than those who were around before the employee buyout, creating two classes of workers. Flight attendants, who elected to take no pay cuts and thus got no stake in the company, often complain that the "employee-owners" treat them just as the old managers did. And now the price of United's stock has soared so much that it would be prohibitively expensive for the flight attendants to buy in.

The real test will likely come when the airline industry moves into one of its cyclical downswings. The company will face pressure from Wall Street—45 percent of United shares are still publicly traded—and in a few years union leaders will be negotiating contracts with their own representatives on the board, whose loyalties will be torn. "There is nothing that insulates us from competitive realities in the long term," said Douglas Hacker, United's chief financial officer. "Can't be done."

When it comes to employee ownership, United is the exception rather than the rule. More typical is Market Forge Industries, a small Boston manufacturer struggling to stay alive with an aging workforce. Like Market Forge, most employee-owned companies are a lot smaller and have a lot less access to money from outside investors than does United. Founded in the old Faneuil Hall marketplace as a family concern, Market Forge grew into a manufacturer of everything from cooking equipment to the shell casings of nuclear bombs. But over the years it became a victim of one buyout after another: For two decades it was part of Beatrice Foods and then became a pawn in several leveraged buyouts. By the early 1990s it was a shell of its former corporate self. No one had invested in the firm in years; research and development had stopped as the owners tried to squeeze more profits out of the company, and the firm's hold over the market for steam cookers, used in institutional kitchens, had withered. The once-brimming factory north of Boston dwindled from 900 employees to 130, with an average age of 55. And when Market Forge's closure seemed imminent, the survivors, most of them high-school-educated blue-collar workers with little prospect of reemployment, were desperate.

At the last minute they won a reprieve by relieving the last owner of the pension liabilities. That left them with the company's name and its aging equipment. "The challenge was to save jobs," said A. Nath Srivastava, the company's president, who was recruited from another firm. "And the first thing I discovered was that no one at the company knew a thing about its financials. So I met everyone in small groups and said 'If we do nothing, we are dead meat in thirty-six months.' "

The workers agreed to scrap most of the union rules about what kind of work they could do. An outside designer was brought in to come up with a state-of-the-art cooker. Mr. Srivastava found some seed money from the National Institute of Standards and Technology, part of the Commerce Department, and a state program. But he has been forced to balance the urge for profitability with the desires of the workers: They have restricted the search for a new factory, something the company desperately needs, to within fifteen miles of the existing factory.

It is still far from clear that the company will prosper, but for now at least no one has been laid off. And the atmosphere is dramatically different. "The hardest part is getting sixty-year-old employees to recognize the current business environment," said Robert F. McGauley, director of marketing projects for the company. "They have to understand every step and why it can save money. That kind of re-education is very, very slow. But suddenly people don't treat the place like a job that you leave at four-thirty."

Rarely do workers own most or all of a company. The more common form of worker ownership in America is when employees own 10 or 15 percent. Joseph Blasi, a fellow at the Institute for Advanced Study in Princeton, and Douglas Kruse, a professor at Rutgers University, studied the employee ownership of public companies and their performance in the 1990s. They found that about 1,500 of the 7,000 companies on the New York Stock Exchange, American Stock Exchange, and Nasdaq market were owned 5 percent or more by their workers. And workers hold more than 20 percent of several major corporations, including Procter & Gamble and Polaroid. But this more limited form of employee ownership does not really change management decisions because workers do not have a controlling interest. Mr. Blasi said the main effect of this kind of employee ownership would probably be to narrow the income gap between executives and workers. "If employees owned a real ownership stake in companies, the distribution of wealth would be more fair," Mr. Blasi said. "But not enough companies have employee stock ownership programs, so workers have the worst of both worlds. They don't benefit from the appreciation in the share values of the companies they work for, and they get laid off."

Retraining

Everybody's first answer when seeking the best defense for workers in an uncertain economy is education and training. And few companies invest more in training than does the Intel Corporation, a maker of the microchips used in personal computers. It spends more than $120 million a year on training, or nearly $3,000 averaged across all of its workers, more than double the national average. Growing and highly profitable, Intel is one of the exceptional companies that can afford the cost. But it is also a matter of survival. Few industries endure

Steve Northup / The New York Times

Intel workers meeting at the company's clean facilities in Rio Rancho, New Mexico. Intel spends double the annual national average on training its workers.

technological change as rapid as in the semiconductor business. Every two or three years, with each new generation of microprocessor, the company requires a new mix of skills.

So five years ago, Intel instituted a system so that its employees can be reprogrammed as fast as its chips. Craig Barrett, Intel's chief operating officer, speaks of the retraining program as "a corporate responsibility but also something that is very much in our long-term self-interest. We have good people and we want to keep them." But Intel offers no guarantees. In the redeployment program, workers are given four months to shop for new jobs within the company. If a worker can't find a new job, he or she has to leave the company. The four-month timetable is not inflexible. An employee can work on engineering, production, or management projects that last a few months, extending the deadline.

To date, 3,600 workers, or 86 percent of the people in the redeployment program, have found jobs within Intel. But much of the responsibility rests with the workers. "Our message to our employees is that they are responsible for gaining new skills so they can continue to be employable either inside or outside the company," said Dorinda Kettmann, in human resources.

Andy Linn has heard the message loud and clear. The former Marine was working the night shift for $4.50 an hour at a convenience store outside Portland, Oregon, in 1988, when he landed a job at an Intel plant nearby. He started as a $15,000-a-year technician monitoring the acid baths in which silicon wafers are dipped as one step in the production of microchips. Since then, Mr. Linn, now 33, has found one job after another at Intel, mainly on his own initiative. He has doubled his yearly income to $30,000, and Intel has paid for his continual training and education, including tuition at a community college and four-year university. His skills have progressed far beyond the acid baths to chip technology and the Internet. He is now a "concept engineer," scouting for new-product ideas at universities.

After eight years at Intel, he observed, "I work for a fine company and I work my butt off for Intel, but there isn't a lot of loyalty in the electronics industry." His father, John, a union foreman, is retiring this year after forty years at Portland General Electric. Mr. Linn views his father as a relic. "I can't even imagine working for a company for that long, or having a company want me for that long," he said. "Man, this is the nineties."

Self-Reliance

A decade ago, Steve Jasik embraced the same ethos of self-reliance, weathered some tough times, and came out a winner. His story resounds with the lesson, heard again and again, that while government and business can do some things, in the end workers have little to fall back on but themselves.

Mr. Jasik is a tall, dark 52-year-old who looks younger than his years. He lives in a two-bedroom tract-style house in Menlo Park, California, modest only by the affluent standards of Silicon Valley. He makes nearly $200,000 a year these days—enough to afford the college educations of his two children, a retirement nest egg, and the red Corvette in his garage. Yet in 1984 Mr. Jasik, a computer programmer, was a downsizing casualty waiting to happen. He worked in Silicon Valley for the Control Data Corporation, a producer of large computers. That fall, Control Data reported a big loss, beginning a long-running retrenchment that eliminated tens of thousands of jobs.

On his own, Mr. Jasik bought an early Apple Macintosh computer. The future, he was convinced, belonged to the personal computer. So in early 1985, he left Control Data and started his own company with $4,000. He had an idea for a software program, a tool to be used by software developers to spot bugs in Macintosh programs. He was recently divorced, paying $1,100 a month in alimony. Mr. Jasik borrowed $5,000 from a friend and $2,000 from his mother. "It was really scary," he recalled. "In the early months, it seemed like a disaster." He came close, he says, to selling his house. Gradually, sales began picking up, and today Mr. Jasik enjoys prosperity.

But he still watches his dollars closely. His company remains a one-man operation, run from his computer-filled den. Being on your own, he says, teaches you to work hard, save, learn new skills, and be prepared to weather some lean times. "I live below my income, and I'm an advocate of that," he said. "Nothing is guaranteed for anybody anymore."

Quid Pro Quo

If technology is the familiar reason companies are forced to retrain workers, Deng Xiaoping is the reason of the future. When China's paramount leader triggered the country's remarkable economic revival, his legions of industrial planners quickly learned to play hardball with American companies vying to get into the Chinese market. They started with the Boeing Company, which now sells one of every seven jets it produces to the People's Republic.

Beijing's new rules are simple: If you want to sell planes in China, you have to make a chunk of them in one of China's four vast aerospace factories, each staffed with 25,000 workers. So starting a few years ago, David Clay and his colleagues in Boeing's giant production hangars in Seattle began watching with growing alarm as parts they once produced—wing ribs and horizontal stabilizers and doors and tail sections— began showing up at the factory in giant crates marked with Chinese characters. Most are produced by workers paid in one month what Mr. Clay makes in two and a half hours— about fifty dollars. "We're turning out more planes today than ever before," said Mr. Clay, a 42-year-old mechanic who maintains the giant equipment that picks up 80-ton plane parts. "We're the country's greatest exporter. But does that mean there are more jobs here? No way. You want a job making Boeing airplanes? Move to Xian."

In fact, Boeing's managers point out, 85 to 90 percent of the content of their planes originates in the United States, far more "local content" than in many American cars. Nevertheless, the Xian conundrum is one of the stickiest—and most politically sensitive—obstacles to creating a "new economy" of companies with high-technology exports that, in President Clinton's oft-repeated phrase, can "compete and win in the global economy."

While export-related jobs are more stable and pay better than their domestic counterparts, the pressure to move more such jobs abroad has been unrelenting. China has proved enormously skilled at playing Boeing, McDonnell Douglas, and Airbus Industrie of Europe against each other to get more jobs for its own workers, as well as better machine tools and more technology.

The union says that as Boeing moves more technology into Chinese hands, it is undercutting new jobs in the United States. Boeing says it has the situation under control. "We don't expect to give away any technology that would harm us," said Larry Clarkson, who heads Boeing's international operations. The most complex jobs—the "systems integration" tasks that put the plane together—have remained in the United States. But clearly the Chinese are seeking to learn those systems-integration skills as well, and few doubt that they will pick them up in the next decade.

Alarmed that Boeing was sending so much work not only to China but also to many American contractors, workers like Mr. Clay demanded that this "outsourcing" slow dramatically. Boeing resisted fiercely, arguing that it is far better to let China produce part of a plane than lose a multibillion-dollar order. The unions held fast. "It's bit by bit by bit," said George J. Kourpias, president of the International Association of Machinists and Aerospace Workers. "And with each piece, you lose another twenty-dollar-an-hour job."

The dispute produced one of the most vituperative strikes in the company's history in 1995. But out of that came an accord that many believe could serve as an early model in the battle against downsizing. Boeing must now inform Mr. Clay and his fellow union members anytime more than fifty jobs will be threatened by moving work outside the company. The workers can make a counterproposal to keep the work in-house. And if the jobs do go, the workers who lost them must be retrained for another job—though perhaps one with lower wages. They can be laid off only if a job cannot be found for them after retraining.

To some the Boeing agreement is a model of how unions can press for real commitments to retraining. But the strike ended without an answer to a fundamental question: Is Boeing's first loyalty to the employment of Americans, as it has long claimed? Or does the company serve the country better by maximizing its profits worldwide so that ultimately it can hire more workers, even if the price of global expansion is shipping some jobs abroad? "This issue of loyalty has become very important," said Michael Sandel, a political philosophy professor at Harvard and author of *Democracy's Discontent: America in Search of a Public Philosophy*. "When the economy was defined by a national market, and corporations had a national purpose, there was a sense that companies had a certain obligation to the nation. When they begin to redefine themselves as citizens of a global economy, the loyalty, the sense of citizenship and obligation, falls away."

Rethinking Attitudes

Abroad, especially in Japan and Europe, many companies see their obligations to employees very differently. If Kunio Motodate had been born American, he would almost certainly have been put out of work when competitive pressures forced his company, Nippon Steel, to close the blast furnace in Kamaishi where he once managed energy usage. Today he still works for Nippon Steel; only now he runs a factory making artificial meat out of soybeans. That business "was set up to create job opportunities," the 59-year-old Mr. Motodate said. "Whether it was profitable or not was not the issue." Indeed, the food factory has never turned a profit.

Japanese executives are now quick to admit what they denied in the 1980s: that many of their employees are unnecessary. Often, they create unrelated businesses simply to keep workers on a payroll. And in other cases, companies keep on workers with largely ceremonial responsibilities, like the many department-store clerks who bow and shout polite greetings to customers. These companies are willing to pay the price—in lower profits, lower stock prices, even slower recoveries from a four-year recession—because of a cultural expectation that they are there to provide jobs.

If that sounds odd to American ears, the downsizing craze in America sounds just as odd to Japanese. "We would be outcasts if we did what many American firms do," the head of one of Japan's major trading companies said recently.

And in fact, American companies once felt similar obligations. During the Great Depression, companies like Kellogg and Sears took steps that seem mind-boggling by the standards of corporate behavior today. They cut the length of the workweek by 25 percent so that they could keep as many employees as possible. Such moves reflected a different sense of national priorities, a recognition that sacrifice had to be distributed—and that loyalty cut both ways.

Today, the Japanese example is not one that American executives, many of whom adoringly studied Japanese management in the 1980s, say they are interested in following. In the last few years, they say, Japan's full-employment practices have exacted a painful toll on the Japanese economy: low growth and continued high prices. Americans, they say, would not tolerate it.

And even in Japan, the Nippon Steel approach is becoming harder to find. More Japanese companies are quietly pressuring workers, particularly older ones, to "retire" early, denying them the lifetime security they thought they earned. In fact, Mr. Motodate's food factory is now feeling pressure from Nippon Steel to become self-supporting. Employment in the factory, once as high as 125 people, is down to 90 workers and will be cut to about 70. But it is still all done by attrition. Layoffs would be a sign of corporate failure.

In Europe, too, businesses are feeling pressure to downsize like their American competitors. But like the Japanese, they face a cultural stigma. "You still cannot think about downsizing," said Carlo De Benedetti, the chairman of Olivetti, the Italian electronics maker. "There is a cultural jump that needs to be made. Only the Germans are making it," he said, citing layoffs at Daimler Benz and elsewhere. "Only the strongest countries can afford to become competitive, and to withstand the pressure that comes from downsizing," Mr. De Benedetti said, with admiration in his voice.

How Much to Pay the Boss

In Japan and many other nations, social pressure also restrains what top executives are paid. Chief executives at the biggest American companies are paid nearly six times their counterparts in Japan, and four times as much as German top executives, estimates Graef Crystal, a compensation consultant. In the United States, more than elsewhere, executives receive bonuses and stock options that become more valuable if a company's stock price rises.

Many people contend that American executives are overpaid—and that they should share the pain in bad times, or when layoffs are made. "I'm sure the CEOs who lay off thousands feel remorse until they pull into their million-dollar homes or fly to Scotland to play golf," said Richard Meyer of White Plains in an electronic-mail comment on downsizing that was typical of many received by *The New York Times*. Often cited is Robert E. Allen, chief executive of AT&T. Since 1986, AT&T has cut its workforce by 125,000 people, but Mr. Allen's salary and bonus have increased fourfold, to $3.3 million. His salary and bonus was trimmed by $200,000 in 1995, but he was also awarded options worth $9.7 million.

AT&T's board says Mr. Allen is the best man to lead AT&T in the new era of deregulated telecommunications. But his critics point out that he also headed AT&T in 1990, when it bought the big computer company NCR for $7.5 billion. The NCR acquisition, AT&T eventually conceded, was all but a complete failure.

In such cases, critics say, the executives responsible should see their paychecks reduced sharply, not just a nominal 5 or 10 percent. "If you are going to lay off a lot of people, you should at least have the decency to cut your pay and cut it way down," Mr. Crystal said. "Be a man and bleed. Lead by example."

Recently, concerns have also been expressed by some owners—major institutional shareholders like pension funds. "What worries us is that many companies seem to be reactive and are just slashing," said Richard H. Koppes, deputy executive director of the California Public Employees' Retirement System, whose $98 billion in assets make it one of America's largest institutional investors. Mr. Koppes said layoffs are often an admission that the past strategies of executives went awry. Still, the victims are workers on the factory floor or middle managers, while executive pay keeps climbing. "Executives should do well when their companies do well," Mr. Koppes said, "but there doesn't seem to be any downside when things go poorly."

A Government Role

In the months before the heat of the 1996 presidential campaign, most of the talk of governmental solutions was not coming from the major candidates themselves. When Robert B. Reich began preaching in late 1995 about the need for "corporate responsibility," many in the administration groaned. Several key members of the Cabinet, from Treasury Secretary Robert E. Rubin to Laura D'Andrea Tyson, the head of the National Economic Council, feared that he would be seen as vilifying corporations with his calls for "some soul searching." When he proposed that the tax code be rewritten to reward companies that promise to avoid layoffs in profitable times and give their employees a stake in the company, good medical coverage, and broad retraining opportunities, Mr. Rubin's office quickly responded that Mr. Reich was talking about blue-sky ideas, not tax policy.

In the Oval Office Mr. Reich may at least have been getting a hearing. The president consistently stopped short of embracing his old friend's solutions. But eager for ideas that both answer and capitalize on the anti-corporate chord that propelled Patrick J. Buchanan's campaign for the Republican nomination, Mr. Clinton several times in early 1996 echoed Mr. Reich's themes. And in early spring he invited business leaders from around the country to the White House for a conference on corporate citizenship. "People are moving past the stage of denying that there is a problem," Mr. Reich said. "We have a lot of people stranded in the old economy, and the transition costs of getting them into the new economy are too high. So who pays? Clearly, the government is constrained. The question is how we allocate these costs—to the companies, to the workers, to the rest of us."

For their part, most Republicans, including the party's nominee, Senator Bob Dole, talk about stimulating economic growth with lower taxes and the end of federal budget deficits. Steve Forbes's campaign was based on the notion that a rising tide will lift all workers. But the evidence of that during the most recent economic expansion has been scarce.

Mr. Buchanan has taken a radically different route, proposing tariffs on all Asian imports to encourage Americans to buy goods made here and to discourage American companies from moving their manufacturing abroad.

But all of these proposals carry consequences, and not all of them are political. The tariffs invite retaliation on goods American companies export. And Mr. Reich's tax proposal raises other questions. Who should judge what constitutes "good" corporate behavior? And should the government, through its tax policy, be subsidizing companies that save jobs at the cost of national economic competitiveness?

Similar questions of standard-setting resonate through the debate over education. Few question that a better-educated workforce is critical if workers are to adjust to the modern economy, and today a college education seems the prerequisite for a growing income that a high school diploma was decades ago.

But that is the end of the common ground. Most discussion about how to change the nation's education system to make it more responsive to the modern economy—setting far higher standards in math and science, lengthening the school year, and improving students' technological literacy—gets bogged down in arguments over who should be setting the rules. During his campaign, Mr. Buchanan got some of his biggest cheers when he denounced "Goals 2000," the Clinton administration's effort to create federal education standards. And the White House has opposed even experimental efforts to provide vouchers to families that want help paying for education outside the public schools, fearing they could undercut public education.

A few executives, led by Louis V. Gerstner Jr., the chairman of IBM, have called for business to help force change by locating their operations in towns where states and local school districts institute high standards; presumably the rest of the country would then pour resources into education in hopes of attracting investment. But most executives say education is the province of the government, not the private sector.

Early Initiatives

Still, there are glimmers of political agreement. While Democrats and Republicans agree that most government-led worker retraining programs have been hopelessly out of touch with the needs of the market, there is growing applause for programs like the North Tennessee Private Industry Council, which turned a failing job-skills training effort into one that has found jobs for hundreds of women who were depending solely on welfare. Of 212 people retraining at the beginning of 1996, 166 now have jobs. Many were unemployed women or downsized textile workers, preparing for new jobs as receptionists or medical technicians.

There are also signs of movement in managing what Mr. Reich calls the "transition costs." As of the end of March 1996, Congress seemed likely to pass legislation that would for the first time assure that workers losing their jobs do not also lose their health insurance. One bill, co-authored by Senator Nancy Landon Kassebaum, Republican of Kansas, and Senator Edward M. Kennedy, Democrat of Massachusetts, required insurance companies to sell individual policies to workers who lost their group health coverage.

Then there is a potpourri of initiatives to make sure that workers propelled out of corporate America can take their assets with them. President Clinton has repeatedly called for "portable pensions" that would accompany workers through layoffs or job switches. Typically, this would require companies to turn over a worker's pension as a lump sum for reinvestment. Mr. Clinton's budget plans for the 1996 election year included a change in the tax code that would permit families to write off up to $10,000 in college tuition costs, or the costs of retraining programs. Such provisions, the administration argued, would fundamentally change the nature of government incentives, investing in workers much as the United States has long helped companies, through tax breaks, to invest in new equipment. It was a proposal that was popular in most polls, but one that may never get out of Congress.

In fact, there is skepticism about the ability or will of government to find a long-term solution. "The truth is that the big initiatives are going to have to start in the business world, and no one wants to face up to that," said Mr. Garten, the Yale dean. "They are hoping that this is some sort of cyclical problem that will go away. And it won't." Mr. Garten questions whether, by their inaction, companies are courting a political backlash, one analogous to the political upheaval of the 1890s that forced the "robber barons" to break up their powerful trusts and submit to regulation.

"In the chaos of the 1890s it was impossible for anyone to foresee the big push for regulation of business, for education to make sure that people were literate, and other measures," said Brad DeLong, an associate professor at the University of California at Berkeley and formerly a senior Treasury Department official. "And yet that's what happened very quickly."

The debate about how American society can respond to the era of downsizing is just beginning. No one can say whether downsizing will remain an issue in the campaign, or whether Congress may act. An easy way to dismiss the problem is that the number of jobs created in February 1996 reached its highest level since late 1983. But the new jobs more often than not do not pay as well as the ones that were lost.

Meanwhile, the odometer keeps clicking. Counting only the layoffs prominent enough to show up in newspapers around the country, the consulting firm Challenger, Gray & Christmas reported that 131,209 workers had been cast out of their jobs in just the first quarter of 1996.

PART II

8

Downsizing and Its Discontents

Editorial

The New York Times

March 10, 1996

MODERN CAPITALISM HAS always dealt its cards unevenly, but over time prosperity and freedom have flowed to almost everyone living under the system. The United States, moreover, is the envy of other industrial democracies because of its recent success in creating jobs and subduing inflation. Why, then, are so many Americans anxious about the future? If you have any doubt that such anxiety exists, read the meticulously reported series of articles in *The Times* last week, with their portrayal of lives, families, workplaces, and communities disrupted by the downsizing in corporate America.

Granted, the series has concentrated on the people who lost jobs, not the many more who have gained jobs in a growing economy. There is also nothing new in churning economic cycles that, over time, have forced Americans from farm to factory, from country to city. As the economist Joseph Schumpeter observed long ago, capitalism embodies a process of "creative destruction" in which outdated enterprises must give way.

But there is something new and disturbing about current economic afflictions.

The middle and upper classes—the very groups benefiting most from the education and training that have for decades been a path upward—are experiencing massive losses of jobs for the first time. Most of these victims have to accept diminished pay and benefits in less secure jobs.

The spread of layoffs in relatively good times and among companies with strong profits has created a searing climate of insecurity as employees accept less, contributing to the leveling off and even decline of wages in the last two decades, the longest period of stagnation since the Civil War.

The anxiety among Americans has become a powerful fact of life in the current election campaign. Although President Clinton has a comparable record on job creation to that of President Ronald Reagan when Mr. Reagan ran for re-election in 1984, it is hard to imagine Mr. Clinton convincing anyone that a new "morning in America" is dawning.

Patrick Buchanan has roiled the scene with his proposals to curb immigration, imports, and the ability of corporations to invest overseas. Fortunately, his prescription seems to have been rejected. But there is an emerging political consensus around a few key points that can show the way forward for voters, presidential candidates, members of Congress and corporations that are smart enough to avoid the backlash whipped up by the unrestrained profit taking of the past fifteen years.

There is, for example, a clear national demand for portable health insurance that follows workers from job to job or into unemployment. Fixing that problem does not have to wait for a 1993-style health care reform effort. Congress should adopt the legislation sponsored by Senators Edward Kennedy and Nancy Kassebaum to preserve health insurance for workers who lose their employer-based coverage and are then turned away by other insurers. The bill commands bipartisan support and Senator Bob Dole can make it happen by allowing a quick vote.

Corporations and financiers must recognize that they cannot forever placate the anxiety of white-collar Americans by saying they are casualties of a righteous effort to squeeze out the last penny of profit for shareholders. American history demonstrates few patterns more clearly than that in which flamboyant corporate callousness leads to government regulation.

When the middle class starts feeling aggrieved, the political system has to respond, as demonstrated by the speed with which Mr. Dole picked up Mr. Buchanan's attack on corporate downsizers. Smart boards of directors will begin to question multimillion-dollar bonuses for CEOs whose main managerial skill is the ability to inflict maximum suffering on senior employees. By the same token, the days of company paternalism are over and skilled workers will have to learn how to save their jobs by navigating in a newly competitive environment.

The point is that neither business nor government lacks the tools to deal with the problems explored in the *Times*'s series. But it is important to remember that, for all the concern about downsizing, the families suffering the most right now are those at the bottom end of the scale, and that the distribution of wealth in the United States is growing increasingly inequitable. This is no time, as this page has said repeatedly, to think that prosperity can be achieved by budget cuts and tax reductions that disproportionately hurt the poor. Washington can play an additional role in investing in more training and education, perhaps through tax breaks, and working hard to open overseas markets for goods and services produced by the highest-paid workers.

However painful the trends of recent years, there is a sinking feeling that they could get worse. The forces of automation and technology, of companies looking for cheaper ways to make products overseas, of immigrants searching for opportunity on our shores, and of consumer demand for less expensive imported goods—these are trends that are almost certain to grow rather than diminish. The United States can no more stop them than it can build up steel and concrete walls along its borders.

Because economic change has always brought dislocation, there are some who feel that the United States should simply accept the current American anxiety as its inevitable lot. That would be a mistake. Exaggerated reverence for the raw justice of the market should not serve as an excuse for inaction. Americans want their leaders to talk sense about their problems. An election year is an excellent place to start. Presidential and congressional candidates who ignore the frozen incomes of the poor and the chilling anxiety of the middle class will have a cold November.

9

Reporters' Postscript:
A Personal View

The Times *asked the writers of the series on downsizing to reflect on how their many months of work on this project had affected the way they looked at their own lives. Here are their thoughts:*

Louis Uchitelle

I REMEMBER THAT afternoon in August three years ago so vividly now. On a day off, my wife and I had gone to the community pool near our home in Scarsdale, New York. Paul was there, an old friend we had not seen in months, and he explained, very carefully, that he was no longer a bank officer. He was a consultant now, working from home, with the "flexibility," as he put it, for afternoon swims. Perhaps he wanted us to behave as if nothing had happened, and the sympathy we offered angered him. For he suddenly converted the pool into a gathering place for the unemployed—the successful who had lost their jobs. "See that fellow over there," he said, pointing to a middle-aged man sitting on the lawn reading a newspaper. "He was the vice president of a major corporation."

Like a museum guide, Paul explained the other exhibits. The fellow with a cigarette, pacing under a huge oak tree, had been pushed out as a partner of a prestigious law firm. The man stretched out on the lawn, sunning himself near the diving pool, had until recently been a busy engineer for a major construction company. There were eight men in all, and I found myself explaining—too emphatically, perhaps—that I had taken the day off, that's why I was at the pool. I had a job.

But the transition began then, and this series of articles completed the process. People who lost jobs had seemed different, apart, somehow to blame for their own downfall. But the men at the pool—nervous, lost in themselves, unhappy—made me listen more closely, and reluctantly I met others, so many others. As an economics writer, I had dealt with the issue as an abstraction, and only gradually did I come to trust the message of those men at the pool, so much more powerful than theory and data. They had been caught in something beyond their control, and so, I realized, could I.

Kirk Johnson and I, doing the early reporting for the series, showed up in late summer at the annual meeting of the American Sociological Association in Washington. Surely among the hundreds of sociologists present there would be some who had explored the layoffs as a powerful social phenomenon. They hadn't. Many acknowledged the probable links to family stress, divorce, depression, violence, self-doubt, altered community life, politics, and so on. And they said, "You explore these links and write your series and we will cite your articles in applying for study grants." I hope they get those grants and do the studies.

N. R. Kleinfield

OVER THE YEARS, I didn't think much about joblessness. Of course, I saw the grim downsizing tabulations in the business headlines, and I read the periodic stories about some despairing out-of-work middle manager gasping for air. And I did begin to sense that this problem had something of the feel of one of those rooms in horror movies where the walls slowly inched closer to each other, and unless someone pulled the right lever they would crush everyone inside. I noticed the walls moving. The thing is, they had not *come* particularly close to me. I kept thinking that before they did someone would pull the lever.

A few weeks after I began reporting about Chase Manhattan Bank and its edgy and despondent workers, my sister called. She told me that she and her colleagues had just been notified by the solidly profitable computer software company that employed her that her division had been sold. She and pretty much everyone else in the division no longer had jobs. She had had an enviable career that had always followed a happily upward trajectory, and suddenly she was downsized for the first time. She felt betrayed. She felt bitter. She felt frightened. (Luckily, she found a good job soon afterward.) A week later, some friends came over for a tree-trimming party. My wife and I had been out of touch with one couple for a month or so. The husband greeted us with the somber news that the big media company he worked for had dispensed with his division. He was jobless. For a while, he thought he might try his hand at consulting. His wife said she was scared to death. Their two young children scampered through the apartment.

Just like that, I felt the walls of the room brushing against me.

They kept hitting me during the weeks, and ultimately months, that I met and spoke with innumerable Chase workers. Now I saw with clarity what was becoming evident to so many: There was no escaping the issue. It was everywhere. Nothing seemed commoner than to see people working from morning until night and then getting told that they were no longer needed. And that seemed to be the way it would go, and so what? There was a torsion that made little sense. As I became intimately exposed to the carapace of suffering encasing the Chase workers, I began to fear that nobody out there was going to pull that lever. And thus the jangled nerves of the Chase people became my jangled nerves. Their fright became my fright. I found myself part of the common doom.

Friends and colleagues would ask me why I seemed morose at times. I would tell them it was because people were losing their jobs. Several of them said I should stop taking work so seriously. Others wondered if perhaps I had a chemical imbalance.

Again and again, people at Chase told me that they were looking for something they had once had—a feeling of peace and certainty. They didn't know if they could get that feeling again, and neither did I. I met one Chase worker at a coin laundry, a refuge for privacy, and he found it hard to complete a full sentence. Sweat had plastered his hair on his forehead. "It's crazy, it's crazy," was how he punctuated almost every sentence. When we were done talking, he said to let him leave and then wait a half hour before I went. If we met again, he told me, bring a bag of laundry. I had not made this rendezvous seem convincing enough. I had never seen a man so terrified.

I had told him about my feeling of the contracting room and the lever, and he had just shaken his head. "Yeah, right," he said. "What lever?" I realized then that he was right. Not only didn't I know if anyone was going to pull the lever, I wasn't sure what the lever looked like and I didn't know where it was.

Rick Bragg

I GREW UP in a blue-collar world in the Deep South. Men worked from dawn till after dark in the cotton fields or the foundries, casting iron pipe. Women worked twelve hours in the sweatshop sewing pants, then went home and patched their childrens' blue jeans. Prospering, it always seemed, was what other people did. The people of my world merely survived. It is an unrealistic yardstick, that kind of life, by which to measure the working world of today. But what it gave me, I believe, was a low tolerance for whining. When editors at *The New York Times* sent me to California to write about two families who had seen their lives altered by layoffs—a prosperous white-collar family and a comfortable blue-collar one—I knew I would feel sympathy for them, but I wondered how much.

The deck was stacked against them in another way. I have made my living by writing, mostly, about what I call "people in trouble." Usually the people in my stories live in poverty, on a kind of sociological high wire, teetering in a stiff breeze. A laid-off executive and a laid-off aircraft worker, I figured, would not even register on the scale of pain I was used to seeing.

I was wrong.

While it is true that the ordeals of the Sharlows and Muses—particularly the white-collar Sharlows—cannot compare with those of an elderly shut-in who is afraid to leave her apartment because of gunfire or a crack baby living out its whole life in a plastic bubble in intensive care, these two families had gone through something that most of America could more easily understand. The two men in these stories had earned their comfortable lives through hard work, by doing all the right things, and had lost anyway. Their stories show us not only the present but the future, and the first thing I did, after finishing them up, was look into opening a new savings account. In case.

All over America, people did the same. Or wished they could spare the money to save. Or just went to sleep feeling a little less secure. One letter, from a woman in Pelham, New York, said it better than I could: "Was I moved to tears because I see my family in this place within a very short time?" she wrote.

I have a high threshold for tears. But I saw Mr. Muse and Mr. Sharlow cry in anger and shame and at their own futility, and while some readers blasted the once-so-prosperous Mr. Sharlow for lamenting his new, downsized existence, or scorned Mr. Muse because he wanted to hold on to a shifting way of life, I could not turn away from them once I had come to know them.

My job was to crawl as deep inside their lives as I could, and lay them open for outsiders. Once, when I saw that one family member was holding back, giving pat answers, I pressed too hard and made her angry, and in the anger was honesty. She was ashamed. But she was ashamed to admit it.

Sara Rimer

THE ECONOMISTS I interviewed by telephone advised me not to go to Dayton. Dayton was the wrong place for the downsizing series, they said. Dayton was doing well, they said. The economic indicators seemed to prove it. My editors told me to go to Dayton and see for myself. I stayed five weeks. The first thing I learned was that the statistics were only part of the story about Dayton. Everyone I met in Dayton talked about their anxiety about jobs and the economy and the fraying of community ties. No one ever brought up Bill Clinton or Whitewater or Newt Gingrich or Bob Dole or the flat tax. No one ever brought up national politics, period.

My first week in town I visited suburban Oakwood High School. I figured if anyone felt safe in today's economy it would be the Oakwood students. The first two students I met, Charlie McElligott and Leslie Woodward, had plenty to say about downsizing, corporate takeovers and declining standards of living. Leslie and Charlie said that everyone had told them that they would not be better off than their parents, that the American Dream was over, that they would have seven different careers in their lifetimes. They worried about how best to prepare themselves for the global economy. The dozen other Oakwood students I spoke with talked pretty much the same way.

I was struck by how Charlie worried about his father—who had been out of work for nearly a year at one point and now, though he was working again, worried constantly about the family's financial security. "He thinks he let us down," Charlie told me. Nothing, he said, could be further from the truth. Charlie's hero is his father.

Listening to Charlie and Leslie, I thought back to my own high school years, in Levittown, Pennsylvania, in the late 1960s and early '70s. I never once worried about my father's job. It never crossed my mind. I knew that his job would pay for college for my two sisters and me. He was vice president for public information at the American Cancer Society in New York City. He commuted by train from Levittown for thirty-three years. My mother's job, as a social worker at a private adoption agency in Trenton, New Jersey, was equally secure. She retired after thirty years.

I did not worry about the economy, or my family's financial stability or my future. I just assumed that if I did reasonably well in college I would get a good job. My friends all felt the same way. My time in Dayton reminded me of how lucky we were, growing up the way we did. It made me grateful, too, that my parents did not have to contend with the indignities and insecurities of today's job market.

Having grown up in Levittown, a postwar instant suburb, where all the houses and all the streets were new, I was impressed by Dayton's history, and how much it mattered to people. When I arrived at the Dayton Marriott in early December of 1995, there was a box of Esther Price chocolates waiting for me. They were from John Gower, a member of the Dayton Planning Department and a local historian, who was to be my guide to the city. He told me that Esther Price had started out making fudge in her kitchen in the 1920s, and that she had sold her company for a lot of money in 1976. And so I quickly learned that Dayton was still a city that made things.

During my time in Dayton, I randomly asked people I met—the woman at the cash register at Meier's grocery store, the man at the convenience store where I bought gas late one night, the woman who cleaned my room at the Marriott, the bellman—if they had two jobs. They all did. They did not seem to think it was unusual. They did not complain. Whatever else it is, Dayton is not a city of whiners.

I feel fortunate, more than ever, to have a job. One good job.

Kirk Johnson

MIDWAY THROUGH REPORTING the story of the Bucknell class of 1970, I read two books that I could never quite get out of my head. The first was *Emotional Intelligence* by Daniel Goleman. The second was *The Winner-Take-All Society* by Robert H. Frank and Philip J. Cook. Mr. Goleman's argument is that traits like optimism and self-discipline—both key indicators of success in life—are largely learned social responses, adaptations to the world around us as the human character is being shaped through early adulthood. Mr. Frank and Mr. Cook summarize the forces that are pulling our society apart and impoverishing our culture by intensifying competition and increasing the concentration of rewards in the hands of those at the pinnacle in almost every field of endeavor.

I was already convinced by then, after more than a hundred interviews with members of the class of 1970, that something fundamental and distinctive had shaped this group. And the more I thought about it, and the more I listened to them, the more I came to see them as time travelers—unintended products of Mr. Goleman's social engineering, happy accidents from an America that every year seems more and more remote from our winner-take-all experience.

In the America of their youth, runners-up got some rewards, too, because there seemed to be plenty for all. That, I think, was the fountainhead of their confidence and their generosity of spirit. They could dream big or they could turn away from the mainstream, and if they fell on their faces, big deal. There was no fear, as there is today in the class of 1996, of falling through the cracks as a result of a misstep.

And the more I began to see them as an anachronism, the more I began to mourn what we have lost. I had come, by then, to admire the members of the class of 1970. More accurately, I admired the traits that I kept encountering over and over—an openness, a particular kind of supple, reflective intelligence, a willingness to see the best in people, a buoyancy. I found them admirable even when—and to a certain degree, especially when—they second-guessed their lives, and their choices, and the compromises that the new economy has in many cases demanded. Only people with real values and principles will do that.

I am too young to have been part of their generation. Their graduation year was the year I turned twelve, old enough to take note of my draft lottery number, 90, but too young for it to mean much except as a symbol of what might have been. I came of age in the 1970s, when gasoline was in short supply and punk rock was tearing down the smiley-face facade that was probably the worst hangover from the 1960s.

But if there is a psychic recipe for what made the class, I'd like to find it. I'd like my twin sons, Anthony and Paul, who are nine, to be open to the world the way the class of 1970 was, to be ready to pursue what seems right, full of the belief that come what may, things will work out somehow. The believing is everything.

There are also some specific places and moments from the reporting of this story that I will always remember: Riding through the snow-packed streets of Aspen in Peter Louthis's pickup truck. The way the waitress greeted Glen Maynard over lunch in downtown Golden, with an affectionate touch on the arm and a "Hi, sweetie," that spoke volumes about one small town and Mr. Maynard's place in it. How Janice Thomas sat, her legs tucked beneath her, through a long late-afternoon conversation in her living room as the rain pounded outside. Christine Dotterer's richly spontaneous laugh. Whatever I may have given the class as a sounding board or a mirror, they gave me more.

Letters to the Editor: A Selection

In the weeks after the publication of the downsizing series, The Times *received hundreds of letters from readers. They came by post and by E-mail. Many applauded the series; more than a few took it to task. Many simply chose to tell their own stories. Here is a selection:*

To the Editor:

Re your front-page series on "The Downsizing of America":

What we are witnessing is a cataclysmic transformation of society, as dislocating as the Industrial Revolution. The work ethic has been supplanted by the gambling ethic, and acquisitiveness and speculation on Wall Street have become the engine that runs our society. Each tale in your series describes the misery in the lives of those who worked hard to deserve something better.

What's next? It won't be another cyclic swing back to normalcy. Faith, trust, loyalty, fair play, compassion, and other maxims we believed constituted America's soul have been trashed.   Sanford A. Marcus
Daly City, California

The World of 1970

To the Editor:

I am about to lose my job after thirty years with the United States Foreign Service. I will retire ten years earlier than colleagues were doing only five years ago. I have a good pension, but I don't know what lies ahead.

I am nevertheless baffled, in your article on the Bucknell University class of 1970, by the reference to "the world that once seemed rich and ripe with potential."

This class graduated into an America mired in a fruitless war in Southeast Asia and torn by race riots and the assassinations of John F. Kennedy, Robert Kennedy, and the Rev. Dr. Martin Luther King Jr. Ahead lay Watergate and double-digit inflation. By those standards, the America into which the class of 1996 will graduate would seem pretty tame.

PHILIP C. BROWN
Vienna, Austria

Bulletproof Logic

To the Editor:

Re your front-page series on "The Downsizing of America": The rationale managers use to justify workforce reduction is rarely mentioned. The logic is almost bulletproof.

Labor costs are the dominant cost of doing business in all but a few endeavors. For most jobs, the variation in individual work-related performance is likely to be greater than the range in compensation; thus it is possible to maintain productivity or work quality and decrease labor costs at the same time.

This situation is most likely to occur where worker output can vary (sales, management, nonproduction-line factory work, skilled labor, and professions), but employment costs like benefits, overhead, and investment are relatively fixed.

In 1993 the output of each full-time worker represented $50,000 of the gross national product. Considering only the economy's commercial sector, the average labor component of this output is 60 percent, or $30,000 a worker. Costs of materials and other business needs like advertising, distribution, and administration are 30 percent, leaving only 10 percent, or $5,000 a worker, for corporate gross profit.

However, if labor costs can be reduced by 10 percent while labor productivity can yet be maintained by improvements in selection, training, or work design, and with all other costs remaining constant, gross profit increases by 60 percent.

To increase profitability quickly, management can reduce labor costs most effectively by replacing older, higher-paid workers with younger workers, by transferring production to lower labor cost areas, and by automation.

LAWRENCE R. ZEITLIN
Peekskill, New York
The writer is professor emeritus of
organizational behavior, CUNY.

Progressive Caucus

To the Editor:

Re "The Downsizing of America": Yes, the economy is booming for the rich and the large corporations. But since 1973, 80 percent of working Americans have seen a decline in their living standard or, at best, economic stagnation. The middle class is working longer hours for lower wages, and the new jobs being created for their children are often low-wage, part-time or temporary jobs.

Your recent article said that "until Patrick J. Buchanan made the issue part of the presidential campaign, it seldom surfaced in political debate." Wrong. The fifty-member House

Progressive Caucus has been discussing this crisis for five years.   (Rep.) BERNARD SANDERS
Chairman, Progressive Caucus
Washington, D.C.

Best for Entrepreneurs

To the Editor:

Re James Sharlow's loss of a $130,000 job at Eastman Kodak: While I'm sympathetic to anyone who loses a good job after so many years of service, one question seems unanswered: Why didn't Mr. Sharlow, a skilled machinist and plant manager, try starting a business of his own? With all its problems and frightening unemployment trends, America is still the best place for an entrepreneur to exercise his or her wings.   VERNON LEWIS
Sparta, New Jersey

Look to Ourselves

To the Editor:

It seems ironic that, at a time when the country is in dire straits and there is real work to be done, so many people can't find jobs. Downsizing *is* a rude awakening for many who have relied on a company, as if on a parent, to take care of them. But maybe it's time we all learned to identify the skills and talents within ourselves that we can take anywhere and apply to society's needs, no matter who is signing our checks.   ILISE BENUM
Hoboken, New Jersey

Not a New Trend

To the Editor:

You treat downsizing as news. Yet this trend has been going on for two decades. The Fortune 500 companies reached a peak in their share of total United States employment in 1969. They reached a peak in absolute terms—total number employed—in 1979.

Meanwhile, as of 1994, 72.5 percent of all jobs in the United States economy were in the service sector, not the Fortune 500 companies. More important, the service sector contained the highest number of best-paid jobs.

It is true that the information revolution, coupled with the lower labor rates overseas, is displacing many industrial jobs, just as manufacturing displaced farm labor a hundred years ago. Those willing to change and learn are being rewarded in the service sector.

BOB DJURDJEVIC
Phoenix, Arizona

Hubris at Chase

To the Editor:

As someone who has spent sixteen years in banking, five at Chase Manhattan Bank, I found your article insightful.

I am no stranger to corporate downsizing, having experienced it at two other banks in my career. At Chase, I read the handwriting on the wall and left for another job well before the merger.

Having joined Chase with ten years' experience, I was shocked at how behind the times it was. While other institutions were downsizing, cutting expenses, and competing for customers, Chase was operating as if it were still the 1950s. Infighting was rampant, with customer needs the last thing on anyone's mind. Management spoke of the corporate "franchise" as if customers were required to bank with Chase.

Expense control was preached but not practiced by management, who deferred raises and cut employees while spending millions of dollars on internal meetings, redecorating offices, and overnight meetings at exclusive locations. At the eleventh hour, management recognized that most of the bank's technology was out of date, having ignored vast changes in the industry for the previous ten years.

In a bizarre twist, Chase managers are congratulating themselves on the enhanced value of the stock and on doing the right thing. How quickly they forget that it was their poor management that kept the stock trading well below book value for many years. Most of these managers retained positions in the "new Chase," while 12,000 people will pay the price for their incompetence.   KATHLEEN ABRUZZO
Forest Hills, Queens

Military Suffers, Too

To the Editor:
While I applaud your front-page series describing the problems facing many Americans in dealing with downsizing, I would like to call your attention to an area not mentioned: the military. The reduction in the workforce of any particular company pales compared with those in the armed forces and civilian Defense Department employees.

The traditional place of employment for former military personnel with leadership experience has been middle management, where their attributes of loyalty, dedication, and self-sacrifice were valued. As your series demonstrates, middle management is an endangered species.

For the jobs that remain, there is fierce competition from unemployed civilians who lost out in the corporate restructuring. Who would more likely be hired for an open position: a former bank vice president from the local area or an infantry major back from three years in Germany?

Military people, generally speaking, are not well equipped upon leaving the service to deal with the financial matters of everyday life. To compensate for lower pay, they have been provided with full services for themselves and their families—medical, educational, housing, recreational—that vanish upon discharge.

I sympathize with those in civilian life who have suffered downsizing. But the "peace dividend" for many people, after having served our country well, has been a particularly bitter pill.   ZEB B. BRADFORD JR.

Atlanta, Georgia

The writer is a retired brigadier general, United States Army.

Do Dropouts Count?

To the Editor:

You state that Bucknell University has produced "few truly famous names," with the writer Philip Roth being an exception. One of baseball's greatest pitchers, and in the first class elected to the Hall of Fame in 1936, Christy Mathewson attended Bucknell from 1898 to 1900, then became the school's most distinguished dropout when he decided to play professional baseball with the New York Giants.

RAY ROBINSON
New York City

High-Tech Contracting

To the Editor:

While I do not wish to minimize anyone's personal hardship; you overlook two points:

First, rather than wring hands, let us recognize that no job is permanent and create incentives to encourage lifelong learning and retraining.

Second, there are positive stories to be told about people who, after the initial shock of losing a job, transformed the experience into an opportunity to re-evaluate life goals. Many are finding positive changes in entrepreneurship and in contract services, with rewards including flexible hours, mobility, and expanded learning potential.

Many companies you describe are high-technology companies—AT&T, IBM, and Digital. Nowhere is there richer opportunity for contract employment than in high-tech services.

According to the Bureau of Labor Statistics, more than 300,000 service jobs were created last year, with more than 110,000 of them in computer-related services. My company employs technical professionals like these, and we are constantly looking for résumés.

At a time when the presidential campaign is focusing the spotlight on the pain of downsizing, you could perform a valuable service by pointing your readers to where the future job opportunities lie, rather than mourning the employment assumptions of the past. JOHN DANIELI
Norwell, Massachusetts

Whither Education?

To the Editor:

The anxiety that heads of households, friends, and relatives feel as they fear for their occupational security is often expressed as "floating anger." This anger manifests in all facets of our lives, including in our schools.

Young people have no faith in our ability to educate for the future. We can no longer proclaim that if you go to school and learn, you will get a good job.

Once we were told that a college education would insure solvency through the retirement years. But our white-collar job force, representing those who received academic high school diplomas and went on to earn college degrees, is feeling the greatest impact from right-sizing, or from simply trying to keep up with changing times.

We can continue to set educational standards based on those set decades ago, or we can take a hard look at the realities that will face our students in the years ahead. Educators are at a crossroads, and schools have an obligation to keep pace with society's demands. STEPHEN J. BUDIHAS
Principal, Park West High School
New York City

The Problem is Capitalism

To the Editor:

In your series, "The Downsizing of America," what I found most surprising was the table that showed that of the people already hard hit by a layoff more (60 percent) put the blame for job loss on "the economic system in this country" than on any other factor. With this result, I expected a discussion of this matter in the accompanying article. But, while the article does deal with other possible sources of job loss—unfair trade, corporate behavior, and inadequate skills—it is completely silent on this one. Yet, if so many people believe that the capitalist system (let's call it by its right name) can't deliver the jobs we need, surely there should have been some discussion of whether this is in fact the case, and, if so, whether the employment situation is likely to get worse no matter what is done about trade, skills, et cetera.

Further, the same problematic would seem to require that we at least raise the question (nowhere mentioned in the whole series) of an alternative economic system, of whether we can reorder the factors of production available to us as a society—machines, raw materials, and skilled workers—to attain full employment and a decent living standard for everyone. After all, ours is not the problem of how to make more of too little (as is the case in Bangladesh and was the case in Russia in 1917), but of how to fairly and democratically allocate too much. We are being drowned in our own surpluses. For a supposedly rational species, this is not only crazy; it is also unnecessary. In short, if capitalism can no longer resolve problems, such as worsening unemployment,

isn't it time to start asking whether some form of democratic socialism can?   PROFESSOR BERTELL OLLMAN
Department of Politics, New York University

Like the Third World

To the Editor:

Your series on downsizing creates a frightening portrait of the future of America. What kind of nation are we becoming, in which the "growing industries are built with the labor of low-paid and desperate people"? That sounds like a third-world nation, one that is perhaps ripe for revolution.

Two of my neighbors, another neighbor's son-in-law, my father, and I have all gone through it. We have found new jobs, although almost all require more work, longer hours, and longer commutes, in return for less money, less prestige, and less security than we believed our old jobs to have held. Three years ago, I would never have believed how terrifying and heartbreaking it can be to lose a job; now I would not wish it on anyone.   MARY CLAIRE LEMING
Stony Brook, Long Island

What Captalism Means

To the Editor:

"Downsizing and Its Discontents," your editorial, makes the astonishing statement that "modern capitalism has always dealt its cards unevenly, but over time prosperity and freedom have flowed to almost everyone living under the system."

The assertion confuses private property, which is fundamental to freedom, with "capitalism," meaning a society in which the disposition of social concerns like health, education, and culture are determined by profit alone.

Capitalism by itself produces only greed and exploitation. The great successes of the modern epoch are due to social movements like populism, progressivism, New Deal liberalism, socialism, feminism, movements for racial equality, and even communism, that have insisted that profit be tempered with social concerns.

ELI ZARETSKY
Visiting Professor, Graduate Faculty
The New School
New York City

CEO Responsibility

To the Editor:

Your editorial referencing the "main managerial skill" of chief executives as "the ability to inflict maximum suffering on senior employees" is an insult to free enterprise. Whether the chief executive is the owner of a small business or is hired, his or her responsibility is to maximize the return on invested capital, using business strategies that encompass short- and long-range goals.

The future of all the employees is affected by the application of the skills of the chief executive.

Free enterprise determines not only the cost of admission to operas, sporting events, etc., as a result of the remuneration paid to the performers, but also the remuneration paid to achievers in the business world.

GERALD M. BONDER
Montreal, Quebec

New Ethical Issue

To the Editor:

The series on the changing patterns of employment and corporate life in America helps explain a number of reactions to the new pleas for isolationist policies. But it does not help explain that masses of new middle classes (although many still lower-middle) are being created around the world. Nor does it help us face the ethical issue of who the "we" is in a post-nationalist era of geo-economics.

Has it not been clear from the effects of the Depression, the alliances formed to fight National Socialism and the more recent fall of the Berlin Wall that fenced-in societies would and should be drawn into new levels of interaction, and that much of the violence of this century is a reaction against some foreign "them" versus "us"?

When we now seek to "protect our own," the "us" is radically expanded and the possibility of a deeper recognition of common humanity is on the horizon.   MAX STACKHOUSE
Professor of Christian Ethics,
Princeton Theological Seminary
Princeton, New Jersey

Blacks and Insecurity

To the Editor:

Your series on corporate downsizing really hit home. Blacks, black men in particular, have known job insecurity since we were emancipated from slavery in America. Today, unemployment has decimated our community to a new nihilism.

How ironic that now that white middle-class America is experiencing what blacks have dealt with all along, the term coined is "downsizing."   SHAWN GRAIN CARTER
South Orange, New Jersey

It Won't Last Forever

To the Editor:

The epidemic of downsizing reflects economywide problems that were decades in the making. The good news is that the downsizing is no more sustainable than the corporate over-expansions and speculative excesses of the 1970s and '80s.

Overexpansion reflected excessive optimism created by the unsustainable postwar boom, powerful unions and oligopolies, too little international competition until the latter 1970s, excessive regulatory protection and complacent managements. Consequently, investment fell in the 1990s to its lowest share of gross domestic product of the postwar era, and speculatively priced fixed assets failed to earn sufficient revenues to repay the debts that financed them.

Overexpansion, technological change and other factors justify much of the downsizing, but not all of it. Job eliminations have come into vogue, especially on Wall Street, where obsession with short-term performance objectives wields far more power than in years past. Downsizing companies are doing themselves more damage than good, to say nothing of their employees, as reductions in morale, loyalty, dynamism, and organizational effectiveness may outweigh payroll savings.

Business can't downsize forever. The era of retrenchments will give way to resurging investment and stronger labor mar-

kets, as has occurred repeatedly in the past. But the "contained depression" is not over yet. DAVID A. LEVY
Vice Chairman, Jerome Levy
Economics Institute, Bard College
Mount Kisco, New York

Who's Fine?

To the Editor:

You quoted Thomas G. Labrecque, the chief executive officer of Chase Manhattan, as saying: ". . . if you're doing what you think is right for everyone involved, then you're fine. So I'm fine." If he thinks he is "doing right by everyone involved," then what are the 10,000 workers whose jobs he has cut in the past ten years? Chopped liver? (Rabbi) ZEV-HAYYIM FEYER
Charleston, South Carolina

A United Response

To the Editor:

The only thing we'd add to your series is the importance of a mutual and united response.

Our group is a coalition of more than fifty labor, religious, and community organizations and individuals with stories like those you featured. In January, we overflowed Faneuil Hall in Boston with more than a thousand people, including half the Massachusetts congressional delegation, to hear from blue-, pink- and white-collar workers, mothers on public assistance, immigrants, and even economists.

Our purpose was to build support for efforts by the Progressive Caucus to require Congress and the President to promote good jobs, and the efforts to eliminate corporate welfare, raise the minimum wage, and cap the tax deductibility of executive compensation.

These proposals are only a start in trying to close the gap between people who are suffering and policy makers. When other states have joined us, we will begin to see things change.

TRUDY BAUER
JIM GOLDBERG
Committee on Economic Insecurity
Watertown, Massachusetts

Stranded in the Nineties

To the Editor:

Peter Finch verbalized it best in *Network*—we are mad as hell. Who are we? We are the fortysomething/fiftysomething generation. We are the ones who have lost our jobs and careers. You can recognize us when you see us on the streets—the men of our generation are the fellows with the short, neat, touched-with-gray haircuts clad in conservative Brooks Brothers suits (the baggy), carrying the polished leather attaché cases. The feminine gender is also attired in conservative "dress for success" suits and professional hairstyles. We are the ones you pass on the sidewalks during the course of the business day, hurrying by with hopeful expressions on our faces as we go to our outplacement centers or on to (for the lucky ones) yet another interview. You can see us after the working day has ended, gathering in clusters in the business district cocktail bars swapping leads or war stories and binding each other's wounds over a quick beer or glass of wine on our way home from one more disappointing day of hunting for nonexistent jobs.

Yes, we are mad as hell, but we have to take it. We've strived hard since our entrance into the workplace—in most cases we started as trainees in our fields in our early twenties and with effort, experience, and a little luck, gained achievement and promotion into senior management when we reached our late thirties to early forties. Now we are into the 1990s and we are told that our faces do not fit in our business environment. We are being outplaced and replaced with the thirtysomething generation and all of the dedication and experience we possess is of no further value. We are the first generation who have had to face this issue, and where do we go from here? What possible guidelines exist for us? How will we survive?

To personalize, my husband and I are only two in a wide circle of friends and acquaintances all going through this fearful and shattering period. My husband was, until over a year ago, a senior executive with an international organization. He had been in his field for over twenty-five years. I was an executive secretary with a worldwide company for twenty years until I was "outplaced" and he was "downsized." Our faces didn't fit anymore. After an extended period of seeking other opportunities to no avail, my husband decided to start his own company in a related field as a Job Search firm. Funding the venture was difficult. However, my husband found a partner—a colleague of his for many years who had held a similar position until, at a similar age, he was let go from his job. Who are our customers? A great many of the same age and background who have been released from their jobs suddenly and replaced by a twentysomething/thirtysomething whiz kid, or an individual whose company was cutting back.

Within my own group of friends, out of four women known as the "Lunchbunch" for nearly twenty years by our colleagues at the office, only one is employed at present. The job market for mature secretaries is bleak and we are getting by, or trying to, by temping, searching for alternative careers, and in my case, assisting my husband in his new venture. Our brother-in-law has been force-retired from a long and distinguished career in engineering at the age of 63 so that he will not be able to avail himself of his full retirement benefits. My sister, a professional administrator with over twenty-five years in her field, cannot find another position because of her age and her experience—do we all recognize the term "overqualified"?

A friend who was a senior executive for an international firm is to open up a delicatessen. Yet another has had to relocate to the South where his parents are retired to run a muffler franchise. The phone at our home rings almost daily with another casualty in the business world reporting in.

The eighties were good to us. We have homes which we worked hard to purchase, and I can tell you that we do not live in mansions or castles. These are homes we bought when we were working our way up the ladder, not when we arrived. These are the homes where we brought up families, and these homes were our investment for our retirement days. Those "golden days" we are not going to realize as those who have come before us were able to do. Those of us with families are having to deal with possible relocation, yanking the kids out of their schools, and wrestling families away from friends and relatives. A terrible and stressful toll is being paid by husbands, wives, and children. Our hopes and plans are being destroyed and we are powerless. The goals we set—work hard with ambition, achieve, earn, and go gracefully into retirement in our sixties, making room for the next business generation—are now valueless. Instead of realizing our plans to give back to the American system by volunteering, teaching, and supporting those in need, we may very well have to take out from our overburdened society via public assistance, food stamps, and food banks, and God help us if we become ill—private medical insurance is astronomical to the unemployed. Dental work, eye care, any ailments accompanying the arrival of our forties and fifties—forget about it. Were our expectations for our lives unrealistic?

- When the "outplaced" and "downsized" generation was employed, we paid our sizeable taxes, i.e. property, schools, government, municipal, etc. Aren't our tax dollars missed?
- Vacations, new cars, new clothing are a thing of the past. We are cutting back on groceries and holiday purchases, and "luxury" items are simply not a consideration. Can this be good for the stimulation of business and the circulation of money?
- IRAs are being cashed in, savings accounts emptied, securities sold rather than purchased. Many of us have taken second mortgages/home equity loans. If we default on our payments we will have no homes and the banks will be left with properties that will not sell quickly or profitably. Isn't this harmful to the economy?
- If we can no longer afford to support the good causes and the needy as we consistently did, who will make those donations in our place?
- If we cannot manage to send our children to college or cannot pay for them to complete their education, then who will be the "bread and butter" support for higher education?

Who cares? No one—unless they happen to be one of us stranded in the nineties.   MARY BERNE
Franklin Lakes, New Jersey

To California and Back

To the Editor:

In early 1990, my husband accepted a job offer in Orange County, California. We sold our home in northern New Jersey, picked up our three children, and went off into the Pacific sunset.

We were convinced this would be a better life of more money and greater opportunity. We bought a beautiful home. I found a great job. Our kids were beginning to call this place with palm trees "home."

In January 1993, the horror that is now our life began. My husband's job was eliminated; the company that relocated us was relocating itself to Colorado.

This wasn't supposed to happen to professional people like us. Out of work for seven months, my husband again relocated—back to New Jersey—the only employment offer he'd had.

The children and I remained in California for one year as we attempted (unsuccessfully) to sell our home in a dying economy. Eventually, once again, I sacrificed my career and uprooted three happy kids to the either cold or humid, albeit familiar, Northeast.

Although the new employer generously funded the moving, no resources were available to us upon our arrival that would allow us to stock up empty cupboards or sign up little boys for the fall soccer season. Because we were unable to recoup our previous salary levels, we have fallen into financial ruin.

No longer yuppies, now we work and work and yet are barely solvent. My marriage is on hold.   SHELLY KAPLAN
Succasunna, New Jersey

Too Many Jobs

To the Editor:

Recently, I saw a political cartoon depicting an affluent older man making a speech at a banquet. He was saying, "Last year, thousands of new jobs were created in this country." The thought balloon over the waiter's head said, "Yeah, and I've got three of them." I didn't know whether to laugh or cry.

You see, for the past year, I've had two jobs instead of the one job I used to have. Together, those two jobs pay approximately 10 percent of what my one job used to pay. I have a Ph.D. in chemistry from a large university with a well-respected chemistry program.

I had entered graduate school with a dream of working for an IBM or an AT&T, doing research that would make a positive difference in people's lives. It took me five years after graduation to land that first industry job. I took great pride in the knowledge that I was working to decrease pollution and produce a useful product. I took my $20,000 sign-on bonus and bought a condominium.

After two and a half years, I was downsized out of the company. I spent eight months writing hundreds of letters, making hundreds of phone calls, and networking at conferences. I got one job offer—800 miles away.

I bid tearful goodbyes to my friends and put my condo on the market. The market wasn't very good that year—everyone else was downsizing too. My $20,000 became $10,000 overnight.

Just before Christmas 1993, I started work at the central research facility of a "good, stable company, heavily committed to research." After one year, things appeared to be going well, so I bought a house. I paid my taxes, bought company stock, and planned for my future.

In 1995, I received a pink slip for Valentine's Day. My new job had lasted all of fifteen months. That was almost a year ago, and I'm still looking for full-time work.

NANCY K.-MCGUIRE
Bay City, Michigan

Happily Unemployed, With Boat

To the Editor:

I too have been downsized, by the World Bank, after more than fifteen years working as an economist. As a matter of fact, my wife and I both lost our jobs in the same month— August 1995—when she was made redundant by a major nongovernmental organization.

Fortunately we had already repaid the mortgage on our large old townhouse in Washington, D.C., the World Bank has given me a more than adequate severance package, and we have managed to save quite a bit since arriving in the United States in 1980. I can also cash in a large part of my pension.

Admittedly, our first reaction when losing two jobs at the same time was confusion and bewilderment. But that soon stopped and we now look at this unexpected situation as a unique chance to change lifestyles, spend more time together, structure our working days differently, and do new things. The first thing we did last year after being made redundant was to buy an old sailboat.

I am also using a small "retraining" grant from the World Bank to do field research on specialized banks that lend to the poor and microenterprises in the Third World, in countries like Bangladesh and Bolivia, as background for a forthcoming book on microfinancing. I will start looking for work as a part-time consultant toward the end of this year.

In the meantime, we'll go sailing, do a lot of writing, and happily get by on my early-retirement pension of about $3,000 a month pretax, compared with our past joint income of about $10,000 posttax. I realize that we are in a privileged situation, but hope that others won't only look at the negative side; trying to "hold on" to the past after being downsized can be destructive and demoralizing.   EUGENE VERSLUYSEN
Washington, D.C.

Downsized and Pregnant

To the Editor:

I worked for the U.S. General Accounting Office, a congressional agency that exposes fraud, waste, abuse, and mismanagement of federal funds. The agency got a 25 percent budget cutback from the Republicans. But no one in my office expected the New York field office to close.

We received the bad news on August 7. At the time, I was eight and a half months pregnant. I was unable to look for a job because no one was interested in interviewing someone in that condition. I appealed to upper management for an extended time with the employment counseling services, but was denied. The exact quote from the Washington lawyer was "GAO didn't get you pregnant."

The office closed on November 10. I have been looking for a job since then. My husband has taken on a second job, often working ninety hours a week. I am having a hard time looking for work while caring for my daughter. I can't hire a sitter until I have income coming in.   DIANA ERANI
                                                    Riverdale, New York

From Electronics to Dialysis

To the Editor:

I was downsized for the first time in my life in November of 1991. Being a fairly sharp guy with an extensive background in electronics and computer programming, I didn't think it would be all that difficult to find a new job. I was somewhat concerned about my eight-month-old baby at home, but optimism was the word of the day.

My first real shock came three months after being laid off: It would cost $598 a month to continue my medical benefits. Due to the fact that we were now living on unemployment compensation of $300 a week, this was impossible.

Of course I could also no longer afford my blood pressure medication either, but I thought that my first obligation was to give my son as good a start in life as I could. I applied for Medicaid when I lost my insurance. The social worker thought it was pretty funny that someone collecting the princely sum of $300 a week would think he was eligible for Medicaid.

Eventually my unemployment ran out and we suffered the indignity of welfare for a month. The one good thing I can say about welfare is it gave me access to a very good career counselor who helped me land a job with a computer consulting firm in the summer of 1993. They kept me for six months, then laid me off. I collected unemployment again for nearly six months, and in the nick of time I got my present job, which seems to be as secure as anything is today.

The reason I mentioned the blood pressure medicine is this. The high blood pressure that I could not afford to treat destroyed my kidneys. I am now on dialysis and am trying to get a transplant. If I lose my job again it will destroy me. My dialysis costs my insurance company $5,000 a month. When I get a transplant, I will have to take anti-rejection drugs for the rest of my life. I cannot change jobs due to this pre-existing condition.   MICHAEL McGINN
                                          Monroe, New York

Education Won't Help

To the Editor:

In the nineteen years since receiving my Ph.D., I have worked full-time for seven colleges and universities in three states. The longest I was able to stay at a single institution was six years, and I stayed at several institutions for periods as brief as one year. I have drawn unemployment compensation five—yes, five—times. I have currently been unemployed for two years. I have applied for close to 2,000 jobs.

At age 45, I have little hope that I will have any more of a career as an academic psychologist. The standard cliché is that we need a better educated workforce. Well, from where I am sitting, having an education is no guarantee that one won't be left behind.   JAMES C. MEGAS
                                          St. Paul, Minnesota

The Ones Who Hang On

To the Editor:

Bell Atlantic, soon to merge with NYNEX, has not had massive layoffs as yet, but many have retired with incentives to leave the payroll. These jobs have not been filled. My story concerns the employees who are left. Many workers have been suspended for minor violations of safety that would have evoked only a warning in the past. Vacation, even though we have earned it, is getting more difficult to schedule. Forced overtime is on the horizon, as well as punishment for sickness.

Downsizing is a catastrophe for those who lose their jobs, and I would not presume to say that the irritations I suffer compare to that. However, downsizing makes life very stressful for the ones who hang on to their jobs a little longer, as well. Mostly, we are living in fear that we are next. We are!!!

PHILLIP RUBY
St. Albans, West Virginia

The Firing

To the Editor:

I am 46 and was employed as the advertising manager of a petroleum company. I lost my job and $65,000 annual salary last month. I was fired during a bitter, late January day. Friday afternoon at 1:45 P.M., to be precise. Behind cautiously closed doors, my boss told me he was regretfully eliminating my job.

My first reaction was to be very professional and emotionally controlled. I was empathetic, understanding, even forgiving. I told him I appreciated how hard it is firing someone. He told me he was protecting himself: there couldn't be two people with the same job responsibilities. Somebody had to go. He told me he was protecting the company. He told me he needed to set an example.

The questions that all newly unemployed people confront bubbled from subconsciousness: Where will I go? What will I do now? How will I pay my bills? My boss left the door open for me to hang around a few days or maybe weeks. I could help finish some of the projects I was working on. Seemed logical—for the company.

What about me? I could get up every day and drag myself into an office where I am no longer wanted. I could use this transition time to look for another job, perhaps convey the half-truth to other would-be employers that I am also securely employed and just interested in career change.

But I was humiliated. I chose to pack my office on Saturday afternoon. I chose to spit in the face of appearance. I wasn't going to become a daily symbol of rejection.

Society is cruel when it comes to the unemployed—especially the fired. Any job interviewer has to suspect someone who has been fired. Thus, there's a clear-cut rule: Everything else being equal between two candidates, don't hire the person who has unwillingly lost a job.

There is a plastic nameplate glued to the wall outside every executive office. It has something to do with company pride. By my office door was my name spelled in crisp, san serif letters. I tried to remove just the upper layer of the nameplate and leave the black plastic base for a future occupant, but the entire plate ripped from the wall. The top layer of wall paint tore with it. For the first time during this 24-hour ordeal, I felt guilt. Is the symbolism of the marred wall too raw? Will

this image become another nail in the coffin holding my credibility? Does it appear I left in rage?   BRENT GREEN
Denver, Colorado

Right and Wronged

To the Editor:

While reading the article in today's *Times*, I cried for the first time after losing my job. I cried because I continue to feel humiliated, frightened, and confused. I did all the right things. I went to college, received an advanced degree, and am currently in a doctoral program in clinical social work . . . and I have no full-time job. I believe I was laid off because the city was forcing cutbacks (Mayor [Rudy] Giuliani's edict). I was an associate director of social work services. However, one month after I lost my job, my ex-boss got a promotion. Two months later she got a salary increase along with all the other senior managers in the agency. My $45,000-a-year job was eliminated so that others could get promotions and raises? I don't understand. I am 53 years old, African American, and out of work. It wasn't supposed to be this way. I did what I was supposed to do . . . didn't I?   CAROL WINSTON
New York City

"You're Too Old"

To the Editor:

This is the third-month anniversary of my unemployment. After 22.917 years (according to my pension) I was let go from Lever Brothers company. I was the only one in my department let go. I was the only female manager over 40. I was paid to the end of 1995 (three weeks) so as to not make it so bad on me for Christmas, I was told! I climbed the corporate ladder the hard way. Started as a clerk, went to school at night to get my BA, took only six weeks off to have my son and worked 80-hour weeks. I held my department together through four senior manager changes in five years. Alas, I am now considered too old at 42 to continue with Lever Brothers. My family income has been cut by 50 percent; I have no health insurance (I carried the family health insurance).

So I start another day. I go to Right Associates (outplacement service—six-month contract), do some networking by phone, call recruiters, answer ads, volunteer for Council of Logistics Management (an organization for those in the logistics field), and pray I find a job before the unemployment payments run out.

I cry at night when the family sleeps. I know they depended on me to bring home the bacon, so to speak, and now I've been told, "You're too old, you didn't go to a top school, you made too much. We're looking for someone like you with three to five years experience, you've done too much, you've done too little," but no job offers. My most recent interview, I was told, "You're perfect for the current position but we're not sure what we would do with you five years from now." I desperately wanted to say, "Take me and let me worry about it five years from now." I have been told that if I get another job, it will be for less money, and I probably will only have it for three to five years before being laid off again.

I know I'm not 26 and right out of Penn State, Michigan State, or Carnegie Mellon. I should be younger and I should have gone to a different school. Hard to change the past. Well, off to outplacement to fight over a cubicle with a window,

computer time, copy machines, and face some more rejection. I know I'll find something because I've been working since I was 14 years old. I'll find something.   ROSE DETWEILER
New York City

The Price of "Synergy"

To the Editor:

On April 1, 1993, we all received E-mail that told us that the place where I used to work had been sold. Another software company had acquired us. The agreement had been signed that day, and the wheels would start to turn, and they hoped that everything would be finished so that they could close the deal by the end of June.

That afternoon we were all called to a meeting at a nearby hotel. At the meeting, the man we had all known as the head of our company told us how great everything was, and how this was just such a good thing, and he was so excited. Excited about the synergy. There was so much synergy. It was all over the place. The company that bought us could see the synergy, he could see the synergy, and he wanted to share all the synergy with us.

Then they asked us if any of us had any questions. People didn't ask so much about the synergy, though. They wanted to know about important things. Were any of us going to lose our jobs because of all this synergy. Stuff like that.

We were told in a rather offhanded way that unfortunately, there would be some small redundancy. It was inevitable, even with all the synergy floating around everywhere, and that the cold reality was that yes, some people would lose their jobs. But it wasn't going to be a big deal. We shouldn't be afraid. They didn't buy us to lay us all off and eliminate the competition. We should not worry about it. And above all, we would be treated fairly. Remember that. We would be treated fairly.

They also told us that the next few months would be a blur of activity as the Decision Makers went around the world to look at our entire company, and made decisions about what the new company would look like. In the meantime, we should just all go back to work and not worry about it, and just focus on having the best darned second quarter there ever was.

For a while, I think we did forget about it. We did focus and concentrate, and do our jobs. We couldn't stand around in the halls and worry for three months. That wouldn't do any good.

But things were changing. We could see the activity. We knew when the Decision Makers were looking at our department position by position. Trying to understand exactly what each of us did, and why we were needed in the new company.

We started having more meetings. Rumor Control meetings, they called them. What had we heard? What were we thinking? What did we want to know?

But I noticed that most of the things we wanted to know had nothing whatsoever to do with what they wanted to tell us. And that's when the rumors started.

I can't remember exactly when they put up the rumor boards. It was after one of the Rumor Control meetings. We had been told that the vice president of our department probably would not be "going on" with the new company. We had whispered about that, and wondered. But then he said it. Right there. Someone had the guts to ask him right to his face, and he said that no, he didn't think he would be "going on." Because no one was talking to him—none of the Decision Makers. And that was a pretty good sign, he said with a smile. He was our leader, and he was upbeat. And he told us not to worry, and to focus and concentrate and keep doing our jobs.

And shortly after that the rumor board went up on the wall in the hallway outside my office. There were two big laminated pieces of white plastic tacked to the wall. One labeled "Substantiated Rumors," the other labeled "Unsubstantiated Rumors."

In the beginning, there were only two Substantiated Rumors. That our vice president would not be "going on," and that there would be a Dress Code. We had a great deal of fun with the Unsubstantiated Rumors. Pretty soon, people were writing all manner of wild and bizarre things on the rumor board under Unsubstantiated Rumors.

One rumor simply said: $900 - 600 = 300$.

We really didn't know what to make of that one. There were roughly 900 employees in the company where I used to work. We got that much. But what did the 600 and the 300 mean? We laughed and put more rumors up.

We elaborated on the Dress Code rumor. It was going to mean plaid jumpers and white blouses with ruffled collars. And black patent leather shoes. (And that was for the men!)

There would be a daily pantyhose check.

Anyone caught starting a rumor would be fired.

It was wonderful. Such a stress reliever. So much fun. So many laughs. At one point, someone with an office near the rumor board actually complained that sometimes it got too loud outside in the hallway by the rumor board. But Management approved of the rumor board. Management said it was a good outlet for stress, and if the noise bothered that woman, she should politely ask people to tone it down, and then close her office door.

One morning I saw two of the Decision Makers outside my office, looking at the rumor board. They weren't laughing like everyone else who looked at it did. They were studying it.

I couldn't figure out if they were checking it to see how accurate the rumor mill was—or reading it trying to get ideas.

We knew that July 1 was the day we would all find out what the new company was going to "look like"—and who would be "going on" and who wouldn't.

And July 1 was coming closer and closer.

Finally, on June 30, the word came down to our department. It still wasn't official, but our vice president (and we already knew he wouldn't be "going on") sent E-mail around asking us to please consider July 1 a "dress up" day. As a favor to him, would we all come in on July 1 dressed up and looking sharp and proud, and show how we could accept change. Even though it would be a short day for some of us.

A short day for some of us?

My God.

So we all talked in the halls about what we were going to do. We thought about what it would mean to be laid off, and have to clean out our offices. And we decided that the best thing to do would be to bring a change of clothes along. If you are going to get laid off, and have to clean out your office, you might as well be comfortable.

So that's what we all did.

We dressed up, and came in . . . and some of us got laid off.

Eight in my department. More than 10 percent. It was a shock to most people, I think, that so many of us got hit, because we thought we were in a really safe department. We thought we would be NEEDED in the new company.

As I was getting ready that morning, I almost didn't bring in my change of clothes. I was that sure I was going to make the cut. But I thought, no . . . better have it, just in case. (I almost thought of it as a good luck charm. If I HAD the casual clothes, I wouldn't NEED them.)

When I got to work, I noticed how out of place everyone looked. For three and a half years, I had seen these same people in this same environment. We all wore whatever we wanted to. We were comfortable.

Not that morning. Everyone was standing around, all dressed up and scared to death. We knew the axe was coming. We knew some of us were going to get hit. But we didn't know who or how many or even, really, when. Everyone just looked so out of place.

And so very Uncomfortable.

At eight-thirty, the Managers went into a meeting. We knew they were getting the word. They were being told. But we didn't know if they were being told THEY were laid off, or who of US they had to lay off.

It was awful. We were all so scared.

Then the Managers came out of their meeting. Nobody said anything. We all just went into our offices. We knew that the word was not going to come right there in the middle of the hall. We went into our offices to wait, and see, and hope we would be passed by.

And in a few minutes, Tim came into my office and invited me to a meeting in Art's office.

Now I am an intelligent person. I know that Art's office is not that big, and I would not be invited to any meeting there unless I was not going to be "going on" with the new company.

After the meeting in Art's office, we all walked back to our offices. By that time, the word had spread like wildfire on the floor, and on our way back to our offices, everyone we met knew that we were not "going on."

And those of us that were not "going on" changed our clothes, just as we had planned, and began to clean out our offices.

They could dress us up.

And they could lay us off.

But, by God, we were comfortable as we cleaned out our offices. BETH WILEY

Herndon, Virginia

Survivor's "Luck"

To the Editor:

My company was proud of its "no layoff" history. In 1991, the first layoffs started in the Manhattan office. We were stunned. Looking back, I felt the sorriest for the victims of the first onslaught . . . but they were the lucky ones.

As the layoffs continued, severance packages shrank, the market became more and more flooded with people with similar skills. I was one of the "lucky ones" and avoided being laid off for four years. As time went by, fewer people were left, but there was even more work to do since the company needed to "rebuild."

It was "strategy du jour" as management's visible panic was manifested in constant reorganizations, new mission statements, revised market strategies . . . products were dropped from the price list, then entire product lines were trashed, as new ones emerged that were more "in tune" with the market.

I, along with the others in my department, worked 70-to-80-hour weeks, trying to do "more with less" while simultaneously trying to second-guess management's next move so we could move with them. I changed jobs (within the company) several times to avoid getting laid off.

The Manhattan office started to resemble a Chicago housing project gone bad as it rapidly deteriorated due to a total lack of office management. Every time someone got laid off, the "vultures" ravaged their office or cubicle for supplies, software, or hardware, since purchase requisitions were being cut off. Basic office supplies couldn't be ordered due to budget cuts. Printers went unrepaired since service contracts were dropped . . . no one appeared to be in charge of keeping the office presentable or assuring we had the fundamental tools to get our jobs done. I made frequent trips to office supply stores to buy binders, quality paper, printer toner, etc., so my client proposals would look like they were coming from a real company.

Piles and piles of trash from "ravaged offices" lined the halls. My office was "vandalized" more than once as remaining employees helped themselves to my computer's memory board, power supply, even my mouse, for God's sake, since no one was allowed to buy anything.

Meantime, the company reported a half-billion-dollar write-down as it paid thousands of people to leave the company.

I rarely left the office before 9 or 10 P.M. My department had virtually no administrative support; market research services had started to vanish; the help desk didn't return calls. The ship was clearly sinking, and time to look for a job was scarce since we had so much work to do.

People were desperate to keep their jobs, especially those with kids in college. Political backstabbing and bitter infighting broke out like wildfire. I watched nice people turn into wild animals desperately clinging to their survival. People spent hours writing memos justifying their existence.

It was so pathetic, and so bizarre.

Many were glad to finally get laid off so they could get a fresh start. Others were devastated. I wondered when a disgruntled employee would "go postal."

Meantime, management continued to assure me that I was critical to the plan to rebuild the company. "Getting laid off is the last thing you need to worry about," my manager said as he heaped on more and more assignments. However, keeping up with the demand was difficult, if not impossible, and more and more customers started to leave.

By 1994, the few talented people left started to voluntarily leave. "Getting the job done" became more and more difficult and management continued to tell me I was needed for the great "re-build." However, the great re-build strategy continued to undergo revision after revision. I wrote at least ten business plans in two years.

In early 1995, the company decided to "decommit" from the market my group was selling to. I was notified by telephone on a Wednesday that Friday would be my last day.

I went to another high-tech company, this time a small startup, but got laid off after ten weeks. I'm now with a very good, very stable consulting company, with a great job, a much higher salary than my old company would have ever granted . . . but, believe me, I take nothing for granted.

And I will never work for a large corporation again.

RICHARD FOUTS
New York City

Just Hanging On

To the Editor:

I am a living example of the day-to-day effects that downsizing has had on a middle-class family in America today. My husband was "downsized/let go" from his executive position at a Manhattan advertising firm five years ago; advertising was all he ever knew in life; he was 50 years old then. Not one day since then did he spend at home; instead, he searched and networked and knocked on doors and waited for phone calls and hoped; after innumerable dead ends and perfunctory "I'm sorries," he joined the training program at New York Life. He is now an insurance agent who works on a commission basis. He has begun from scratch. During the last five years, we exhausted his retirement and our savings, sold some belongings, and then had to be taxed and penalized for using such funds. Throughout it all, our goal was to keep our house, the only asset we have and the only home our daughter has ever known.

Last year, we were forced into bankruptcy, and presently we face the imminent danger of having our home seized by the bank. The sleepless nights are nightmarish and the morning light holds hope only in the sense that I can get up and hope that the dawn of a new day may bring with it some luck. I have taught English, happily, to seventh and eighth graders at Rye Country Day School for the last seventeen years, and I tutor after school hours, yet my $40,000 salary seems to count for nothing when it comes to contributing to the mortgage on our modest home in Port Chester (no pool, no air conditioning, just a normal home). It is a fact that my family literally has nowhere to go; on my salary, I could not even rent a two-bedroom apartment in this area. Where can we turn for help? As my husband works diligently to build his clientele, his monthly income is sporadic, yet the bank does not seem to care to work with any families such as mine to help them keep their home and, ultimately, their dignity and pride. They will not accept partial payments or even consider lowering our monthly payments. I live in fear, and grasp for the strength to shade my pain with a smile for my students every day.   GINNY BLACK
Port Chester, New York

Two *New York Times* Polls

THE *NEW YORK TIMES* POLL on issues of economic insecurity was based on telephone interviews conducted December 3–6, 1995, with 1,265 adults throughout the United States.

The sample of telephone exchanges called was randomly selected by a computer from a complete list of active residential exchanges in the country. The list of more than 36,000 residential exchanges is maintained by Marketing Systems Group of Philadelphia.

Within each exchange, random digits were added to form a complete telephone number, thus permitting access to both listed and unlisted numbers. Within each household, one adult was designated by a random procedure to be the respondent for the survey.

The results have been weighted to take account of household size and number of telephone lines into the residence and to adjust for variations in the sample relating to geographic region, race, sex, age, and education.

In theory, in nineteen cases out of twenty the results based on such samples will differ by no more than three percentage points in either direction from what would have been obtained by seeking out all American adults. For smaller subgroups the potential sampling error is larger. For example, it is plus or minus seven percentage points for those who are very worried about losing their job in the coming year. It is plus or minus nine percentage points for those who have experienced a layoff in the past that created a major crisis in their life.

In addition to sampling error, the practical difficulties of conducting any survey of public opinion may introduce other sources of error into the poll. Variations in question wording or the order of questions, for instance, can lead to somewhat different results.

Responses labeled "12/95 TOTAL" are based on the entire sample.

Responses labeled "crisis layoff" (Sample size = 132) are of respondents with a layoff, either their own or someone else's in the household, that created a *major* crisis in their life.

Responses labeled "non-crisis layoff" (Sample size = 290) are of respondents with a layoff, either their own or someone else's in the household, that did *not* create a major crisis in their life.

Responses labeled "friend layoff" (Sample size = 492) are those respondents who had a friend, relative, or neighbor laid off.

Responses labeled "no layoff" (Sample size = 351) are those respondents that have no layoff experience.

Responses labeled "worried" (Sample size = 177) are those respondents who are *very* worried that they or someone in their household will be out of a job in the next twelve months.

Responses labeled "extra job" (Sample size = 238) are employed respondents who have had to take on an extra job in the last three years.

Percentages labeled "omitted" are those respondents who were skipped out of the question.

DK means "Don't Know," and NA stands for "No Answer."

The *Times*' National Economic Insecurity Survey

1. *Do you approve or disapprove of the way Bill Clinton is handling his job as president?*

	APPROVE	DISAPPROVE	DK/NA
12/95 TOTAL	47%	40%	13%
Crisis layoff	50	40	10
Non-crisis layoff	44	41	15
Friend layoff	47	41	12
No layoff	47	38	15
Worried	44	37	18
Extra job	45	42	13

2. *Do you feel things in this country are generally going in the right direction today, or do you feel things have pretty seriously gotten off on the wrong track?*

	RIGHT DIRECTION	WRONG TRACK	DK/NA
12/95 TOTAL	25%	64%	10%
Crisis layoff	18	76	6
Non-crisis layoff	26	68	7
Friend layoff	25	64	11
No layoff	29	58	14
Worried	15	76	9
Extra job	19	72	10

3. *How would you rate the condition of the national economy these days? Is it very good, fairly good, fairly bad, or very bad?*

	VERY GOOD	FAIRLY GOOD	FAIRLY BAD	VERY BAD	DK/NA
12/95 TOTAL	4%	47%	33%	13%	3%
Crisis layoff	—	33	42·	24	1
Non-crisis layoff	3	46	36	13	2
Friend layoff	4	49	34	11	2

	VERY GOOD	FAIRLY GOOD	FAIRLY BAD	VERY BAD	DK/NA
No layoff	5	52	26	12	5
Worried	—	29	47	22	2
Extra job	2	34	45	18	1

4. *Do you think the economy is getting better, getting worse, or staying about the same?*

	BETTER	WORSE	SAME	DK/NA
12/95 TOTAL	15%	31%	53%	2%
Crisis layoff	14	42	43	1
Non-crisis layoff	14	33	51	2
Friend layoff	13	28	58	2
No layoff	18	28	52	2
Worried	8	46	42	5
Extra job	12	41	46	1

5. *In the past couple of years would you say you have been getting ahead financially, just staying even financially, or falling behind financially?*

	GETTING AHEAD	STAYING EVEN	FALLING BEHIND	DK/NA
12/95 TOTAL	20%	51%	28%	1%
Crisis layoff	15	38	47	
Non-crisis layoff	19	53	28	—
Friend layoff	21	52	26	1
No layoff	22	53	23	1
Worried	6	37	55	2
Extra job	16	44	40	—

6. *In your community these days, how easy is it for someone who is trying to find a job to get a good job at good wages—very easy, somewhat easy, somewhat hard, or very hard?*

	VERY EASY	SOMEWHAT EASY	SOMEWHAT HARD	VERY HARD	IMPOSSIBLE	DK/NA
12/95 TOTAL	3%	13%	42%	36%	1%	5%
Crisis layoff		7	34	57		2

	VERY EASY	SOMEWHAT EASY	SOMEWHAT HARD	VERY HARD	IMPOSSIBLE	DK/NA
Non-crisis layoff	3	14	41	39	—	2
Friend layoff	3	14	44	33	1	5
No layoff	4	14	41	31	—	9
Worried	—	3	26	67	1	3
Extra job	2	7	43	46	—	1

7. *Are you at least as well off financially today as you expected to be at this point in your life?*

	YES	NO	DK/NA
12/95 NYT	44%	53%	3%
Crisis layoff	28	71	1
Non-crisis layoff	36	61	3
Friend layoff	48	49	3
No layoff	50	46	4
Worried	23	75	1
Extra job	30	69	1

8. *In America, each generation has tried to have a better life than their parents, with a better living standard, better homes, a better education, etc. How likely do you think it is that today's youth will have a better life than their parents—very likely, somewhat likely, somewhat unlikely, or very unlikely?*

	VERY LIKELY	SOMEWHAT LIKELY	SOMEWHAT UNLIKELY	VERY UNLIKELY	DK/NA
12/95 NYT	11%	38%	32%	17%	2%
Crisis layoff	9	34	33	23	1
Non-crisis layoff	9	38	32	19	3
Friend layoff	12	36	34	16	1
No layoff	12	41	29	14	4
Worried	6	31	31	28	5
Extra job	4	35	38	22	1

9. *Would you agree or disagree with the following statement: I'm angry at both political parties.*

	AGREE	DISAGREE	DK/NA
12/95 TOTAL	58%	38%	4%
Crisis layoff	69	26	5
Non-crisis layoff	61	35	4
Friend layoff	60	37	2
No layoff	49	45	6
Worried	67	29	4
Extra job	68	28	4

10. *Would you agree or disagree with the following statement: It makes no real difference who is elected—things go on just as they did before.*

	AGREE	DISAGREE	DK/NA
12/95 TOTAL	48%	49%	3%
Crisis layoff	43	53	4
Non-crisis layoff	50	46	3
Friend layoff	49	49	2
No layoff	47	50	3
Worried	59	39	2
Extra job	52	47	1

11. *Would you agree or disagree with the following statement: People like me don't have any say about what the government does.*

	AGREE	DISAGREE	DK/NA
12/95 NYT	50%	47%	2%
Crisis layoff	51	49	1
Non-crisis layoff	52	46	2
Friend layoff	50	48	2
No layoff	49	47	4
Worried	59	40	—
Extra job	55	45	—

12. *When it comes to the availability of good jobs for American workers, some say that America's best years are behind us. Others say that the best times are yet to come. What do you think?*

	BEST YEARS BEHIND	BEST YET TO COME	DK/NA
12/95 TOTAL	49%	40%	11%
Crisis layoff	62	27	10
Non-crisis layoff	52	38	11
Friend layoff	48	44	8
No layoff	45	41	14
Worried	62	30	8
Extra job	56	32	13

13. *Looking ahead for the next few years, which political party—the Republican or the Democratic—do you think will do the best job of keeping the country prosperous?*

	REPUBLICAN	DEMOCRATIC	NO DIFFERENCE	DK/NA
12/95 NYT	38%	37%	10%	15%
Crisis layoff	27	43	13	17
Non-crisis layoff	39	36	11	14
Friend layoff	42	33	11	15
No layoff	35	40	9	16
Worried	31	40	15	15
Extra job	35	35	12	18

14. *Regardless of how you usually vote, do you think the Republican Party or the Democratic Party is better able to handle unemployment?*

	REPUBLICAN	DEMOCRATIC	BOTH	NEITHER	DK/NA
12/95 NYT	34%	42%	1%	9%	14%
Crisis layoff	34	43		11	12
Non-crisis layoff	34	41	1	10	14
Friend layoff	33	40	2	10	14
No layoff	33	45	1	5	16
Worried	31	44	2	12	11
Extra job	29	44	1	11	15

15. *Regardless of how you usually vote, do you think the Republican Party or the Democratic Party is better able to stop layoffs and the loss of jobs in this country?*

	REPUBLICAN	DEMOCRATIC	BOTH	NEITHER	DK/NA
12/95 NYT	33%	40%	1%	11%	15%
Crisis layoff	28	45	2	13	13
Non-crisis layoff	36	41	1	9	13
Friend layoff	35	38	1	11	15
No layoff	28	40	1	12	18
Worried	32	38	1	13	16
Extra job	31	41	1	11	16

16. *Do you agree or disagree that there is a need for a new third political party to compete with the Democrats and Republicans?*

	AGREE	DISAGREE	DK/NA
12/95 TOTAL	57%	36%	7%
Crisis layoff	61	34	5
Non-crisis layoff	58	34	8
Friend layoff	60	34	6
No layoff	50	43	7
Worried	58	36	6
Extra job	71	23	6

17. *Do you favor or oppose national health insurance, which would be financed by tax money, paying for most forms of health care?*

	FAVOR	OPPOSE	DK/NA
12/95 NYT	53%	39%	8%
Crisis layoff	64	29	7
Non-crisis layoff	59	36	5
Friend layoff	52	42	6
No layoff	47	42	12
Worried	66	29	5
Extra job	67	29	4

18. *Do you believe that where there has been job discrimination against women in the past, preference in hiring or promotion should be given to women today? (Note: The ordering of questions 18 and 19 were rotated.)*

	YES, PREFERENCE	NO	DEPENDS	DK/NA
12/95 TOTAL	32%	62%		6%
Crisis layoff	42	51		7
Non-crisis layoff	32	65		3
Friend layoff	29	65		6
No layoff	34	60		7
Worried	46	50		4
Extra job	35	63		2

19. *Do you believe that where there has been job discrimination against blacks in the past, preference in hiring or promotion should be given to blacks today? (Note: The ordering of questions 18 and 19 were rotated.)*

	YES, PREFERENCE	NO	DEPENDS	DK/NA
12/95 TOTAL	29%	66%		6%
Crisis layoff	39	55		6
Non-crisis layoff	26	68		6
Friend layoff	27	68		5
No layoff	30	64		6
Worried	41	55		4
Extra job	32	65		3

20. *Would you agree or disagree: It is the responsibility of the government to take care of people who can't take care of themselves.*

	AGREE	DISAGREE	DK/NA
12/95 NYT	64%	30%	6%
Crisis layoff	64	30	6
Non-crisis layoff	64	29	7
Friend layoff	63	30	6
No layoff	64	29	6
Worried	67	26	7
Extra job	61	33	6

21. *Do you think that immigration into the United States should be increased, decreased, or kept about the same?*

	INCREASED	DECREASED	PRESENT LEVEL	DK/NA
12/95 NYT	2%	64%	31%	3%
Crisis layoff	5	74	20	1
Non-crisis layoff	3	69	26	3
Friend layoff	2	59	38	2
No layoff	1	64	34	4
Worried	4	65	28	4
Extra job	3	73	21	2

22. *Do you think the immigrants coming to this country today mostly take jobs away from American citizens, or do they mostly take jobs Americans don't want?*

	TAKE JOBS FROM AMERICAN CITIZENS	TAKE JOBS AMERICANS DON'T WANT	BOTH	DK/NA
12/95 TOTAL	36%	55%		10%
Crisis layoff	49	47		4
Non-crisis layoff	40	50		10
Friend layoff	31	59		10
No layoff	34	55		11
Worried	49	39		11
Extra job	41	50		9

23. *In recent years, has the amount of money you give to charity increased, decreased, or stayed about the same?*

	INCREASED	DECREASED	STAYED SAME	DK/NA
12/95 TOTAL	26%	16%	57%	1%
Crisis layoff	17	20	63	
Non-crisis layoff	28	14	56	1
Friend layoff	29	16	55	1
No layoff	25	17	57	1
Worried	19	22	58	1
Extra job	23	20	57	

24. *In recent years, has the amount of time you devote to doing volunteer work increased, decreased, or stayed about the same?*

	INCREASED	DECREASED	STAYED SAME	DK/NA
12/95 TOTAL	24%	21%	53%	2%
Crisis layoff	31	26	44	
Non-crisis layoff	23	22	54	1
Friend layoff	24	21	53	4
No layoff	21	20	56	2
Worried	16	26	57	1
Extra job	29	24	46	—

25. *In recent years, has your involvement or participation in civic or community groups increased, decreased, or stayed about the same?*

	INCREASED	DECREASED	STAYED SAME	DK/NA
12/95 TOTAL	21%	20%	57%	1%
Crisis layoff	24	20	55	
Non-crisis layoff	24	22	51	3
Friend layoff	21	19	59	1
No layoff	18	20	61	1
Worried	15	23	60	2
Extra job	23	22	55	—

26. *In recent years, have you attended religious services more often or less often, or has there been no change?*

	MORE OFTEN	LESS OFTEN	NO CHANGE	DK/NA
12/95 TOTAL	20%	21%	58%	1%
Crisis layoff	21	22	57	
Non-crisis layoff	23	21	56	1
Friend layoff	21	23	55	1
No layoff	17	19	64	1
Worried	18	28	53	1
Extra job	17	28	55	—

27. *Other than labor unions and professional societies, do you belong to any group that helps you with employment opportunities or business contacts?*

	YES	NO	DK/NA
12/95 TOTAL	11%	88%	1%
Crisis layoff	19	81	
Non-crisis layoff	12	87	1
Friend layoff	14	86	—
No layoff	4	94	2
Worried	11	88	1
Extra job	18	81	1

28. *How worried are you that in the next twelve months you or someone else in your household might be out of work and looking for a job for any reason—very worried, somewhat worried, or not worried at all?*

	VERY	SOMEWHAT	NOT AT ALL	DK/NA
12/95 TOTAL	15%	31%	52%	2%
Crisis layoff	39	32	29	
Non-crisis layoff	19	38	42	—
Friend layoff	12	33	54	2
No layoff	9	23	65	3
Worried	100			
Extra job	32	37	31	—

29. *Are you currently employed, or are you temporarily out of work, or are you not in the market for work at all?*

	CURRENTLY EMPLOYED	TEMPORARILY OUT OF WORK	NOT IN THE MARKET FOR WORK	RETIRED	DK/NA
12/95 TOTAL	63%	7%	16%	13%	
Crisis layoff	64	16	13	7	
Non-crisis layoff	64	9	16	11	
Friend layoff	67	5	15	12	
No layoff	57	6	20	18	
Worried	57	23	16	4	
Extra job	87	13			

a. *If not in the market for work: Are you currently retired, or not? (Note: Percentages include retired results from question 29.)*

	RETIRED	NOT RETIRED	DK/NA
12/95 TOTAL	20%	9%	—
Crisis layoff	11	9	—
Non-crisis layoff	17	10	—
Friend layoff	20	8	—
No layoff	28	10	—
Worried	12	8	—

30. *Is there anyone else in your household who is currently employed? If no: Is there anyone else in your household who is temporarily out of work?*

	OTHER EMPLOYED	TEMPORARILY OUT OF WORK	NOT IN THE MARKET FOR WORK	DK/NA
12/95 TOTAL	61%	1%	38%	—
Crisis layoff	67	3	30	
Non-crisis layoff	69	1	30	—
Friend layoff	61	1	38	
No layoff	51	1	47	2
Worried	66	4	30	
Extra job	73	1	25	

31. *How satisfied are you with your job—very satisfied, somewhat satisfied, somewhat dissatisfied, or very dissatisfied?**

	VERY SATISFIED	SOMEWHAT SATISFIED	SOMEWHAT DISSATISFIED	VERY DISSATISFIED	DK/NA
12/95 NYT	43%	42%	11%	4%	
Crisis layoff	37	39	20	5	
Non-crisis layoff	38	45	16	1	
Friend layoff	45	44	8	4	
No layoff	46	39	8	6	
Worried	25	37	29	8	
Extra job	33	38	22	6	

*Based on employed respondents (sample size = 808)

32. *In the past three years, have you been forced to work reduced hours or forced to take a cut in pay?**

	REDUCED HOURS	CUT IN PAY	NO	BOTH	DK/NA
12/95 TOTAL	10%	15%	69%	5%	1%
Crisis layoff	13	22	46	18	—
Non-crisis layoff	13	19	61	6	1
Friend layoff	9	11	76	3	1
No layoff	7	13	77	3	
Worried	14	26	48	13	
Extra job	17	23	48	13	1

*Based on those in labor market (sample size = 887)

33. *In the past three years, have you frequently had to work* more *hours than usual at your job?**

	YES, MORE HOURS	NO	DK/NA
12/95 TOTAL	42%	57%	1%
Crisis layoff	45	55	
Non-crisis layoff	45	54	1
Friend layoff	44	54	2
No layoff	33	67	—
Worried	52	48	
Extra job	55	44	1

*Based on those in labor market (sample size = 887)

34. *In the past three years, have you had to take on an extra job?**

	YES, EXTRA JOB	NO	DK/NA
12/95 TOTAL	28%	72%	—
Crisis layoff	47	52	—
Non-crisis layoff	29	71	
Friend layoff	26	74	
No layoff	21	79	
Worried	50	49	—
Extra job	100		

*Based on those in labor market (sample size = 887)

35. *In the past three years, was there anyone else in your household who was forced to work reduced hours or forced to take a cut in pay?**

	REDUCED HOURS	CUT IN PAY	NO	BOTH	DK/NA
12/95 TOTAL	11%	11%	72%	5%	1%
Crisis layoff	21	18	48	11	1
Non-crisis layoff	12	10	69	8	1
Friend layoff	11	12	75	2	1
No layoff	7	7	84	3	
Worried	25	13	51	10	1
Extra job	13	13	62	10	1

*Based on those with some other household member in labor market (sample size = 682)

36. *In the past three years, has anyone else in your household frequently had to work more hours than usual at their job?**

	YES, MORE HOURS	NO	DK/NA
12/95 TOTAL	41%	58%	1%
Crisis layoff	50	50	
Non-crisis layoff	53	45	1
Friend layoff	38	62	—
No layoff	29	70	1
Worried	56	44	
Extra job	61	39	

*Based on those with some other household member in labor market (sample size = 682)

37. *In the past three years, has anyone else in your household had to take on an extra job?**

	YES, EXTRA JOB	NO	DK/NA
12/95 TOTAL	23%	77%	1%
Crisis layoff	46	54	
Non-crisis layoff	28	71	1
Friend layoff	18	82	1
No layoff	13	87	—
Worried	43	57	
Extra job	40	59	1

*Based on those with some other household member in labor market (sample size = 682)

38. *What is your occupation? If necessary: What exactly do you do for a living? What is your job title?**

	12/95 NYT
Executive/high-level management	2%
Professional/other managers/artists	19
Technical/administrative	15
Clerical	9
Skilled labor	11
Unskilled labor	10
Service workers/protective services	31
Other	3
Nothing	—
Refused	1

	CRISIS LAYOFF	NON-CRISIS LAYOFF	FRIEND LAYOFF	NO LAYOFF
Executive/high-level management	2%	2%	2%	3%
Professional/other managers/ artists	16	15	23	18
Technical/administrative	21	11	16	13
Clerical	7	13	6	8
Skilled labor	10	18	8	10
Unskilled labor	13	8	8	12
Service workers/protective services	28	29	32	30
Other	2	2	3	3
Nothing	1			
Refused		1	1	2

*Based on those in labor market (sample size = 887)

	WORRIED	EXTRA JOB
Executive/high-level management	1%	1%
Professional/other managers/artists	13	18
Technical/administrative	11	14
Clerical	10	9

	WORRIED	EXTRA JOB
Skilled labor	14	10
Unskilled labor	13	8
Service workers/protective services	33	38
Other	4	2
Nothing		—
Refused	1	2

*Based on those in labor market (sample size = 887)

39. *What is the other person's occupation in your household? If necessary: What exactly do they do for a living? What is their job title?**

	12/95 TOTAL
Executive/high-level management	3%
Professional/other managers/artists	20
Technical/administrative	19
Clerical	6
Skilled labor	13
Unskilled labor	8
Service workers/protective services	26
Other	3
Nothing	—
Refused	2

*Based on those with some other household member in labor market (sample size = 682)

	CRISIS LAYOFF	NON-CRISIS LAYOFF	FRIEND LAYOFF	NO LAYOFF
Executive/high-level management	1%	2%	4%	2%
Professional/other managers/artists	22	24	20	16
Technical/administrative	17	18	19	20
Clerical	1	5	7	5
Skilled labor	13	17	9	16
Unskilled labor	10	4	10	8

	CRISIS LAYOFF	NON-CRISIS LAYOFF	FRIEND LAYOFF	NO LAYOFF
Service workers/protective services	32	23	27	23
Other	2	4	3	3
Nothing		—		
Refused	2	4	1	3

*Based on those with some other household member in labor market (sample size = 682)

	WORRIED	EXTRA JOB
Executive/high-level management	1%	2%
Professional/other managers/artists	23	19
Technical/administrative	10	15
Clerical	5	6
Skilled labor	16	17
Unskilled labor	11	6
Service workers/protective services	31	34
Other	2	1
Refused	3	

*Based on those with some other household member in labor market (sample size = 682)

40. *In the past couple of years, would you say you have felt* more *secure and confident that you can continue in your job as long as you want, or* less *secure and confident, or has there been no change?**

	MORE	LESS	NO CHANGE	DK/NA
12/95 TOTAL	29%	28%	42%	—
Crisis layoff	18	57	24	1
Non-crisis layoff	27	33	38	1
Friend layoff	28	22	50	
No layoff	38	21	41	
Worried	9	61	29	1
Extra job	24	40	35	1

*Based on employed respondents (sample size = 808)

41. *How worried are you about not having enough savings for retirement—very worried, somewhat worried, or not worried at all?**

	VERY WORRIED	SOMEWHAT WORRIED	NOT WORRIED AT ALL	DK/NA
12/95 TOTAL	35%	42%	22%	—
Crisis layoff	66	28	6	
Non-crisis layoff	41	40	19	—
Friend layoff	30	44	25	—
No layoff	23	48	29	—
Worried	73	23	3	—
Extra job	54	35	11	—

*Based on respondents who are not retired (sample size = 995)

42. *In recent years, has uncertainty or insecurity about your economic future caused you to make cutbacks in your day-to-day spending?*

	YES	NO	DK/NA
12/95 TOTAL	65%	34%	1%
Crisis layoff	91	9	1
Non-crisis layoff	72	28	—
Friend layoff	63	36	1
No layoff	53	45	2
Worried	91	8	—
Extra job	86	14	1

a. *If yes: Would you call those cutbacks severe, or not so severe?*

	SEVERE	NOT SEVERE	DK/NA
12/95 TOTAL	20%	44%	1%
Crisis layoff	50	40	1
Non-crisis layoff	21	49	1
Friend layoff	16	46	—
No layoff	15	37	1
Worried	49	42	1
Extra job	41	44	1

43. *Generally speaking, do you think companies are more, or less, loyal to their employees than they were ten years ago, or hasn't this changed?*

	MORE LOYAL	LESS LOYAL	NO CHANGE	DK/NA
12/95 NYT	6%	75%	13%	6%
Crisis layoff	4	89	3	4
Non-crisis layoff	6	74	14	6
Friend layoff	6	78	11	5
No layoff	6	66	18	10
Worried	6	79	10	5
Extra job	5	84	8	3

44. *Generally speaking, do you think workers are more, or less, loyal to their employers than they were ten years ago, or hasn't this changed?*

	MORE LOYAL	LESS LOYAL	NO CHANGE	DK/NA
12/95 NYT	9%	64%	22%	5%
Crisis layoff	13	70	13	4
Non-crisis layoff	8	66	21	5
Friend layoff	9	67	22	3
No layoff	10	55	27	9
Worried	14	62	21	4
Extra job	11	69	17	3

45. *Compared to the way things used to be, do you think most working people today cooperate more with one another at the place where they work, or that they compete more with one another at the place where they work?*

	COOPERATE MORE	COMPETE MORE	NO CHANGE	DK/NA
12/95 TOTAL	20%	70%	2%	8%
Crisis layoff	15	83	—	1
Non-crisis layoff	23	71	1	6
Friend layoff	19	71	2	8
No layoff	22	64	3	11
Worried	20	74	2	4
Extra job	17	79	1	3

46. *And compared to the way things used to be, do you think the mood at many workplaces today is a more angry mood, or a more friendly mood, or has there been no change?*

	MORE ANGRY	MORE FRIENDLY	NO CHANGE	DK/NA
12/95 TOTAL	53%	8%	31%	8%
Crisis layoff	75	4	20	2
Non-crisis layoff	53	8	31	8
Friend layoff	56	8	30	6
No layoff	41	10	35	14
Worried	64	9	25	2
Extra job	67	8	23	2

a. *If more angry: What do you think workers are most angry about?*

	12/95 NYT
Job security/lack of certainty	12%
Opportunity	2
Layoffs/restructuring	2
Benefits	2
Don't trust managers, employers, administration	3
Too much work/exploitation/ working conditions/stress/pressure	9
Wages/money	13
Competition in the workplace	1
Lazy co-workers	—
Jobs leaving the country	—
Other	3
DK/NA	4

	CRISIS LAYOFF	NON-CRISIS LAYOFF	FRIEND LAYOFF	NO LAYOFF
Job security/lack of certainty	25%	10%	12%	7%
Opportunity	2	2	2	3
Layoffs/restructuring	2	1	3	1
Benefits	2	5	2	2

	CRISIS LAYOFF	NON-CRISIS LAYOFF	FRIEND LAYOFF	NO LAYOFF
Don't trust managers, employers, administration	10	4	3	1
Too much work/exploitation/ working conditions/stress/pressure	10	8	10	9
Wages/money	17	15	14	10
Competition in the workplace	—	1	2	2
Lazy co-workers		1		
Jobs leaving the country	1	—		
Other	2	3	4	2
DK/NA	4	3	5	4

	WORRIED	EXTRA JOB
Job security/lack of certainty	15%	15%
Opportunity	2	1
Layoffs/restructuring	3	3
Benefits	2	2
Don't trust managers, employers, administration	6	2
Too much work/exploitation/ working conditions/stress/pressure	8	13
Wages/money	21	21
Competition in the workplace	1	1
Lazy co-workers	—	—
Jobs leaving the country	1	—
Other	2	2
DK/NA	2	6

b. *If more angry: Are you more angry at work these days, or not?**

	MORE ANGRY	NOT MORE ANGRY	DK/NA	OMITTED
12/95 TOTAL	19%	37%	1%	44%
Crisis layoff	43	34	1	23
Non-crisis layoff	21	36	—	43
Friend layoff	17	39	—	43

296

	MORE ANGRY	NOT MORE ANGRY	DK/NA	OMITTED
No layoff	10	35	1	55
Worried	40	31	3	26
Extra job	29	37	2	32

*Based on employed respondents (sample size = 808)

47. *My next questions are about what are often called "job layoffs"—by that we don't mean temporary or seasonal layoffs. We mean people losing their jobs due to employer downsizing, reductions in force, corporate restructuring, permanent plant closings, jobs moving overseas, or jobs just permanently disappearing. In the past fifteen years—since 1980—was there any time when you experienced that type of job layoff?*

	YES	NO	DK/NA
12/95 TOTAL	20%	79%	1%
Crisis layoff	55	44	1
Non-crisis layoff	59	40	—
Friend layoff		99	1
No layoff		99	1
Worried	34	65	
Extra job	34	66	

48. *How many different jobs have you been laid off from?*

	12/95 TOTAL	CRISIS LAYOFF	NON-CRISIS LAYOFF
One	52	41	56
Two	28	38	24
Three	9	10	8
Four	4	5	4
Five	1	4	1
More than five	1		1
DK/NA	5	2	7

*Based on respondents with layoff experience (sample size = 242)

49. *If laid off from one job: How many years had you worked for that employer before the layoff happened? If more than one: My next question will refer to the most recent layoff. How many years had you worked for that employer before the layoff happened?**

	12/95 TOTAL	CRISIS LAYOFF	NON-CRISIS LAYOFF
Less than a year	13%	17%	12%
One year	12	9	13
Two years	17	20	16
Three to five years	20	17	21
Six to nine years	15	16	14
Ten to fifteen years	11	9	12
Sixteen years or more	10	12	9
DK/NA	2		3

*Based on respondents with layoff experience (sample size = 242)

50. *If no layoff experience: In the past fifteen years—since 1980—was there anyone else in your household who has ever experienced that type of job layoff?*

	YES	NO	DK/NA	OMITTED
12/95 TOTAL	14%	66%	1%	20%
Crisis layoff	45			55
Non-crisis layoff	41	—		59
Friend layoff		99	1	
No layoff		99	1	
Worried	20	45	1	34
Extra job	11	55	1	34

51. *How many different jobs has that person been laid off from?**

	12/95 TOTAL	CRISIS LAYOFF	NON-CRISIS LAYOFF
One	61%	66%	58%
Two	22	20	22
Three	7	9	7
Four	3		4

	12/95 TOTAL	CRISIS LAYOFF	NON-CRISIS LAYOFF
Five and over	2	5	
DK/NA	6		9

*Based on those with some other household member with layoff experience (sample size = 180)

52. *If laid off from one job: How many years had the person worked for that employer before the layoff happened? If more than one: My next question will refer to the most recent layoff. How many years had that person worked for that employer before the layoff happened?**

	12/95 TOTAL	CRISIS LAYOFF	NON-CRISIS LAYOFF
Less than a year	4%	1%	6%
One year	13	12	14
Two years	8	7	9
Three to five years	26	18	29
Six to nine years	11	13	10
Ten to fifteen years	19	27	14
Sixteen years or more	14	20	11
DK/NA	5	2	6

*Based on those with some other household member with layoff experience (sample size = 180)

53. *If neither respondent nor any other household member with layoff experience: In the past fifteen years—since 1980—was there anyone you know well—like a neighbor, close friend, or relative—who experienced that type of job layoff?*

	YES	NO	DK/NA	OMITTED
12/95 TOTAL	38%	27%	1%	34%
Crisis layoff				100
Non-crisis layoff				100
Friend layoff	100			
No layoff		96	4	
Worried	29	16		54
Extra job	36	19	1	44

54. *Did (you/that person) find another permanent job?**

	YES	NO	DK/NA
12/95 TOTAL	69%	30%	1%
Crisis layoff	70	30	
Non-crisis layoff	69	30	1
Worried	56	44	—
Extra job	72	27	—

*Based on households with layoff experience (sample size = 422)

a. *If new job: How long did (you/that person) have to look for the new job?**

	12/95 TOTAL	CRISIS LAYOFF	NON-CRISIS LAYOFF	WORRIED	EXTRA JOB
One month or less	17%	11%	20%	11%	20%
Two months	6	7	6	3	4
Three months	8	12	7	12	14
Four months	2			1	1
Five months	3	3	3	3	3
Six months	7	4	4	3	8
Seven months to one year	14	18	12	9	13
Over one year	7	14	5	7	6
DK/NA	1	2	5	6	1

*Based on households with layoff experience (sample size = 422)

b. *If new job: Did the new job involve the same kind of work, or a slightly different kind of work, or a very different kind of work as compared to the previous job?**

	SAME KIND	SLIGHTLY DIFFERENT	VERY DIFFERENT	OMITTED
12/95 TOTAL	24%	19%	27%	31%
Crisis layoff	21	20	29	30
Non-crisis layoff	25	18	26	31
Worried	16	9	32	44
Extra job	16	16	41	28

*Based on households with layoff experience (sample size = 422)

c. *If new job: Did the new job pay a wage or salary that was better, about the same, or worse than the previous job?**

	BETTER	ABOUT THE SAME	WORSE	DK/NA	OMITTED
12/95 TOTAL	21%	19%	29%	—	31%
Crisis layoff	9	16	44		30
Non-crisis layoff	25	20	23	—	31
Worried	12	10	34		44
Extra job	10	24	38		28

*Based on households with layoff experience (sample size = 422)

55. *As a result of the layoff, did you or someone in your household take money out of any retirement account that required you to pay a penalty?**

	YES	NO	DK/NA
12/95 TOTAL	15%	84%	2%
Crisis layoff	24	75	1
Non-crisis layoff	11	88	2
Worried	15	84	2
Extra job	15	84	—

*Based on households with layoff experience (sample size = 422)

56. *As a result of the layoff, did you or someone in your household receive unemployment checks?**

	YES	NO	DK/NA
12/95 TOTAL	58%	41%	1%
Crisis layoff	70	30	
Non-crisis layoff	53	46	2
Worried	62	38	
Extra job	65	35	

*Based on households with layoff experience (sample size = 422)

a. *If yes: Did the unemployment checks run out during the layoff?**

	YES	NO	DK/NA	OMITTED
12/95 TOTAL	29%	28%	1%	42%
Crisis layoff	43	25	3	30

	YES	NO	DK/NA	OMITTED
Non-crisis layoff	23	29	1	46
Worried	35	27	1	38
Extra job	35	30	1	35

*Based on households with layoff experience (sample size = 422)

57. *During the period of the layoff, how often did you feel embarrassed or ashamed about the layoff—most of the time, some of the time, hardly ever, or never?**

	MOST OF THE TIME	SOME OF THE TIME	HARDLY EVER	NEVER	DK/NA
12/95 TOTAL	22%	19%	18%	39%	2%
Crisis layoff	41	25	11	23	—
Non-crisis layoff	14	16	21	45	3
Worried	42	18	13	27	
Extra job	28	25	17	30	

*Based on households with layoff experience (sample size = 422)

58. *During the period of the layoff, how often did you feel angry because of the layoff—most of the time, some of the time, hardly ever, or never?**

	MOST OF THE TIME	SOME OF THE TIME	HARDLY EVER	NEVER	ALL OF THE TIME	DK/NA
12/95 TOTAL	36%	29%	15%	17%	1%	2%
Crisis layoff	58	26	8	5	3	—
Non-crisis layoff	27	30	19	22	—	3
Worried	58	21	7	12	2	
Extra job	40	36	12	8	3	

*Based on households with layoff experience (sample size = 422)

59. *All in all, would you say that your experience with the layoff created a major crisis in your life, a minor crisis, or no crisis at all?**

	MAJOR	MINOR	NO CRISIS	DK/NA
12/95 TOTAL	29%	47%	22%	1%
Crisis layoff	100			
Non-crisis layoff		66	32	2

	MAJOR	MINOR	NO CRISIS	DK/NA
Worried	46	38	16	
Extra job	43	40	17	

*Based on households with layoff experience (sample size = 422)

60. *During the period of the layoff, did you discuss the situation with friends and relatives, or did you keep it pretty much to yourself?*

	DISCUSSED	KEPT TO SELF	DK/NA
12/95 TOTAL	64%	34%	2%
Crisis layoff	58	42	
Non-crisis layoff	66	31	3
Worried	57	43	
Extra job	64	36	

*Based on households with layoff experience (sample size = 422)

61. *To what extent would you say that the overall experience with the layoff has changed your life—has it changed your life completely, or in at least one serious way, or not much, or not at all?*

	COMPLETELY	AT LEAST A SERIOUS WAY	NOT MUCH	NOT AT ALL	DK/NA
12/95 TOTAL	14%	34%	34%	15%	3%
Crisis layoff	24	52	19	4	2
Non-crisis layoff	10	26	41	20	3
Worried	20	46	24	6	4
Extra job	17	48	31	4	—

*Based on households with layoff experience (sample size = 422)

a. *If completely or serious way: In what way has it changed your life?*

	12/95 TOTAL	CRISIS LAYOFF	NON-CRISIS LAYOFF
Relocation	3%	4%	3%
Less time with family/less time for personal life	1	2	1
Financial/wages/not enough money	14	34	5

	12/95 TOTAL	CRISIS LAYOFF	NON-CRISIS LAYOFF
Caused divorce	1	2	1
Depression	2	3	2
Create budget	5	8	5
Rethink my future/get more training	7	10	6
Uncertainty	2	—	2
Job Security/lack of job security	1	3	1
More awareness of things in general/ less compliant	1	1	1
Everything	—	1	
Other	7	7	8
DK/NA	2	2	3

	WORRIED	EXTRA JOB
Relocation	1%	5%
Less time with family/less time for personal life	1	3
Financial/wages/not enough money	28	14
Caused divorce	4	4
Depression	1	1
Create budget	7	8
Rethink my future/get more training	7	7
Uncertainty		3
Job security/lack of job security	3	3
More awareness of things in general/ less compliant	1	
Everything		1
Other	7	13
DK/NA	6	3

62. *How much blame for the layoff would you place on (yourself/the person who was laid off)—a lot, some, or not much?**

	A LOT	SOME	NOT MUCH	NONE	DK/NA
12/95 TOTAL	2%	6%	50%	39%	2%
Crisis layoff	4	9	53	33	
Non-crisis layoff	1	5	49	41	3

	A LOT	SOME	NOT MUCH	NONE	DK/NA
Worried	1	11	42	42	3
Extra job	1	8	64	27	

*Based on households with layoff experience (sample size = 422)

63. *How much blame for the layoff would you place on (your/that person's) employers—a lot, some, or not much?**

	A LOT	SOME	NOT MUCH	NONE	DK/NA
12/95 TOTAL	56%	15%	22%	5%	3%
Crisis layoff	70	10	17	2	1
Non-crisis layoff	50	16	24	6	4
Worried	63	11	20	5	1
Extra job	60	14	23	2	2

*Based on households with layoff experience (sample size = 422)

64. *Have you ever belonged to any group that has helped you adjust to and deal with being laid off?**

	YES	NO	DK/NA
12/95 TOTAL	9%	90%	1%
Crisis layoff	13	87	
Non-crisis layoff	7	92	2
Worried	8	92	
Extra job	12	88	

*Based on respondent with layoff experience (sample size = 242)

65. *Have you ever changed jobs because you expected you would be laid off, or would soon be out of work?*

	YES	NO	DK/NA
12/95 TOTAL	14%	85%	—
Crisis layoff	25	75	
Non-crisis layoff	16	83	1
Friend layoff	13	86	—
No layoff	10	90	1
Worried	23	77	
Extra job	28	72	

66. *My next few questions are about what is often called "early retirement" or a "buy-out" or a "golden handshake"—where people are given a cash settlement to induce them to voluntarily give up a job. In the past fifteen years—since 1980— have you accepted an early retirement offer or a buy-out offer to give up your job?*

	YES	NO	DK/NA
12/95 TOTAL	4%	95%	1%
Crisis layoff	4	95	1
Non-crisis layoff	6	94	
Friend layoff	3	96	1
No layoff	2	97	1
Worried	5	94	2
Extra job	3	97	

a. *If no: In the past fifteen years—since 1980—has anyone else in your household accepted an early retirement offer or a buy-out offer to give up their job?*

	YES	NO	DK/NA
12/95 TOTAL	6%	90%	1%
Crisis layoff	6	90	—
Non-crisis layoff	8	86	
Friend layoff	5	90	1
No layoff	4	93	1
Worried	8	88	—
Extra job	5	91	1

b. *If no: In the past fifteen years—since 1980—was there anyone you know well—like a neighbor, close friend, or relative—who accepted an early retirement offer or a buy-out offer to give up their job?*

	YES	NO	DK/NA
12/95 TOTAL	46%	43%	1%
Crisis layoff	50	40	
Non-crisis layoff	46	38	2
Friend layoff	58	32	—
No layoff	29	61	3
Worried	43	42	3
Extra job	53	39	

67. *How worried are you that in the next twelve months someone might be out of work whom you will have to provide financial support for—very worried, somewhat worried, or not worried at all?*

	VERY	SOMEWHAT	NOT AT ALL	DK/NA
12/95 TOTAL	9%	27%	65%	—
Crisis layoff	20	41	39	
Non-crisis layoff	10	30	60	
Friend layoff	7	27	67	—
No layoff	6	19	75	—
Worried	34	40	26	
Extra job	13	36	51	

68a. *If it might increase your chances of keeping a job, would you work more hours each week than in the past?**

	YES	NO	DEPENDS	DK/NA
12/95 TOTAL	82%	‾15%	1%	1%
Crisis layoff	87	11	1	1
Non-crisis layoff	83	15	1	—
Friend layoff	84	14	1	1
No layoff	77	20	1	3
Worried	92	7	1	
Extra job	89	10	1	

*Based on those in labor market (sample size = 887)

68b. *If it might increase your chances of keeping a job, would you accept a smaller wage than in the past?**

	YES	NO	DEPENDS	DK/NA
12/95 TOTAL	44%	50%	3%	2%
Crisis layoff	59	33	7	2
Non-crisis layoff	50	45	4	1
Friend layoff	42	54	1	2
No layoff	35	56	4	5
Worried	54	41	4	1
Extra job	46	48	2	4

*Based on those in labor market (sample size = 887)

68c. *If it might increase your chances of keeping a job, would you take fewer vacation days than in the past?**

	YES	NO	DEPENDS	DON'T HAVE NOW	DK/NA
12/95 TOTAL	71%	26%	1%	1%	1%
Crisis layoff	80	14	2	2	2
Non-crisis layoff	72	22	2	4	—
Friend layoff	70	29	—	—	1
No layoff	67	29	1	1	2
Worried	84	15		1	—
Extra job	79	18	1	2	1

*Based on those in labor market (sample size = 887)

68d. *If it might increase your chances of keeping a job, would you accept smaller benefits than in the past?**

	YES	NO	DEPENDS	DON'T HAVE NOW	DK/NA
12/95 TOTAL	53%	39%	3%	3%	1%
Crisis layoff	69	18	7	5	2
Non-crisis layoff	58	34	2	5	1
Friend layoff	49	44	4	1	1
No layoff	49	45	3	1	2
Worried	62	30	4	4	—
Extra job	57	38	2	2	1

*Based on those in labor market (sample size = 887)

68e. *If it might increase your chances of keeping a job, would you challenge the boss less often than in the past?**

	YES	NO	DEPENDS	DK/NA
12/95 TOTAL	49%	46%	1%	3%
Crisis layoff	66	31	1	2
Non-crisis layoff	54	42	1	3
Friend layoff	44	51	2	3
No layoff	45	51	1	4
Worried	59	40		1
Extra job	53	44		2

*Based on those in labor market (sample size = 887)

68f. *If it might increase your chances of keeping a job, would you get more job training or education than in the past?**

	YES	NO	DEPENDS	DK/NA
12/95 TOTAL	93%	5%	—	1%
Crisis layoff	95	2	2	1
Non-crisis layoff	93	6		—
Friend layoff	95	5		1
No layoff	90	8	—	2
Worried	96	2	1	
Extra job	97	3	1	—

*Based on those in labor market (sample size = 887)

69a. *How much blame for the loss of jobs in this country would you place on automation, computers, and technology—a lot, some, or not much?*

	A LOT	SOME	NOT MUCH	NONE	DK/NA
12/95 TOTAL	35%	39%	22%	1%	3%
Crisis layoff	39	37	22		2
Non-crisis layoff	34	38	24	1	2
Friend layoff	36	43	19	—	2
No layoff	31	36	24	1	8
Worried	43	34	20		3
Extra job	35	40	23	—	2

69b. *How much blame for the loss of jobs in this country would you place on the economic system in this country—a lot, some, or not much?*

	A LOT	SOME	NOT MUCH	NONE	DK/NA
12/95 TOTAL	38%	46%	13%	1%	3%
Crisis layoff	60	35	5		
Non-crisis layoff	43	46	8	2	2
Friend layoff	38	48	11	1	2
No layoff	26	46	23	—	5
Worried	55	33	9		3
Extra job	48	45	6		1

69c. *How much blame for the loss of jobs in this country would you place on business corporations—a lot, some, or not much?*

	A LOT	SOME	NOT MUCH	NONE	DK/NA
12/95 TOTAL	37%	44%	14%	—	4%
Crisis layoff	47	43	4	1	5
Non-crisis layoff	42	44	11	—	3
Friend layoff	37	48	12	—	3
No layoff	30	40	24	—	6
Worried	43	42	10		4
Extra job	43	48	7	1	2

69d. *How much blame for the loss of jobs in this country would you place on foreign competition—a lot, some, or not much?*

	A LOT	SOME	NOT MUCH	NONE	DK/NA
12/95 TOTAL	48%	38%	12%	—	1%
Crisis layoff	59	31	9		—
Non-crisis layoff	49	35	14	1	1
Friend layoff	46	42	11	—	1
No layoff	45	38	14		3
Worried	54	29	14		2
Extra job	51	38	11		—

69e. *How much blame for the loss of jobs in this country would you place on the federal government—a lot, some, or not much?*

	A LOT	SOME	NOT MUCH	NONE	DK/NA
12/95 TOTAL	31%	48%	17%	—	3%
Crisis layoff	44	42	12		2
Non-crisis layoff	31	50	14	1	4
Friend layoff	32	50	16	—	2
No layoff	26	47	22	—	5
Worried	44	40	12	1	3
Extra job	42	46	10		2

70. *All in all, how economically secure do you feel—very secure, somewhat secure, somewhat insecure, or very insecure?*

	VERY SECURE	SOMEWHAT SECURE	SOMEWHAT INSECURE	VERY INSECURE	DK/NA
12/95 TOTAL	13%	50%	28%	9%	—
Crisis layoff	4	28	38	29	
Non-crisis layoff	9	48	34	8	1
Friend layoff	14	55	24	7	
No layoff	17	54	24	5	—
Worried	4	17	52	27	—
Extra job	6	37	39	18	

71. *Do you think that layoffs and loss of jobs in this country are just temporary problems, or do you think they will continue permanently?*

	TEMPORARY	PERMANENT	DEPENDS	DK/NA
12/95 TOTAL	22%	72%	3%	3%
Crisis layoff	8	88	3	1
Non-crisis layoff	19	77	2	3
Friend layoff	24	70	2	4
No layoff	26	64	5	5
Worried	19	76	2	3
Extra job	14	82	2	2

72. *Do you think the government should step in to do something about layoffs and loss of jobs, or is this something the government should stay out of?*

	DO SOMETHING	STAY OUT	DK/NA
12/95 TOTAL	47%	46%	8%
Crisis layoff	63	29	8
Non-crisis layoff	52	42	6
Friend layoff	43	51	6
No layoff	42	47	11
Worried	65	29	7
Extra job	57	38	5

73. *Do you think layoffs and the loss of jobs are something labor unions can do something about, or do you think these problems are beyond their control?*

	CAN DO SOMETHING ABOUT	BEYOND THEIR CONTROL	DK/NA
12/95 TOTAL	44%	49%	7%
Crisis layoff	44	52	4
Non-crisis layoff	45	47	7
Friend layoff	42	50	8
No layoff	46	48	7
Worried	54	40	7
Extra job	53	42	5

74. *Do you think layoffs and the loss of jobs are something President Clinton can do something about, or do you think these problems are beyond the president's control?*

	CAN DO SOMETHING ABOUT	BEYOND HIS CONTROL	DK/NA
12/95 TOTAL	41%	54%	4%
Crisis layoff	48	46	6
Non-crisis layoff	41	57	2
Friend layoff	39	56	5
No layoff	42	53	5
Worried	57	38	6
Extra job	47	49	4

75. *Do you think layoffs and the loss of jobs are something Congress can do something about, or do you think these problems are beyond the control of Congress?*

	CAN DO SOMETHING ABOUT	BEYOND THEIR CONTROL	DK/NA
12/95 TOTAL	64%	32%	4%
Crisis layoff	78	21	1
Non-crisis layoff	66	32	2
Friend layoff	63	32	4
No layoff	57	35	8
Worried	75	20	5
Extra job	74	24	2

76. *Do you think layoffs and the loss of jobs are something any of the Republicans currently running for president can do something about, or do you think these problems are beyond their control?*

	CAN DO SOMETHING ABOUT	BEYOND THEIR CONTROL	DK/NA
12/95 TOTAL	40%	49%	11%
Crisis layoff	45	41	14
Non-crisis layoff	40	49	11
Friend layoff	42	48	10
No layoff	35	54	11
Worried	48	39	13
Extra job	48	42	10

a. *If can do something: Which Republican presidential candidate do you think can do something?*

	12/95 TOTAL	CRISIS LAYOFF	NON-CRISIS LAYOFF	FRIEND LAYOFF	NO LAYOFF
Dole	12%	17%	16%	8%	11%
Gramm	1		2	—	1
Forbes	1	—	1	2	—
Buchanan	1	2	1	1	—
Most of them	—	1	—	—	—
Any/all of them	1	—		1	1
Others	1	1	1	5	1
None	3	4	3	4	2
DK/NA	20	19	16	24	18

	WORRIED	EXTRA JOB
Dole	12%	13%
Gramm	—	1
Forbes	1	—
Buchanan	2	1
Most of them	1	1
Any/All of them	2	2
Others	2	2
None	3	3
DK/NA	23	24

77a. *How much blame for the loss of jobs in this country would you place on labor unions—a lot, some, or not much?*

	A LOT	SOME	NOT MUCH	NONE	DK/NA
12/95 TOTAL	16%	46%	33%	1%	4%
Crisis layoff	18	41	35	1	5
Non-crisis layoff	19	48	28	2	3
Friend layoff	15	48	32	2	4
No layoff	13	42	38	1	6
Worried	12	45	38	1	4
Extra job	17	47	32	1	3

77b. *How much blame for the loss of jobs in this country would you place on the lower labor costs overseas—a lot, some, or not much?*

	A LOT	SOME	NOT MUCH	NONE	DK/NA
12/95 TOTAL	46%	39%	12%	—	3%
Crisis layoff	47	32	15		5
Non-crisis layoff	49	36	13	—	2
Friend layoff	46	42	10	—	2
No layoff	44	39	13		4
Worried	47	34	14		6
Extra job	49	36	13		3

77c. *How much blame for the loss of jobs in this country would you place on American workers themselves—a lot, some, or not much?*

	A LOT	SOME	NOT MUCH	NONE	DK/NA
12/95 TOTAL	18%	57%	22%	1%	2%
Crisis layoff	17	56	26	1	—
Non-crisis layoff	16	60	21	1	2
Friend layoff	19	56	23	1	1
No layoff	21	54	21	1	3
Worried	13	56	29	1	1
Extra job	21	57	21	1	1

77d. *How much blame for the loss of jobs in this country would you place on Wall Street—a lot, some, or not much?*

	A LOT	SOME	NOT MUCH	NONE	DK/NA
12/95 TOTAL	10%	40%	36%	1%	13%
Crisis layoff	11	46	30	1	13
Non-crisis layoff	12	34	42	1	11
Friend layoff	9	44	34	2	11
No layoff	7	37	36	3	19
Worried	14	42	28	1	14
Extra job	10	55	27		8

78a. *Congress has passed legislation to scale back welfare programs for the poor. Do you think this is a good idea or a bad idea?*

	GOOD IDEA	BAD IDEA	DK/NA
12/95 TOTAL	54%	37%	9%
Crisis layoff	45	46	8
Non-crisis layoff	52	39	9
Friend layoff	58	33	9
No layoff	53	38	9
Worried	41	55	4
Extra job	51	43	7

78b. *Congress has passed legislation to scale back Medicare programs, which provide health insurance for the elderly. Do you think this is a good idea or a bad idea?*

	GOOD IDEA	BAD IDEA	DK/NA
12/95 TOTAL	22%	75%	3%
Crisis layoff	13	82	5
Non-crisis layoff	22	75	3
Friend layoff	22	76	3
No layoff	26	70	4
Worried	17	79	3
Extra job	15	83	2

78c. *Congress has passed legislation to scale back Medicaid programs, which provide health insurance for the poor. Do you think this is a good idea or a bad idea?*

	GOOD IDEA	BAD IDEA	DK/NA
12/95 TOTAL	26%	69%	6%
Crisis layoff	17	78	5
Non-crisis layoff	23	73	4
Friend layoff	28	67	4
No layoff	28	63	9
Worried	21	76	3
Extra job	22	76	2

79. *The Republicans in Congress have said that scaling back these social programs is necessary to safeguard the future for the next generation of Americans. Do you agree or disagree?*

	AGREE	DISAGREE	DK/NA
12/95 TOTAL	35%	59%	6%
Crisis layoff	26	67	7
Non-crisis layoff	33	60	7
Friend layoff	37	59	4
No layoff	38	56	7
Worried	28	65	7
Extra job	27	70	4

80. *Now think about the next two or three years. How concerned are you that you or someone else in your household might be laid off from work—are you very concerned, somewhat concerned, or not concerned at all?*

	VERY	SOMEWHAT	NOT AT ALL	DK/NA
12/95 TOTAL	16%	35%	48%	1%
Crisis layoff	41	36	22	—
Non-crisis layoff	20	41	38	1
Friend layoff	13	37	50	—
No layoff	10	26	63	1
Worried	61	30	7	1
Extra job	29	46	25	—

81. *How likely is it that in the next two or three years you or someone else in your household might be offered early retirement or a buy-out—very likely, somewhat likely, or not likely at all?*

	VERY	SOMEWHAT	NOT AT ALL	DK/NA
12/95 TOTAL	7%	14%	78%	1%
Crisis layoff	9	15	76	
Non-crisis layoff	5	17	77	2
Friend layoff	9	14	77	1
No layoff	6	10	82	2
Worried	15	19	65	1
Extra job	9	18	73	1

82. *Some people are registered to vote and others are not. Are you registered to vote in the precinct or election district where you now live, or aren't you?*

	YES	NO	DK/NA
12/95 TOTAL	79%	21%	—
Crisis layoff	77	23	
Non-crisis layoff	80	20	
Friend layoff	81	19	
No layoff	77	23	—
Worried	76	24	
Extra job	74	26	

83. *Do you consider yourself part of the religious right political movement, or not?*

	YES	NO	DK/NA
12/95 TOTAL	12%	81%	7%
Crisis layoff	8	82	10
Non-crisis layoff	15	77	7
Friend layoff	9	86	5
No layoff	13	78	9
Worried	15	74	11
Extra job	9	89	2

84. *If you were asked to use one of four names to describe your social class, would you say you were in the upper class, the middle class, the working class, or the lower class?*

	UPPER CLASS	MIDDLE CLASS	WORKING CLASS	LOWER CLASS	DK/NA
12/95 NYT	2%	36%	55%	6%	1%
Crisis layoff	1	25	63	10	1
Non-crisis layoff	2	36	57	5	1
Friend layoff	3	41	52	4	—
No layoff	2	35	54	6	2
Worried	1	22	67	10	—
Extra job	1	25	69	5	

a. *If middle class: Do you ever feel as if you're at risk of falling out of the middle class?*

	YES	NO	DK/NA	OMITTED
12/95 TOTAL	13%	23%	1%	64%
Crisis layoff	11	14		75
Non-crisis layoff	14	19	2	64
Friend layoff	16	25	—	59
No layoff	8	26	1	65
Worried	14	7		78
Extra job	11	13		75

85. *Are you or any other member of your household—that is, any other adult living in your home or apartment—a member of a labor union? If yes: Is that person you or someone else?*

	YES	SOMEONE ELSE	NO	DK/NA
12/95 TOTAL	9%	10%	81%	1%
Crisis layoff	6	12	81	1
Non-crisis layoff	11	12	77	—
Friend layoff	12	8	79	1
No layoff	4	9	86	—
Worried	11	7	81	1
Extra job	12	12	75	2

86. *In this household, are there any children? If yes: Are they under or over the age of 18?*

	UNDER 18	OVER 18	BOTH	NO	DK/NA
12/95 TOTAL	38%	5%	3%	55%	—
Crisis layoff	39	6	2	53	
Non-crisis layoff	39	4	3	53	
Friend layoff	40	4	3	52	
No layoff	32	5	1	61	—
Worried	48	3	2	47	
Extra job	50	4	3	43	

87. *Do you frequently listen to political call-in radio shows, or don't you?*

	YES	NO	DK/NA
12/95 TOTAL	27%	72%	—
Crisis layoff	36	64	
Non-crisis layoff	26	74	
Friend layoff	29	71	—
No layoff	24	76	—
Worried	33	67	
Extra job	26	74	

88. *Did you vote for U.S. House of Representatives in the elections held in 1994, or did something prevent you from voting, or did you choose not to vote for U.S. House of Representatives in 1994? If voted: Did you vote for the Republican candidate or the Democratic candidate in your district?*

	REPUBLICAN	DEMOCRATIC	WON'T SAY OR OTHER	DIDN'T VOTE	DK/NA
12/95 TOTAL	24%	23%	5%	44%	4%
Crisis layoff	23	27	5	42	3
Non-crisis layoff	24	19	7	44	5
Friend layoff	26	24	5	42	3
No layoff	21	25	3	46	5
Worried	16	24	5	52	2
Extra job	20	21	4	52	4

89. *If voted Republican or Democratic: Do you usually vote for the (Republican/ Democratic) candidate for U.S. House of Representatives, or not?*

	USUALLY VOTE THAT WAY	DON'T USUALLY	FIRST-TIME VOTER	DEPENDS	DK/NA
12/95 TOTAL	32%	9%	—	6%	—
Crisis layoff	24	15	1	9	—
Non-crisis layoff	28	10	—	6	—
Friend layoff	35	8		6	
No layoff	34	6		6	—
Worried	26	10	1	4	
Extra job	25	11	—	4	—

b. *If don't usually vote that way: What's the main reason you voted differently last year?*

	12/95 NYT
Candidate's position	5%
Vote differently each year/time for change	1
Economic philosophy	—
Angry at other party	1
DK/NA	1

	CRISIS LAYOFF	NON-CRISIS LAYOFF	FRIEND LAYOFF	NO LAYOFF
Candidate's position	5%	6%	5%	4%
Vote differently each year/time for change	4	—	1	
Economic philosophy	1	—		
Angry at other party	4	2	1	1
DK/NA	1	1	1	1

	WORRIED	EXTRA JOB
Candidate's position	6%	5%
Vote differently each year/time for change	2	2
Economic philosophy		1
Angry at other party	2	2
DK/NA		2

90. *Did you vote for president in 1992, did something prevent you from voting, or did you choose not to vote for president in 1992? If voted: Did you vote for George Bush, Bill Clinton, or Ross Perot?*

	BUSH	CLINTON	PEROT	WON'T SAY OR OTHER	DIDN'T VOTE	DK/NA
12/95 TOTAL	25%	33%	10%	3%	28%	1%
Crisis layoff	22	32	15	4	25	2
Non-crisis layoff	29	30	12	2	26	1
Friend layoff	26	33	11	3	27	—
No layoff	21	35	7	2	33	2
Worried	21	31	6	3	37	2
Extra job	19	29	18	3	30	1

91. *Generally speaking, do you usually consider yourself a Republican, a Democrat, an Independent, or what?*

	REPUBLICAN	DEMOCRAT	INDEPENDENT	DK/NA
12/95 TOTAL	27%	33%	33%	7%
Crisis layoff	23	36	33	7
Non-crisis layoff	24	31	40	5
Friend layoff	28	32	32	8
No layoff	30	35	28	6
Worried	16	38	40	6
Extra job	23	28	43	6

a. *If Independent or DK/NA: Do you think of yourself as closer to the Republican Party or to the Democratic Party? (Note: These percentages are based on the results of questions 91 AND 91a.)*

	REPUBLICAN	DEMOCRAT	DK/NA
12/95 TOTAL	40%	48%	12%
Crisis layoff	35	52	13
Non-crisis layoff	39	49	12
Friend layoff	41	47	12
No layoff	42	47	11
Worried	31	57	12
Extra job	40	49	11

92. *How would you describe your views on most political matters? Generally, do you think of yourself as liberal, moderate, or conservative?*

	LIBERAL	MODERATE	CONSERVATIVE	DK/NA
12/95 TOTAL	15%	46%	34%	5%
Crisis layoff	21	46	26	7
Non-crisis layoff	15	44	36	5
Friend layoff	14	49	34	3
No layoff	15	45	35	6
Worried	17	44	33	6
Extra job	22	45	32	2

93. *Are you currently married, widowed, divorced, or separated, or have you never been married?*

	MARRIED	WIDOWED	DIVORCED	SEPARATED	NEVER MARRIED	DK/NA
12/95 TOTAL	62%	7%	8%	2%	20%	—
Crisis layoff	65	3	14	3	16	—
Non-crisis layoff	67	5	6	2	19	
Friend layoff	62	6	9	1	21	
No layoff	57	11	7	3	22	1
Worried	54	4	13	5	23	
Extra job	56	1	11	5	27	

94. *What was the last grade in school you completed?*

	NOT A HIGH SCHOOL GRAD	HIGH SCHOOL GRAD	SOME COLLEGE	COLLEGE GRAD	REFUSED
12/95 TOTAL	15%	39%	25%	20%	—
Crisis layoff	17	31	26	26	
Non-crisis layoff	14	40	29	17	
Friend layoff	12	36	28	24	1
No layoff	20	45	19	16	1
Worried	17	43	24	15	—
Extra job	10	36	31	23	

95. *How old are you?*

	18–29	30–44	45–64	OVER 64	REFUSED
12/95 TOTAL	23%	33%	26%	17%	—
Crisis layoff	20	37	35	8	
Non-crisis layoff	21	39	27	13	
Friend layoff	25	33	27	15	—
No layoff	23	27	22	28	—
Worried	28	36	26	10	—
Extra job	34	47	18	1	

96. *Are you white, black, or some other race?*

	WHITE	BLACK	OTHER	REFUSED
12/95 TOTAL	81%	12%	6%	1%
Crisis layoff	75	16	7	2
Non-crisis layoff	81	13	5	1
Friend layoff	81	12	6	1
No layoff	84	9	6	1
Worried	67	23	10	
Extra job	76	14	9	1

97. *Are you of Hispanic origin or descent, or not?*

	HISPANIC	NOT HISPANIC	DK/NA
12/95 TOTAL	6%	93%	1%
Crisis layoff	8	87	5
Non-crisis layoff	7	93	1
Friend layoff	6	94	—
No layoff	7	93	1
Worried	11	88	2
Extra job	11	88	1

98. *Was your total family income in 1994 under or over $30,000? If under: Was it under or over $15,000? If over: Was it between $30,000 and $50,000, or between $50,000 and $75,000, or was it over $75,000?*

	UNDER $15,000	$15,000— $29,999	$30,000— $49,999	$50,000— $75,000	OVER $75,000	REFUSED
12/95 TOTAL	12%	30%	31%	14%	10%	4%
Crisis layoff	13	42	18	17	4	6
Non-crisis layoff	13	21	36	17	9	5
Friend layoff	8	30	35	11	13	3
No layoff	16	33	24	14	9	4
Worried	15	41	24	8	5	6
Extra job	9	39	29	12	7	4

Demographic Breakdown

SEX	MALE	FEMALE
12/95 TOTAL	48%	52%
Crisis layoff	46	54
Non-crisis layoff	49	51
Friend layoff	47	53
No layoff	48	52
Worried	43	57
Extra job	48	52

REGION	NORTHEAST	NORTH CENTRAL	SOUTH	WEST
12/95 TOTAL	24%	24%	31%	21%
Crisis layoff	24	25	26	25
Non-crisis layoff	24	24	37	15
Friend layoff	28	22	29	20
No layoff	18	25	32	25
Worried	26	24	29	22
Extra job	31	24	24	21

SIZE OF PLACE	500,000+	50–500,000	SUBURBS	RURAL
12/95 TOTAL	9%	25%	37%	28%
Crisis layoff	10	23	47	21
Non-crisis layoff	8	27	35	29
Friend layoff	10	26	38	26
No layoff	9	24	35	22
Worried	13	16	37	33
Extra job	14	27	34	25

LABOR MARKET STATUS	SELF ONLY	SELF AND OTHER	OTHER ONLY	NO ONE
12/95 TOTAL	19%	51%	11%	19%
Crisis layoff	18	62	8	12
Non-crisis layoff	17	55	15	12
Friend layoff	20	52	10	18
No layoff	20	42	9	29
Worried	20	60	10	10
Extra job	25	75		

The Bucknell University Class of 1970 Poll

The Bucknell University Class of 1970 Poll was conducted December 1–9, 1995; the national economic insecurity survey occurred December 3–6, 1995. The national total sample size equaled 1,265 persons; the Bucknell total sample size was 503 persons.

1. *Do you approve or disapprove of the way Bill Clinton is handling his job as president?*

	APPROVE	DISAPPROVE	DK/NA
National	47%	40%	13%
Bucknell	52	34	14

2. *Do you feel things in this country are generally going in the right direction today, or do you feel things have pretty seriously gotten off on the wrong track?*

	RIGHT DIRECTION	WRONG TRACK	DK/NA
National	25%	64%	10%
Bucknell	31	55	14

3. *How would you rate the condition of the national economy these days? Is it very good, fairly good, fairly bad, or very bad?*

	VERY GOOD	FAIRLY GOOD	FAIRLY BAD	VERY BAD	DK/NA
National	4%	47%	33%	13%	3%
Bucknell	4	65	26	3	2

4. *Do you think the economy is getting better, getting worse, or staying about the same?*

	BETTER	WORSE	SAME	DK/NA
National	15%	31%	53%	2%
Bucknell	24	22	51	2

5. *In the past couple of years would you say you have been getting ahead financially, just staying even financially, or falling behind financially?*

	GETTING AHEAD	STAYING EVEN	FALLING BEHIND	DK/NA
National	20%	51%	28%	1%
Bucknell	45	39	15	1

6. *In your community these days, how easy is it for someone who is trying to find a job to get a good job at good wages—very easy, somewhat easy, somewhat hard, or very hard?*

	VERY EASY	SOMEWHAT EASY	SOMEWHAT HARD	VERY HARD	IMPOSSIBLE	DK/NA
National	3%	13%	42%	36%	1%	5%
Bucknell	2	12	57	25		4

7. *Are you at least as well off financially today as you expected to be at this point in your life?*

	YES	NO	DK/NA
National	44%	53%	3%
Bucknell	69	27	4

8. *In America, each generation has tried to have a better life than their parents, with a better living standard, better homes, a better education, etc. How likely do you think it is that today's youth will have a better life than their parents—very likely, somewhat likely, somewhat unlikely, or very unlikely?*

	VERY LIKELY	SOMEWHAT LIKELY	SOMEWHAT UNLIKELY	VERY UNLIKELY	DK/NA
National	11%	38%	32%	17%	2%
Bucknell	2	24	58	14	2

9. *Would you agree or disagree with the following statement: I'm angry at both political parties.*

	AGREE	DISAGREE	DK/NA
National	58%	38%	4%
Bucknell	67	31	2

10. *Would you agree or disagree with the following statement: It makes no real difference who is elected—things go on just as they did before.*

	AGREE	DISAGREE	DK/NA
National	48%	49%	3%
Bucknell	37	61	1

11. *Would you agree or disagree with the following statement: People like me don't have any say about what the government does.*

	AGREE	DISAGREE	DK/NA
National	50%	47%	2%
Bucknell	26	72	2

12. *When it comes to the availability of good jobs for American workers, some say that America's best years are behind us. Others say that the best times are yet to come. What do you think?*

	BEST YEARS BEHIND	BEST YET TO COME	DK/NA
National	49%	40%	11%
Bucknell	39	39	21

13. *Looking ahead for the next few years, which political party—the Republican or the Democratic—do you think will do the best job of keeping the country prosperous?*

	REPUBLICAN	DEMOCRATIC	NO DIFFERENCE	DK/NA
National	38%	37%	10%	15%
Bucknell	44	31	13	12

14. *Regardless of how you usually vote, do you think the Republican Party or the Democratic Party is better able to handle unemployment?*

	REPUBLICAN	DEMOCRATIC	BOTH	NEITHER	DK/NA
National	34%	42%	1%	9%	14%
Bucknell	35	50	1	7	7

1 5. *Regardless of how you usually vote, do you think the Republican Party or the Democratic Party is better able to stop layoffs and the loss of jobs in this country?*

	REPUBLICAN	DEMOCRATIC	BOTH	NEITHER	DK/NA
National	33%	40%	1%	11%	15%
Bucknell	36	41	2	13	8

1 6. *Do you agree or disagree that there is a need for a new third political party to compete with the Democrats and Republicans?*

	AGREE	DISAGREE	DK/NA
National	57%	36%	7%
Bucknell	62	35	3

1 7. *Do you favor or oppose national health insurance, which would be financed by tax money, paying for most forms of health care?*

	FAVOR	OPPOSE	DK/NA
National	53%	39%	8%
Bucknell	54	44	2

1 8. *Do you believe that where there has been job discrimination against women in the past, preference in hiring or promotion should be given to women today? (Note: The ordering of questions 18 and 19 were rotated.)*

	YES, PREFERENCE	NO	DK/NA
National	32%	62%	6%
Bucknell	34	62	4

1 9. *Do you believe that where there has been job discrimination against blacks in the past, preference in hiring or promotion should be given to blacks today? (Note: The ordering of questions 18 and 19 were rotated.)*

	YES, PREFERENCE	NO	DK/NA
National	29%	66%	6%
Bucknell	36	60	4

20. *Would you agree or disagree: It is the responsibility of the government to take care of people who can't take care of themselves.*

	AGREE	DISAGREE	DK/NA
National	64%	30%	6%
Bucknell	71	23	6

21. *Do you think that immigration into the United States should be increased, decreased, or kept about the same?*

	INCREASED	DECREASED	PRESENT LEVEL	DK/NA
National	2%	64%	31%	3%
Bucknell	5	35	54	6

22. *Do you think the immigrants coming to this country today mostly take jobs away from American citizens, or do they mostly take jobs Americans don't want?*

	TAKE JOBS FROM AMERICAN CITIZENS	TAKE JOBS AMERICANS DON'T WANT	DK/NA
National	36%	55%	10%
Bucknell	11	78	11

23. *In recent years, has the amount of money you give to charity increased, decreased, or stayed about the same?*

	INCREASED	DECREASED	STAYED SAME	DK/NA
National	26%	16%	57%	1%
Bucknell	55	8	37	—

24. *In recent years, has the amount of time you devote to doing volunteer work increased, decreased, or stayed about the same?*

	INCREASED	DECREASED	STAYED SAME	DK/NA
National	24%	21%	53%	2%
Bucknell	32	21	47	—

25. *In recent years, has your involvement or participation in civic or community groups increased, decreased, or stayed about the same?*

	INCREASED	DECREASED	STAYED SAME	DK/NA
National	21%	20%	57%	1%
Bucknell	31	17	52	—

26. *In recent years, have you attended religious services more often, less often, or has there been no change?*

	MORE OFTEN	LESS OFTEN	NO CHANGE	DK/NA
National	20%	21%	58%	1%
Bucknell	18	16	65	1

27. *Other than labor unions and professional societies, do you belong to any group that helps you with employment opportunities or business contacts?*

	YES	NO	DK/NA
National	11%	88%	1%
Bucknell	21	78	—

28. *How worried are you that in the next twelve months you or someone else in your household might be out of work and looking for a job for any reason—very worried, somewhat worried, or not worried at all?*

	VERY	SOMEWHAT	NOT AT ALL	DK/NA
National	15%	31%	52%	2%
Bucknell	6	33	60	—

29. *Are you currently employed, or are you temporarily out of work, or are you not in the market for work at all?*

	CURRENTLY EMPLOYED	TEMPORARILY OUT OF WORK	NOT IN THE MARKET FOR WORK	RETIRED	DK/NA
National	63%	7%	16%	13%	
Bucknell	94	1	5	—	

a. *If not in the market for work: Are you currently retired, or not? (Note: Percentages include retired results from question 29.)*

	RETIRED	NOT RETIRED	DK/NA
National	20%	9%	—
Bucknell	1	4	—

30. *Is there anyone else in your household who is currently employed? If no: Is there anyone else in your household who is temporarily out of work?*

	OTHER EMPLOYED	TEMPORARILY OUT OF WORK	NOT IN THE MARKET FOR WORK	DK/NA
National	61%	1%	38%	—
Bucknell	70	2	29	

31. *How satisfied are you with your job—very satisfied, somewhat satisfied, somewhat dissatisfied, or very dissatisfied?**

	VERY SATISFIED	SOMEWHAT SATISFIED	SOMEWHAT DISSATISFIED	VERY DISSATISFIED	DK/NA
National	43%	42%	11%	4%	
Bucknell	50	35	10	2	2

*Based on employed respondents (sample size = 808/471)

32. *In the past three years, have you been forced to work reduced hours or forced to take a cut in pay?**

	REDUCED HOURS	CUT IN PAY	BOTH	NO	DK/NA
National	10%	15%	5%	69%	1%
Bucknell	2	10	2	85	1

*Based on those in labor market (sample size = 887/477)

33. *In the past three years, have you frequently had to work more hours than usual at your job?**

	YES, MORE HOURS	NO	DK/NA
National	42%	57%	1%
Bucknell	54	46	1

*Based on those in labor market (sample size = 887/477)

34. *In the past three years, have you had to take on an extra job?**

	YES, EXTRA JOB	NO	DK/NA
National	28%	72%	—
Bucknell	12	88	—

*Based on those in labor market (sample size = 887/477)

35. *In the past three years, was there anyone else in your household who was forced to work reduced hours or forced to take a cut in pay?**

	REDUCED HOURS	CUT IN PAY	BOTH	NO	DK/NA
National	11%	11%	5%	72%	1%
Bucknell	1	6	1	91	1

*Based on those with some other household member in labor market (sample size = 682/359)

36. *In the past three years, has anyone else in your household frequently had to work more hours than usual at their job?**

	YES, MORE HOURS	NO	DK/NA
National	41%	58%	1%
Bucknell	36	64	—

*Based on those with some other household member in labor market (sample size = 682/359)

37. *In the past three years, has anyone else in your household had to take on an extra job?**

	YES, EXTRA JOB	NO	DK/NA
National	23%	77%	1%
Bucknell	8	92	—

*Based on those with some other household member in labor market (sample size = 682/359)

38. *What is your occupation? If necessary: What exactly do you do for a living? What is your job title?**

	NATIONAL	BUCKNELL
Executive/high-level management	2%	7%
Professional/other managers/artists	19	65

	NATIONAL	BUCKNELL
Technical/administrative	15	20
Clerical	9	1
Skilled labor	11	1
Unskilled labor	10	
Service workers/protective services	31	6
Other	3	—
Refused	1	

*Based on those in labor market (sample size = 887/477)

39. *What is the other person's occupation in your household? If necessary: What exactly do they do for a living? What is their job title?* *

	NATIONAL	BUCKNELL
Executive/high-level management	3%	8%
Professional/other managers/artists	20	50
Technical/administrative	19	27
Clerical	6	3
Skilled labor	13	2
Unskilled labor	8	1
Service workers/protective services	26	7
Other	3	1
Refused	2	1

*Based on those with some other household member in labor market (sample size = 682/359)

40. *In the past couple of years, would you say you have felt more secure and confident that you can continue in your job as long as you want, or less secure and confident, or has there been no change?*

	MORE	LESS	NO CHANGE	DK/NA
National	29%	28%	42%	—
Bucknell	23	36	41	1

*Based on employed respondents (sample size = 808/471)

41. *How worried are you about not having enough savings for retirement—very worried, somewhat worried, or not worried at all?* *

	VERY WORRIED	SOMEWHAT WORRIED	NOT WORRIED AT ALL	DK/NA
National	35%	42%	22%	—
Bucknell	16	58	26	

*Based on respondents who are not retired (sample size = 995/499)

42. *In recent years, has uncertainty or insecurity about your economic future caused you to make cutbacks in your day-to-day spending?*

	YES	NO	DK/NA
National	65%	34%	1%
Bucknell	41	58	—

a. *If yes: Would you call those cutbacks severe, or not so severe?*

	SEVERE	NOT SEVERE	DK/NA
National	20%	44%	1%
Bucknell	7	35	

43. *Generally speaking, do you think companies are more, or less, loyal to their employees than they were ten years ago, or hasn't this changed?*

	MORE LOYAL	LESS LOYAL	NO CHANGE	DK/NA
National	6%	75%	13%	6%
Bucknell	1	91	4	4

44. *Generally speaking, do you think workers are more, or less, loyal to their employers than they were ten years ago, or hasn't this changed?*

	MORE LOYAL	LESS LOYAL	NO CHANGE	DK/NA
National	9%	64%	22%	5%
Bucknell	3	78	14	5

45. *Compared to the way things used to be, do you think most working people today cooperate more with one another at the place where they work, or that they compete more with one another at the place where they work?*

	COOPERATE MORE	COMPETE MORE	NO CHANGE	DK/NA
National	20%	70%	2%	8%
Bucknell	29	49	2	17

46. *And compared to the way things used to be, do you think the mood at many workplaces today is a more angry mood, or a more friendly mood, or has there been no change?*

	MORE ANGRY	MORE FRIENDLY	NO CHANGE	DK/NA
National	53%	8%	31%	8%
Bucknell	60	5	22	13

a. *If more angry: What do you think workers are most angry about?*

	NATIONAL	BUCKNELL
Job security/lack of certainty	12%	31%
Opportunity	2	2
Layoffs/restructuring	2	3
Benefits	2	3
Don't trust managers, employers, administration	3	3
Too much work/exploitation/ working conditions/stress/pressure	9	11
Wages/money	13	3
Competition in the workplace	1	—
Lazy co-workers	—	
Jobs leaving the country	—	—
Other	3	2
DK/NA	4	1

b. *If more angry: Are you more angry at work these days, or not?**

	MORE ANGRY	NOT MORE ANGRY	DK/NA	OMITTED
National	19%	37%	1%	44%
Bucknell	22	39		39

*Based on employed respondents (sample size = 808/471)

47. *My next questions are about what are often called "job layoffs"—by that we don't mean temporary or seasonal layoffs. We mean people losing their jobs due to employer downsizing, reductions in force, corporate restructuring, permanent plant closings, jobs moving overseas, or jobs just permanently disappearing. In the past fifteen years— since 1980—was there any time when you experienced that type of job layoff?*

	YES	NO	DK/NA
National	20%	79%	1%
Bucknell	11	89	

48. *How many different jobs have you been laid off from?**

	12/95 LAYOFF	BUCKNELL
One	52%	77%
Two	28	14
Three	9	5
Four	4	4
Five	1	
More than five	1	
DK/NA	5	

*Based on respondents with layoff experience (sample size = 242/56)

49. *If laid off from one job: How many years had you worked for that employer before the layoff happened? If more than one: My next question will refer to the most recent layoff. How many years had you worked for that employer before the layoff happened?**

	12/95 LAYOFF	BUCKNELL
Less than a year	13%	5%
One year	12	20
Two years	17	5
Three to five years	20	35
Six to nine years	15	11
Ten to fifteen years	11	14
Sixteen years or more	10	12
DK/NA	2	

*Based on respondents with layoff experience (sample size = 242/56)

50. *If no layoff experience: In the past fifteen years—since 1980—was there anyone else in your household who has ever experienced that type of job layoff?*

	YES	NO	DK/NA	OMITTED
National	14%	66%	1%	20%
Bucknell	9	80		11

51. *How many different jobs has that person been laid off from?**

	12/95 LAYOFF	BUCKNELL
One	61%	77%
Two	22	20
Three	7	
Four	3	
Over five	2	
DK/NA	6	

*Based on those with some other household member with layoff experience (sample size = 180/44)

52. *If laid off from one job: How many years had the person worked for that employer before the layoff happened? If more than one: My next question will refer to the most recent layoff. How many years had that person worked for that employer before the layoff happened?**

	12/95 LAYOFF	BUCKNELL
Less than a year	4%	7%
One year	13	11
Two years	8	20
Three to five years	26	41
Six to nine years	11	2
Ten to fifteen years	19	16
Sixteen years or more	14	2
DK/NA	5	

*Based on those with some other household member with layoff experience (sample size = 180/44)

53. *If neither respondent nor any other household member with layoff experience: In the past fifteen years—since 1980—was there anyone you know well—like a neighbor, close friend, or relative—who experienced that type of job layoff?*

	YES	NO	DK/NA	OMITTED
National	38%	27%	1%	34%
Bucknell	62	18		20

54. *Did (you/that person) find another permanent job?*

	YES	NO	DK/NA
12/95 Layoff	69%	30%	1%
Bucknell	82	18	

*Based on households with layoff experience (sample size = 422/100)

a. *If new job: How long did (you/that person) have to look for the new job?**

	12/95 LAYOFF	BUCKNELL
One month or less	17%	19%
Two months	6	7
Three months	8	13
Four months	2	6
Five months	3	3
Six months	7	10
Seven months to one year	14	6
Over one year	7	13
DK/NA	1	4

*Based on households with layoff experience (sample size = 422/100)

b. *If new job: Did the new job involve the same kind of work, or a slightly different kind of work, or a very different kind of work as compared to the previous job?**

	SAME KIND	SLIGHTLY DIFFERENT	VERY DIFFERENT	DK/NA	OMITTED
12/95 Layoff	24%	19%	27%		31%
Bucknell	29	37	16		18

*Based on households with layoff experience (sample size = 422/100)

c. *If new job: Did the new job pay a wage or salary that was better, about the same, or worse than the previous job?* *

	BETTER	ABOUT THE SAME	WORSE	DK/NA	OMITTED
12/95 Layoff	21%	19%	29%	—	31%
Bucknell	23	32	26	1	18

*Based on households with layoff experience (sample size = 422/100)

55. *As a result of the layoff, did you or someone in your household take money out of any retirement account that required you to pay a penalty?* *

	YES	NO	DK/NA
12/95 Layoff	15%	84%	2%
Bucknell	10	90	

*Based on households with layoff experience (sample size = 422/100)

56. *As a result of the layoff, did you or someone in your household receive unemployment checks?* *

	YES	NO	DK/NA
12/95 Layoff	58%	41%	1%
Bucknell	41	58	1

*Based on households with layoff experience (sample size = 422/100)

a. *If yes: Did the unemployment checks run out during the layoff?* *

	YES	NO	DK/NA	OMITTED
12/95 Layoff	29%	28%	1%	42%
Bucknell	12	29		59

*Based on households with layoff experience (sample size = 422/100)

57. *During the period of the layoff, how often did you feel embarrassed or ashamed about the layoff—most of the time, some of the time, hardly ever, or never?* *

	MOST OF THE TIME	SOME OF THE TIME	HARDLY EVER	NEVER	DK/NA
12/95 Layoff	22%	19%	18%	39%	2
Bucknell	10	20	29	40	1

*Based on households with layoff experience (sample size = 422/100)

58. *During the period of the layoff, how often did you feel angry because of the layoff—most of the time, some of the time, hardly ever, or never?**

	MOST OF THE TIME	SOME OF THE TIME	HARDLY EVER	NEVER	ALL OF THE TIME	DK/NA
12/95 Layoff	36%	29%	15%	17%	1%	2%
Bucknell	25	35	21	18		1

*Based on households with layoff experience (sample size = 422/100)

59. *All in all, would you say that your experience with the layoff created a major crisis in your life, a minor crisis, or no crisis at all?**

	MAJOR	MINOR	NO CRISIS	DK/NA
12/95 Layoff	29%	47%	22%	1%
Bucknell	30	46	23	1

*Based on households with layoff experience (sample size = 422/100)

60. *During the period of the layoff, did you discuss the situation with friends and relatives, or did you keep it pretty much to yourself?**

	DISCUSSED	KEPT TO SELF	DK/NA
12/95 Layoff	64%	34%	2%
Bucknell	74	23	3

*Based on households with layoff experience (sample size = 422/100)

61. *To what extent would you say that the overall experience with the layoff has changed your life—has it changed your life completely, or in at least one serious way, or not much, or not at all?**

	COMPLETELY	AT LEAST A SERIOUS WAY	NOT MUCH	NOT AT ALL	DK/NA
12/95 Layoff	14%	34%	34%	15%	3%
Bucknell	16	39	34	11	

*Based on households with layoff experience (sample size = 422/100)

a. *If completely or serious way: In what way has it changed your life?*

	12/95 LAYOFF	BUCKNELL
Relocation	3%	9%
Less time with family/less time for personal life	1	1
Financial/wages/not enough money	14	8
Caused divorce	1	1
Depression	2	2
Create budget	5	
Rethink my future/get more training	7	14
Uncertainty	2	2
Job security/lack of job security	1	2
More awareness of things in general/ less compliant	1	7
Other	7	6
DK/NA	2	3

62. *How much blame for the layoff would you place on (yourself/the person who was laid off)—a lot, some, or not much?**

	A LOT	SOME	NOT MUCH	NONE	DK/NA
12/95 Layoff	2%	6%	50%	39%	2%
Bucknell	3	11	59	26	1

*Based on households with layoff experience (sample size = 422/100)

63. *How much blame for the layoff would you place on (your/that person's) employers—a lot, some, or not much?**

	A LOT	SOME	NOT MUCH	NONE	DK/NA
12/95 Layoff	56%	15%	22%	5%	3%
Bucknell	59	23	14	1	1

*Based on households with layoff experience (sample size = 422/100)

64. *Have you ever belonged to any group that has helped you adjust to and deal with being laid off?**

	YES	NO	DK/NA
12/95 Layoff	9%	90%	1%
Bucknell	25	75	

*Based on respondents with layoff experience (sample size = 422/100)

65. *Have you ever changed jobs because you expected you would be laid off, or would soon be out of work?*

	YES	NO	DK/NA
National	14%	85%	—
Bucknell	11	89	

66. *My next few questions are about what is often called "early retirement" or a "buy-out" or a "golden handshake," where people are given a cash settlement to induce them to voluntarily give up a job. In the past fifteen years—since 1980—have you accepted an early retirement offer or a buy-out offer to give up your job?*

	YES	NO	DK/NA
National	4%	95%	1%
Bucknell	2	98	

   a. *If no: In the past fifteen years—since 1980—has anyone else in your household accepted an early retirement offer or a buy-out offer to give up their job?*

	YES	NO	DK/NA
National	6%	90%	1%
Bucknell	1	97	

   b. *If no: In the past fifteen years (since 1980) was there anyone you know well—like a neighbor, close friend, or relative—who accepted an early retirement offer or a buy-out offer to give up their job?*

	YES	NO	DK/NA
National	46%	43%	1%
Bucknell	67	30	

67. *How worried are you that in the next twelve months someone might be out of work that you will have to provide financial support for—very worried, somewhat worried, or not worried at all?*

	VERY	SOMEWHAT	NOT AT ALL	DK/NA
National	9%	27%	65%	—
Bucknell	4	20	76	

68a. *If it might increase your chances of keeping a job, would you work more hours each week than in the past?**

	YES	NO	DEPENDS	DK/NA
National	82%	15%	1%	1%
Bucknell	84	13	1	2

*Based on those in labor market (sample size = 887/477)

68b. *If it might increase your chances of keeping a job, would you accept a smaller wage than in the past?**

	YES	NO	DEPENDS	DK/NA
National	44%	50%	3%	2%
Bucknell	71	21	5	3

*Based on those in labor market (sample size = 887/477)

68c. *If it might increase your chances of keeping a job, would you take fewer vacation days than in the past?**

	YES	NO	DEPENDS	DON'T HAVE NOW	DK/NA
National	71%	26%	1%	1%	1%
Bucknell	75	19	1	1	3

*Based on those in labor market (sample size = 887/477)

68d. *If it might increase your chances of keeping a job, would you accept smaller benefits than in the past?**

	YES	NO	DEPENDS	DON'T HAVE NOW	DK/NA
National	53%	39%	3%	3%	1%
Bucknell	76	16	5	1	3

*Based on those in labor market (sample size = 887/477)

68e. *If it might increase your chances of keeping a job, would you challenge the boss less often than in the past?**

	YES	NO	DEPENDS	DK/NA
National	49%	46%	1%	3%
Bucknell	44	45	2	8

*Based on those in labor market (sample size = 887/477)

68f. *If it might increase your chances of keeping a job, would you get more job training or education than in the past?**

	YES	NO	DEPENDS	DK/NA
National	93%	5%	—	1%
Bucknell	93	5	—	2

*Based on those in labor market (sample size = 887/477)

69a. *How much blame for the loss of jobs in this country would you place on automation, computers, and technology—a lot, some, or not much?*

	A LOT	SOME	NOT MUCH	NONE	DK/NA
National	35%	39%	22%	1%	3%
Bucknell	18	46	32	2	1

69b. *How much blame for the loss of jobs in this country would you place on the economic system in this country—a lot, some, or not much?*

	A LOT	SOME	NOT MUCH	NONE	DK/NA
National	38%	46%	13%	1%	3%
Bucknell	37	41	18	1	3

69c. *How much blame for the loss of jobs in this country would you place on business corporations—a lot, some, or not much?*

	A LOT	SOME	NOT MUCH	NONE	DK/NA
National	37%	44%	14%	—	4%
Bucknell	46	40	12	—	2

69d. *How much blame for the loss of jobs in this country would you place on for-eign competition—a lot, some, or not much?*

	A LOT	SOME	NOT MUCH	NONE	DK/NA
National	48%	38%	12%	—	1%
Bucknell	30	59	10	—	1

69e. *How much blame for the loss of jobs in this country would you place on the federal government—a lot, some, or not much?*

	A LOT	SOME	NOT MUCH	NONE	DK/NA
National	31%	48%	17%	—	3%
Bucknell	18	51	30	—	1

70. *All in all, how economically secure do you feel—very secure, somewhat secure, somewhat insecure, or very insecure?*

	VERY SECURE	SOMEWHAT SECURE	SOMEWHAT INSECURE	VERY INSECURE	DK/NA
National	13%	50%	28%	9%	—
Bucknell	25	56	16	3	

71. *Do you think that layoffs and loss of jobs in this country are just temporary problems, or do you think they will continue permanently?*

	TEMPORARY	PERMANENT	DEPENDS	DK/NA
National	22%	72%	3%	3%
Bucknell	23	68	3	6

72. *Do you think the government should step in to do something about layoffs and loss of jobs, or is this something the government should stay out of?*

	DO SOMETHING	STAY OUT	DK/NA
National	47%	46%	8%
Bucknell	32	63	5

73. *Do you think layoffs and the loss of jobs are something labor unions can do something about, or do you think these problems are beyond their control?*

	CAN DO SOMETHING ABOUT	BEYOND THEIR CONTROL	DK/NA
National	44%	49%	7%
Bucknell	41	55	4

74. *Do you think layoffs and the loss of jobs are something President Clinton can do something about, or do you think these problems are beyond the president's control?*

	CAN DO SOMETHING ABOUT	BEYOND HIS CONTROL	DK/NA
National	41%	54%	4%
Bucknell	36	60	4

75. *Do you think layoffs and the loss of jobs are something Congress can do something about, or do you think these problems are beyond the control of Congress?*

	CAN DO SOMETHING ABOUT	BEYOND THEIR CONTROL	DK/NA
National	64%	32%	4%
Bucknell	62	34	3

76. *Do you think layoffs and the loss of jobs are something any of the Republicans currently running for president can do something about, or do you think these problems are beyond their control?*

	CAN DO SOMETHING ABOUT	BEYOND THEIR CONTROL	DK/NA
National	40%	49%	11%
Bucknell	35	56	9

a. *If can do something: Which Republican presidential candidate do you think can do something?*

	NATIONAL	BUCKNELL
Dole	12%	15%
Gramm	1	1
Forbes	1	—
Buchanan	1	1
Most of them	—	1

	NATIONAL	BUCKNELL
Any/all of them	1	3
Others	1	2
None	3	4
DK/NA	20	9

77a. *How much blame for the loss of jobs in this country would you place on labor unions—a lot, some, or not much?*

	A LOT	SOME	NOT MUCH	NONE	DK/NA
National	16%	46%	33%	1%	4%
Bucknell	16	55	26	1	2

77b. *How much blame for the loss of jobs in this country would you place on the lower labor costs overseas—a lot, some, or not much?*

	A LOT	SOME	NOT MUCH	NONE	DK/NA
National	46%	39%	12%	—	3%
Bucknell	36	53	9	—	1

77c. *How much blame for the loss of jobs in this country would you place on American workers themselves—a lot, some, or not much?*

	A LOT	SOME	NOT MUCH	NONE	DK/NA
National	18%	57%	22%	1%	2%
Bucknell	16	62	21	—	1

77d. *How much blame for the loss of jobs in this country would you place on Wall Street—a lot, some, or not much?*

	A LOT	SOME	NOT MUCH	NONE	DK/NA
National	10%	40%	36%	1%	13%
Bucknell	15	47	32	1	6

78a. *Congress has passed legislation to scale back welfare programs for the poor. Do you think this is a good idea or a bad idea?*

	GOOD IDEA	BAD IDEA	DK/NA
National	54%	37%	9%
Bucknell	51	39	10

78b. *Congress has passed legislation to scale back Medicare programs, which provide health insurance for the elderly. Do you think this is a good idea or a bad idea?*

	GOOD IDEA	BAD IDEA	DK/NA
National	22%	75%	3%
Bucknell	33	59	8

78c. *Congress has passed legislation to scale back Medicaid programs, which provide health insurance for the poor. Do you think this is a good idea or a bad idea?*

	GOOD IDEA	BAD IDEA	DK/NA
National	26%	69%	6%
Bucknell	27	67	6

79. *The Republicans in Congress have said that scaling back these social programs is necessary to safeguard the future for the next generation of Americans. Do you agree or disagree?*

	AGREE	DISAGREE	DK/NA
National	35%	59%	6%
Bucknell	46	50	4

80. *Now think about the next two or three years. How concerned are you that you or someone else in your household might be laid off from work—are you very concerned, somewhat concerned, or not concerned at all?*

	VERY	SOMEWHAT	NOT AT ALL	DK/NA
National	16%	35%	48%	1%
Bucknell	7	39	54	—

81. *How likely is it that in the next two or three years you or someone else in your household might be offered early retirement or a buy-out—very likely, somewhat likely, or not likely at all?*

	VERY	SOMEWHAT	NOT AT ALL	DK/NA
National	7%	14%	78%	1%
Bucknell	4	16	80	—

b1. *Has the nature of your job or profession—such as how you work, where you work, or the issues you deal with—changed a lot in recent years, or changed somewhat, or has it been fairly stable?**

	A LOT	SOMEWHAT	STABLE	DK/NA
Bucknell	42%	29%	27%	2%

*Based on those in labor market (sample size = 477)

b2. *Do you see the effects of layoffs and loss of jobs in people you deal with on your job?**

	YES	NO	DK/NA
Bucknell	68%	29%	2%

*Based on those in labor market (sample size = 477)

b3. *Have you or your spouse ever participated in a management role in planning or conducting a downsizing or layoff in a company?*

	YES, SELF	YES, SPOUSE	NO
Bucknell:	27%	6%	67%

b4. *Looking back on the past twenty-five years, would you say that your working life has turned out about how you expected and planned?*

	YES	NO	DK/NA
Bucknell	52%	44%	4%

b4a. *If no: Were unexpected developments generally positive, negative, or neutral?*

	POSITIVE	NEGATIVE	NEUTRAL	DK/NA
Bucknell	18%	13%	12%	1%

b5. *Do you think that young people entering the job market today with the same education you had in 1970 will face more career obstacles and competition than you did, or fewer obstacles and competition, or do you think it's about the same?*

	MORE	LESS	SAME	DK/NA
Bucknell	74%	2%	24%	1%

b6. *Do you think that young people today generally need more help getting started in a career than your generation did, less help, or about the same?*

	MORE	LESS	SAME	DK/NA
Bucknell	63%	1%	33%	2%

b7. *Do you have any children attending Bucknell now, or who have already graduated from Bucknell?*

	ATTENDING	GRADUATED	NO
Bucknell	3%	2%	95%

b8. *Would you encourage any young people you know to follow your career example, or go into your line of work?*

	YES	NO	DK/NA
Bucknell	81%	17%	2%

b8a. *If yes: Would you encourage any young people you know to take a job at the company where you work?*

	YES	NO	DON'T WORK FOR A COMPANY	DK/NA
Bucknell	62%	8%	5%	1%

82. *Some people are registered to vote and others are not. Are you registered to vote in the precinct or election district where you now live, or aren't you?*

	YES	NO	DK/NA
National	79%	21%	—
Bucknell	96	4	

83. *Do you consider yourself part of the religious right political movement, or not?*

	YES	NO	DK/NA
National	12%	81%	7%
Bucknell	2	97	1

84. *If you were asked to use one of four names to describe your social class, would you say you were in the upper class, the middle class, the working class, or the lower class?*

	UPPER CLASS	MIDDLE CLASS	WORKING CLASS	LOWER CLASS	DK/NA
National	2%	36%	55%	6%	1%
Bucknell	20	76	4		—

a. *If middle class: Do you ever feel as if you're at risk of falling out of the middle class?*

	YES	NO	DK/NA	OMITTED
National	13%	23%	1%	64%
Bucknell	13	63	1	24

85. *Are you or any other member of your household—that is, any other adult living in your home or apartment—a member of a labor union? If yes: Is that person you or someone else?*

	YES	SOMEONE ELSE	NO	DK/NA
National	9%	10%	81%	1%
Bucknell	11	8	81	—

86. *In this household, are there any children? If yes: Are they under or over the age of 18?*

	UNDER 18	OVER 18	BOTH	NO	DK/NA
National	38%	5%	3%	55%	—
Bucknell	40	11	19	31	

87. *Do you frequently listen to political call-in radio shows, or don't you?*

	YES	NO	DK/NA
National	27%	72%	—
Bucknell	17	83	

88. *Did you vote for U.S. House of Representatives in the elections held in 1994, or did something prevent you from voting, or did you choose not to vote for U.S. House of Representatives in 1994? If voted: Did you vote for the Republican candidate or the Democratic candidate in your district?*

	REPUBLICAN	DEMOCRATIC	WON'T SAY OR OTHER	DIDN'T VOTE	DK/NA
National	24%	23%	5%	44%	4%
Bucknell	38	45	4	11	1

89. *If voted Republican or Democratic: Do you usually vote for the (Republican/ Democratic) candidate for U.S. House of Representatives, or not?*

	USUALLY VOTE THAT WAY	DON'T USUALLY	FIRST-TIME VOTER	DEPENDS	DK/NA
National	32%	9%	—	6%	—
Bucknell	62	14		7	1

b. *If don't usually vote that way: What's the main reason you voted differently last year?*

	NATIONAL	BUCKNELL
Candidate's position	5%	7%
Vote differently each year/time for change	1	1

	NATIONAL	BUCKNELL
Economic philosophy	—	I
Angry at other party	I	3
Other		I
DK/NA	I	I

90. *Did you vote for president in 1992, did something prevent you from voting, or did you choose not to vote for president in 1992? If voted: Did you vote for George Bush, Bill Clinton, or Ross Perot?*

	BUSH	CLINTON	PEROT	WON'T SAY OR OTHER	DIDN'T VOTE	DK/NA
National	25%	33%	10%	3%	28%	1%
Bucknell	29	58	9	2	2	—

91. *Generally speaking, do you usually consider yourself a Republican, a Democrat, an Independent, or what?*

	REPUBLICAN	DEMOCRAT	INDEPENDENT	DK/NA
National	27%	33%	33%	7%
Bucknell	31	37	31	I

a. *If Independent or DK/NA: Do you think of yourself as closer to the Republican Party or to the Democratic Party?*
(Note: These percentages are based on the results of questions 91 and 91a.)

	REPUBLICAN	DEMOCRAT	DK/NA
National	40%	48%	12%
Bucknell	41	52	7

92. *How would you describe your views on most political matters? Generally, do you think of yourself as liberal, moderate, or conservative?*

	LIBERAL	MODERATE	CONSERVATIVE	DK/NA
National	15%	46%	34%	5%
Bucknell	27	52	19	2

93. *Are you currently married, widowed, divorced, separated, or have you never been married?*

	MARRIED	WIDOWED	DIVORCED	SEPARATED	NEVER MARRIED	DK/NA
National	62%	7%	8%	2%	20%	—
Bucknell	78	1	11	2	8	—

94. *What was the last grade in school you completed?*

	NOT A HIGH SCHOOL GRAD	HIGH SCHOOL GRAD	SOME COLLEGE	COLLEGE GRAD	REFUSED
National	15%	39%	25%	20%	—
Bucknell				100	

95. *How old are you?*

	18–29	30–44	45–64	OVER 64	REFUSED
National	23%	33%	26%	17%	—
Bucknell		100			—

96. *Are you white, black, or some other race?*

	WHITE	BLACK	OTHER	REFUSED
National	23%	33%	26%	17%
Bucknell	98	1	—	—

97. *Are you of Hispanic origin or descent, or not?*

	HISPANIC	NOT HISPANIC	DK/NA
National	6%	93%	1%
Bucknell	1	99	

98. *Was your total family income in 1994 under or over $30,000? If under: Was it under or over $15,000? If over: Was it between $30,000 and $50,000, or between $50,000 and $75,000, or was it over $75,000?*

	UNDER $15,000	$15,000–$29,999	$30,000–$49,999	$50,000–$75,000	OVER $75,000	REFUSED
National	12%	30%	31%	14%	10%	4%
Bucknell	—	3	9	20	66	2

SEX	MALE	FEMALE
National	48%	52%
Bucknell	56	44